Winnicott on the Child

Winnicott on the Child

D. W. WINNICOTT

Introductions by

T. Berry Brazelton, M.D.
Stanley I. Greenspan, M.D.
Benjamin Spock, M.D.

A Merloyd Lawrence Book

PERSEUS PUBLISHING
A Member of the Perseus Books Group

Copyright © 2002 by The Winnicott Trust

Talking to Parents copyright © 1993 by The Winnicott Trust by arrangement with Mark Paterson

Babies and Their Mothers copyright © 1987 by The Winnicott Trust by arrangment with Mark Paterson

"The Child in the Family Group," "Children Learning," "The Mother's Contribution to Society," from *Home is Where We Start From; Essays by a Psychoanalyst* by D.W. Winnicott. Copyright © 1986 by the Estate of D.W. Winnicott. Used by permission of W.W. Norton & Company, Inc.

"The Development of the Capacity for Concern" from *Deprivation and Delinquency* by D.W. Winnicott. Copyright © 1965 by D.W. Winnicott. Used by permission of Routledge.

"The Family and Emotional Maturity" and "Advising Parents" from *The Family and Individual Development*, copyright © 1965 by D. W. Winnicott, used by permission of Routledge.

Cataloging-in-Publication Data is available from the Library of Congress.
ISBN 0-7382-0764-0

Perseus Publishing is a member of the Perseus Books Group.
Find us on the World Wide Web at http://www.perseuspublishing.com

Perseus Publishing books are available at special discounts for bulk purchases in the U.S. by corporations, institutions, and other organizations. For more information, please contact the Special Markets Department at the Perseus Books Group, 11 Cambridge Center, Cambridge, MA 02142, or call (617)252-5298, (800) 255-1514, or email j.mccrary@perseusbooks.com

Set in 11-point Adobe Caslon by the Perseus Books Group

First printing, September, 2002

1 2 3 4 5 6 7 8 9 10—04 03 02

Contents

PART ONE: BABIES AND THEIR MOTHERS

Introduction by Benjamin Spock, M.D.   *3*
Editors' Preface   *9*

1   The Ordinary Devoted Mother   *11*
2   Knowing and Learning   *19*
3   Breast-feeding as Communication   *24*
4   The Newborn and His Mother   *32*
5   The Beginning of the Individual   *43*
6   Environmental Health in Infancy   *49*
7   The Contribution of Psychoanalysis to Midwifery   *56*
8   Dependence in Child Care   *65*
9   Communication Between Infant and Mother,
    and Mother and Infant, Compared and Contrasted   *70*

PART TWO: TALKING TO PARENTS

On Reading Winnicott by T. Berry Brazelton, M.D.   *85*
Editors' Preface   *89*

10 Health Education through Broadcasting   *95*
11 For Stepparents   *99*
12 What Do We Know about Babies as Cloth Suckers?   *104*
13 Saying "No"   *108*
14 Jealousy   *122*
15 What Irks?   *139*
16 Security   *155*
17 Feeling Guilty   *160*

18 The Development of a Child's Sense of
     Right and Wrong   *167*
19 Now They Are Five   *171*
20 The Building Up of Trust   *178*

PART THREE: THE CHILD IN THE FAMILY

Introduction by Stanley I. Greenspan, M.D.   *191*

21 Advising Parents   *193*
22 The Mother's Contribution to Society   *202*
23 The Family and Emotional Maturity   *207*
24 The Development of the Capacity for Concern   *215*
25 The Child in the Family Group   *221*
26 Children Learning   *232*

Original Source of Each Chapter   *239*
The Works of D. W. Winnicott   *245*
Index   *247*
Biographical Note   *265*

PART ONE

Babies and Their Mothers

Introduction

by Benjamin Spock, M.D.

I well remember, back in the 1930s when I was starting pediatric practice in New York, my excitement in finding Dr. Winnicott's first book *Disorders of Childhood.* Here were words of wisdom from a psychoanalyst in London who had begun as a pediatrician and therefore had special insights into the mother-infant relationship.

At the time, I was groping and frustrated. During my pediatric residency I had picked up the idea somewhere—certainly not from any of my teachers or colleagues—that I should have some kind of psychological training in order to practice pediatrics in a way that would satisfy mothers, and also to satisfy myself that my advice was sound. (I was of an overly conscientious and teacherish make-up.) Perhaps this idea grew from the feeling that there must be a pleasanter way to raise children than my tyrannical mother's. Though she loved babies and devoted her life exclusively to her six children, she nevertheless oppressed us all with her stern Victorian morality and left us as adults feeling guilty until proved innocent.

I had written to three professors of pediatrics about psychological training for a pediatrician, but they all replied that there was no such thing. So, following medical tradition, I applied for a psychiatric residency at New York Hospital–Cornell Medical School (a university department of child development might have been more appropriate), where I spent a year caring mainly for schizophrenic and manic-depressive adults. The only usable thing I learned was that the attending staff members who made our case discussions interesting were those trained in psychoanalysis. So I resolved, as I started pediatric practice, to get that training: a personal analysis, five years of evening seminars, analysis of a patient under supervision. (I might, like Winnicott, have moved on to the practice of psychoanalysis had I succeeded in turning my patient into a happy person. I learned a lot but didn't help my patient.)

Psychoanalytic training gave me a sound theoretical framework but no practical advice for anxious mothers worried about thumb sucking, resistance to weaning and toilet training, or feeding and sleep problems. Still feeling unsure and uneasy, I gave the best advice I could think of and then listened attentively to what mothers reported at the next visit—and the next.

After five years of practice I was asked by a publisher to write a book for parents. I said unhesitatingly that I didn't know enough. Five years later came a droll editor from Pocket Books who said the book they wanted didn't have to be very good because, at twenty-five cents a copy, they could sell tens of thousands. That appealed to me both as a do-gooder and as a person afraid to claim too much expertise, and I set to work. The reason these publishers had come to me was not because I was well known—I was utterly unknown except for a small clientele of psychologically minded mothers. The publishers came because their inquiries revealed that I was the only pediatrician with any psychiatric and psychoanalytic training.

Even though Winnicott's books and articles were more concerned with meanings than with the practical answers for mothers, I had a great interest and trust in them. His psychoanalytic training and his analytic work with adults, children, and borderline psychotic patients gave him new, deeper insights into the subtleties of the mother-child relationship and of the stages each was going through. Because of this special expertise, he became one of the major theoreticians of the British psychoanalytic movement, and most of his publications focused on this subject. For me, he helped to bridge the gap between pediatrics and the dynamics of child development.

This book is composed of talks given by Winnicott, not to psychoanalysts, but to pediatricians, general practitioners, nurses, midwives, nursery school teachers and parents, not only in Britain but in international meetings. A few examples show his focus.

In "The Ordinary Devoted Mother" he expresses his deep faith (which crops up in other talks, too) in the broad capability and correctness of a mother's intuition about what her baby feels and needs, and how this enables the baby's trust to form and his or her increasingly complex development to proceed.

The mother acquires this intuition primarily through her extraordinary capability to identify with her baby. And the baby gets carried along by identifying with her. First the baby assumes that he and his mother are one and the same. Then gradually he senses and asserts his autonomy. The early relationship between mother and baby must not be interfered with by anybody—physicians, nurses, baby nurses in the home, untrained in psychodynamics—for they may undermine the mother's self-confidence and, secondarily, the baby's integrity.

In a radio broadcast to mothers, on whose side he is *always* firmly planted, Winnicott comes back to his emphasis on the great differences between *knowing* and *learning*. A mother knows or soon finds out, by intuition, how to hold and handle a baby so that the baby and she are comfortable and secure. Another example: when an older child gets hurt, climbs in her mother's lap and cries miserably, like an infant, the mother knows, without wondering or asking, that for ten minutes the child must be a baby again and will then revert to her proper age.

Learning from the doctor what vitamins are necessary, and in what dosage, is an entirely different matter. Winnicott says firmly: Don't let the professionals, when they give you information to learn, take away from you your confidence in your natural knowledge.

In "Breast-feeding as Communication" Winnicott first dissociates himself from those who try to *make* mothers breast-feed. (I feel the same way.) The most that doctors and nurses can do is create an atmosphere in which the mother can believe in herself, and then depend on her own intuitive reactions. He speaks approvingly, though, about the taste, smell, and other sensuous experiences of breast-feeding for the baby, and the sense of achievement for the mother. Then he moves on to a two-sided aspect of breast-feeding, the older baby's impulse to bite the nipple occasionally, which the baby himself learns to inhibit and which the mother also can inhibit, without vindictiveness, just by protecting herself. In a sense the baby has thus learned a new dimension of love, through aggressiveness; he has learned that a valued object such as the breast can survive his hostile impulses. These are the kinds of insights, gained from the psychoanalysis of adults and children, that show us the complexities of emotional development.

In "The Contribution of Psychoanalysis to Midwifery" Winnicott calls attention to the many disturbances in women's genital functioning, in menstruation and childbearing, that are at least partially due to emotional factors, and he congratulates midwives on being increasingly aware of these factors. He points out that a woman in labor cannot turn control of herself over to a professional unless she has come to know and trust her during the perinatal period.

The patient in labor and afterwards is highly sensitive to a too-dominating attitude on the part of midwife, nurse or baby nurse, often a carryover from a critical mother. With this in mind he begs the professionals not to try to take over the management of breast-feeding but leave it to the intuitive knowledge of the mother.

In a lecture called "Communication Between Infant and Mother, and Mother and Infant, Compared and Contrasted" Winnicott starts with the newborn baby's absolute dependence and matches this with the new mother's extraordinary, total preoccupation with him. It is so intense that it sometimes frightens a mother into thinking she has turned into a vegetable, but it only lasts a few weeks. It enables her to make a deep and crucial identification with her baby at the start. But she has also been prepared for this stage by having been a baby, played at being a baby and a mother, and regressed to babyhood during illness. For the baby it is all new; he recognizes no words, no time. He is ready to become human but must depend on an "ordinary devoted mother" to achieve it. She communicates by the inflections in her voice (the words don't matter), by her holding and handling and rocking. She communicates even by her breathing and her heartbeat, by meeting her baby's daily and gradually changing needs.

All this adds up to reliability and to love. But as Winnicott points out, even the best of human beings fail and fail often. In a sense this is how the infant comes to recognize the existence of reliability—by its occasional lapses. At the same time, mothers keep promptly mending their failures, and this, to mother and baby, adds up to adaptation and success. (Failures that are not mended constitute serious deprivations and bring developmental distortions.) Mother and baby also communicate on the common ground of playfulness and, most effectively, by the expressions on the mother's face, by the intuitive way the mother brings to the baby just what the baby is wanting—a change of position, a breast, a bottle—from which the baby acquires a sense of control, a sense of omnipotence and creativity.

As for the newborn baby's communication with the mother, Winnicott singles out the power of the baby's appearance of helplessness which renders the parent helpless to resist.

Finally I want to single out, as one source of *my* pleasure in reading Winnicott, the surprising contrasts in his language. It is predominately grave, deeply thoughtful and analytical. Then suddenly he gives way to earthy folk talk: "There is more to the baby than blood and bones." "She feels like shoving the breast into the baby's mouth or shoving the baby's mouth into the breast." "Then one day they [mothers] find they have become hostess to a new human being who has decided to take up lodging." "Damn you, you little bugger."

Editors' Preface to
Babies and Their Mothers

In the years following Donald Winnicott's death in 1971 it was decided that the papers that he had left unpublished, together with those that had appeared only in journals and anthologies, should be published in collections under his own name.

The papers brought together in *Babies and Their Mothers* were written specifically about the psychological processes that take place in the infant around the time of birth and shortly thereafter, when "the baby and the mother are not yet separated out in the baby's rudimentary mind"; and they examine the implications that ensue for those who have care of newborn babies and their mothers.

We hope in particular that professional workers in this field will find the selection valuable and enjoyable, and that it will reach a new generation of readers who can make use of Winnicott's ability to see the everlasting in the ephemeral.

RAY SHEPHERD
MADELEINE DAVIS
London, 1986

ONE

The Ordinary
Devoted Mother

How to say something new on a well-worn subject? My name has become linked with these words, and first perhaps I should explain this.

I was walking, in the summer of 1949, to have drinks with the B.B.C. producer, Miss Isa Benzie, who now has retired and whose name I like to remember, and she was telling me that I could give a series of nine talks on any subject that might please me. She was, of course, on the lookout for a catchphrase, but I did not know this. I told her that I had no interest whatever in trying to tell people what to do. To start with, I didn't know. But I would like to talk to mothers about the thing that they do well, and that they do well simply because each mother is devoted to the task in hand, namely the care of one infant, or perhaps twins. I said that ordinarily this just happens, and it is the exception when a baby has to do without being cared for at the start by a specialist. Isa Benzie picked up the clue in a matter of twenty yards, and she said: "Splendid! The Ordinary Devoted Mother." So that was that.

You can imagine that I have been ragged somewhat on account of this phrase, and there are many who assume that I am sentimental about mothers and that I idealise them, and that I leave out fathers, and that I can't see that some mothers are pretty awful if not in fact impossible. I have to put up with these small inconveniences because I am not ashamed of what is implied by these words.

There is another criticism that comes from those who have also heard me say that failure of mothers at the Ordinary Devoted Mother level is one

---

Note: Information about sources, previous publication, or the original audience for each chapter can be found on p. 239.

factor in the aetiology of autism. It is felt to be an accusation when one really goes on logically and refers to the effects of Ordinary Devoted Mother failure. But is it not natural that if this thing called devotion is really important, then its absence or a relative failure in this area should have consequences that are untoward? I shall return to this theme when I come to discuss what is meant by the word *blame*.

I see that I cannot avoid saying the obvious. It is a trite remark when I say that by devoted I simply mean devoted. You have the job of doing the altar flowers for your church at the end of every week. If you take it on you simply do not forget. On Fridays you find yourself making sure the flowers are there to be arranged; or if you have the flu you begin telephoning round, or sending a message to someone by the milkman, even though you don't like to see them done well by someone else. It just doesn't happen that the congregation congregates on Sunday and the altar is bare or there are dead flowers in dirty vases disgracing instead of gracing the sanctuary. Yet, at the same time, it cannot be said, I hope, that you spend Monday to Thursday getting all worked up or worrying. The matter is simply lying asleep in the back of your mind, and it wakes up and wakes you up on Friday, or perhaps Saturday.

In a similar way women are not all the time fussing around thinking they ought to be looking after a baby. They play golf, they have a job that they lose themselves in, they quite naturally do all sorts of male things like being irresponsible, or taking everything for granted, or motor-racing. This is Monday to Friday, in terms of the altar flowers.

Then, one day, they find they have become hostess to a new human being who has decided to take up lodgings, and like the character played by Robert Morley in *The Man Who Came to Dinner*, to exercise a crescendo of demands till some date in the far-extended future when there will once again be peace and quiet; and they, these women, may return to self-expression of a more direct kind. During this prolonged Friday–Saturday–Sunday, they have been in a phase of self-expression through identification with what with luck grows into a baby, and becomes autonomous, biting the hand that fed it.

There happens to be this useful nine-months period in which there is time for a gradual change-over in the woman from the one kind of selfishness to the other. The same thing can be observed in fathers; also it is like this with people who decide to adopt a baby, who come round to the idea of adopting, and who get worked up, and who reach a point at which the baby must materialise—unfortunately for adopters there is sometimes a disappointment here, and by the time the baby is found they have gone over into not being so sure that they want one.

I want to stress the importance of this period of preparation. When I was a medical student, I had a friend who was a poet. He was one of several of us who shared some very good digs in the slums of North Kensington. This is how we found the digs:

My friend the poet, who was very tall and indolent and always smoking, walked down a terrace till he saw a house that looked friendly. He rang the bell. A woman came to the door and he liked the look of her face. So he said: "I want lodgings here." She said: "I have a vacancy. When will you be coming?" He said: "I have come." So he went in, and when he was shown the bedroom he said: "It happens that I am ill, so I will go straight to bed. What time can I have tea?" And he went to bed and stayed in bed for six months. In the course of a few days we had all settled in nicely, but the poet remained the landlady's favourite.

But nature has decreed that babies do not choose their mothers. They just turn up, and the mothers have time to re-orientate, to find that for a few months their orient is not in the east but is in the centre (or is it a bit off-centre?).

I suggest, as you know I do, and I suppose everyone agrees, that *ordinarily* the woman enters into a phase, a phase from which she *ordinarily* recovers in the weeks and months after the baby's birth, in which to a large extent she is the baby and the baby is her. There is nothing mystical about this. After all, she was a baby once, and she has in her the memories of being a baby; she also has memories of being cared for, and these memories either help or hinder her in her own experiences as a mother.

I think that by the time the baby is ripe for birth the mother, if properly cared for herself by her man or by the Welfare State or both, is ready for an experience in which she knows extremely well what are the baby's needs. You will understand I am not simply referring to her being able to know whether the baby is or is not hungry, and all that sort of thing; I am referring to innumerable subtle things, things that only my friend the poet could properly put into words. For my part, I am contented to use the world *hold*, and to extend its meaning to cover all that a mother is and does at this time. I believe it is a critical time, but I scarcely dare say this because it would be a pity to make a woman feel self-conscious just here where she is and where she acts naturally *naturally*. It is here that she cannot learn from books. She cannot use even Spock just at this point where she feels that the baby needs to be picked up, or put down, to be left alone or to be turned over, or where she knows that what is essential is the simplest of all experiences, that based on contact without activity, where there is opportunity for the feeling of oneness between two persons who are in fact two and not one. These things give the baby the opportunity to be, out of which there can arise the next things that have to do with action, doing and being done to. Here is the basis for what gradually becomes, for the infant, the self-experiencing being.

All this is highly tenuous, but repeated and repeated adds up to the foundation of the capacity in the baby to feel real. With this capacity the baby can face the world, or (I should say) can go ahead with the maturational processes which he or she inherits.

When these conditions obtain, as they usually do, the baby becomes able to develop the capacity to have feelings that correspond to some extent with those of the mother who is identified with her baby; or shall I say, heavily invested in her baby and in his or her care. At three or four months after being born the baby may be able to show that he or she knows what it is like to be a mother, that is a mother in her state of being devoted to something that is not in fact herself.

It must be remembered that what first appears at an early age needs a long period of time to become established as a more or less fixed mechanism in the child's mental processes. What can be shown to have been present can indeed be lost, as is to be expected. But what I am concerned with here is that the more complex cannot arise except out of the most simple, and in health the complexity of the mind and personality develops gradually and by steady growth, always from simple to complex.

In time the baby begins to need the mother to fail to adapt—this failure being also a graduated process that cannot be learned from books. It would be irksome for a human child to go on experiencing omnipotence when the apparatus has arrived which can cope with frustrations and relative environmental failures. There is much satisfaction to be got from anger that does not go over into despair.

Any parent here will know what I mean when I say that although you subjected your baby to the most awful frustrations you never once let him (or her) down—that is, your ego support to the baby's ego was reliable. The baby never woke and cried and there was no one to hear. In later language you found you did not try to put your child off with lies.

But, of course, all this implies not only that the mother was able to give herself over to this preoccupation with the care of her infant, but also that she was lucky. I need not start to enumerate the things that may happen even in the best-regulated families. I will give three examples, however, to illustrate three types of trouble. The first is pure chance—a mother gets ill and dies, and she has to let her baby down exactly in the way that she hates to do. Or she starts up a new pregnancy before the time that she had thought out as appropriate. She might be to some extent responsible for this complication, but these things are not as simple as winking. Or a mother becomes depressed and she can feel herself depriving her child of what the child needs, but she cannot help the onset of a mood swing, which may quite easily be reactive to something that has impinged in her private life. Here she is causing trouble, but no one would blame her.

In other words there are all manner of reasons why some children do get let down before they are able to avoid being wounded or maimed in personality by the fact.

Here I must go back to the idea of blame. It is necessary for us to be able to look at human growth and development, with all its complexities that are internal or personal to the child, and we must be able to say: here the ordinary devoted mother factor failed, without blaming anyone. For my part I have no interest whatever in apportioning blame. Mothers and fathers blame themselves, but that is another matter, and indeed they blame themselves for almost anything, for having a mongol child, for instance, which they certainly could not be held responsible for.

But we must be able to look at aetiology and be able if necessary to say that some of the failures of development that we meet sprang from a failure of the ordinary devoted mother factor at a certain point or over a phase. This has nothing to do with moral responsibility. It is another subject. In any case, what good would I have been as a mother?

But I have one special reason why I feel we must be able to apportion aetiological significance (not blame), and that is that in no other way can we recognise the positive value of the ordinary devoted mother factor—the vital necessity for every baby that someone should facilitate the earliest stages of the processes of psychological growth, or psychosomatic growth, or shall I say the growth of the most immature and absolutely dependent human personality.

In other words, I do not believe in the story of Romulus and Remus, much as I respect wolf bitches. Someone who was human found and cared for the founders of Rome, if indeed we are to allow any truth at all to this myth. I do not go on further and say we as men and women *owe* anything to the women who did this for each one of us severally. We owe nothing. But to ourselves we owe an intellectual recognition of the fact that at first we were (psychologically) absolutely dependent, and that absolutely means absolutely. Luckily we were met by ordinary devotion.

⌇

Is it possible to say something about the reasons why it is necessary that a mother should be able to make this very close adaptation to her child's needs at the beginning?[1] It is easy to say quite a lot about the more obvious although more complicated needs of older children and of children making the grade from being related simply to mother to triangular relationships. It is easy to see that children need a firm setting in which to work out their conflicts of love and hate and their two main trends, one based on an orientation to the parent of the same sex and the other based on an orientation to the parent of the other sex. This can be referred to as the hetero- and homosexual strivings in object-relating.

You will want me, however, to try to make a statement about the infant's needs in this very early stage where there nearly always is a mother-figure who is in the position of having nothing much else on her mind over a phase in which the baby's dependence is absolute. Elsewhere I have written quite a lot on this subject, and I cannot hope to do more than sum up if I am to refer to it in a few words. I want to say that in these early, most significant weeks of the baby's life the initial stages of the maturational processes have their first opportunity to become experiences of the baby. Where there is good enough quality in the facilitating environment, which has to be a human one and a personal one, the inherited tendencies of the baby to grow have their first important achievements. One can give names to these things. The main thing is covered by the word *integration*. All the bits and pieces of activity and sensation which go to form what we come to know as this particular baby begin to come together at times so that there are moments of integration in which the baby is a unit although of course a highly dependent one. We say that the mother's ego support facilitates the ego organization of the baby. Eventually the baby becomes able to assert his or her own individuality and even to feel a sense of identity. The whole thing looks very simple when it goes well, and the basis for all this is in the very early relationship in which the baby and the mother are at one. There is nothing mystical about this. The mother has one kind of identification with the baby, a highly sophisticated one, in that she feels very much identified with the baby, but of course she remains adult. The baby, on the other hand, has an identity with the mother in the quiet moments of contact which is not so much an achievement of the baby as of the relationship which the mother makes possible. From the baby's point of view there is nothing else but the baby, and therefore the mother is at first part of the baby. In other words, there is something here which people call primary identification. There is the beginning of everything, and it gives meaning to very simple words like *being*.

We could use a Frenchified word *existing* and talk about existence, and we can make this into a philosophy and call it existentialism, but somehow or other we like to start with the word *being* and then with the statement *I am*. The important thing is that *I am* means nothing unless *I* at the beginning *am along with another human being* who has not yet been differentiated off. For this reason it is more true to talk about *being* than to use the words *I am*, which belong to the next stage. It cannot be overemphasized that being is the beginning of everything, without which *doing* and *being done to* have no significance. It is possible to seduce a baby into feeding and into the functioning of all the bodily processes, but the baby does not feel these things as an experience unless it is built on a quantity of simple being which is enough to establish the self that is eventually a person.

The opposite of integration is a failure of integration or disintegration from a state of integration. This is unbearable. It is one of the most basic unthinkable anxieties of infancy which are prevented by ordinary care of the kind that nearly all infants do, in fact, get from an adult human being. I will enumerate very briefly one or two other similar basic growth processes. It is not possible to take for granted that the infant's psyche will form satisfactorily in partnership with the soma, that is to say with the body and its functioning. Psycho-somatic existence is an achievement, and although its basis is an inherited growth tendency, it cannot become a fact without the active participation of a human being who is holding and handling the baby. A breakdown in this area has to do with all the difficulties affecting bodily health which actually stem from uncertainty in personality structure. You will see that the breakdown of these very early growth processes takes us immediately to the kind of symptomatology which we find in our mental hospitals so that the prevention of mental hospital disorder belongs initially to infant care and the things that come naturally to mothers who like having a baby to look after.

Another thing that I could mention has to do with the beginnings of object-relating. This is already getting on towards a sophisticated view of psychology. You will recognise, however, the way in which, when the relationship between the baby and the mother is satisfactory, objects begin to turn up which the baby can use symbolically; not only the thumb for sucking but also something to catch hold of which eventually may become a doll or a toy. A breakdown here has to be measured in terms of a failure of the capacity for object-relating.

It will be observed that though at first we were talking about very simple things, we were also talking about matters that have vital importance, matters that concern the laying down of the foundations for mental health. A great deal of course is done at later stages, but it is when the beginning is good that all that is done at later stages can take effect. Sometimes mothers find it alarming to think that what they are doing is so important and in that case it is better not to tell them. It makes them self-conscious and then they do everything less well. It is not possible to learn these matters, and anxiety is no substitute for this very simple kind of love which is almost physical. It might be asked, why then bother to point all this out? But I do want to emphasize that someone must bother about these things because otherwise we forget the importance of the very early relationships and we interfere too easily. This is something we must absolutely never do. When a mother has a capacity quite simply to be a mother we must never interfere. She will not be able to fight for her rights because she will not understand. All she will know is that she has been wounded. Only the wound is not a broken bone or a gash in her arm. It is the maimed personality of the baby. How often a mother spends years of her life trying to mend this wound which in fact was caused by us when we unnecessarily interfered with something that was so simple that it seemed to be unimportant.

1966

Notes

1. The passages that follow were found with the foregoing talk in Dr. Winnicott's papers.

TWO

Knowing and Learning

There is much for a young mother to learn. She gets told useful things by experts, about the introduction of solids into the diet, about vitamins, and about the use of the weight chart: and then sometimes she gets told about quite a different kind of thing, for instance, about her reaction to her infant's refusal of food.

It seems to me to be important for you[1] to be quite clear about the difference between these two types of knowledge. What you do and know, simply by virtue of the fact that you are the mother of an infant, is as far apart from what you know by learning as is the east from the west coast of England. I cannot put this too strongly. Just as the professor who found out about the vitamins that prevent rickets really has something to teach you, so you really have something to teach him about the other kind of knowledge, that which comes to you naturally.

The mother who breast-feeds her baby simply does not have to bother about fats and proteins while she is thoroughly caught up in the management of the early stages. By the time she weans at nine months or so and the baby is making fewer demands on her, she is becoming free to study facts and advice which doctors and nurses offer. Obviously there is a great deal that she could not know intuitively, and she does want to be told about the giving of solids, and about how to use the sort of foods that are available in such a way that the baby will be able to grow and keep healthy. But she must wait for such instruction until she is in a state of mind to receive it.

We can easily see that years of brilliant research have gone into the doctor's bit of advice about vitamins, and we can look with awe at the scientist's work and at the self-discipline that such work entails, and be grateful when, by the results of scientific research, a great deal of suffering can be avoided, perhaps by some quite simple advice like adding a few drops of cod-liver oil to the diet.

At the same time the scientist, if he cares to do so, may look with awe at the mother's intuitive understanding, which makes her able to care for her infant without learning. In fact, the essential richness of this intuitive understanding, I would say, is that it *is* natural and unspoiled by learning.

The difficult task, in preparing a series of talks and books on infant care, is to know how to avoid disturbance of what comes naturally to mothers while getting them informed accurately as to the useful facts that emerge from scientific research.

I want you to be able to feel confident about your capacity as mothers, and not feel that because you could not know about vitamins, you also could not know about, for instance, how to hold your infant.

How to hold your infant; that would be a good example for me to follow up.

The phrase "holding the baby" has a definite meaning in the English language; someone was co-operating with you over something, and then waltzed off, and you were left "holding the baby." By this we can see that everybody knows that mothers naturally have a sense of responsibility, and if they have a baby in their arms they are involved in some special way. Of course, some women get left holding the baby literally, in the sense that the father is unable to enjoy the part he has to play, and unable to share with the mother the great responsibility which a baby must always be to someone.

Or perhaps there is no father. Ordinarily, however, the mother feels supported by her husband and so is free to be a mother properly, and when she holds her baby she does it naturally, and without thinking it out. Such a mother will be surprised if I talk about such a thing as holding a baby as a skilled job.

When people see a baby they love to be able to be allowed to experience just this thing, of holding the baby in their arms. You don't let people hold your baby if you feel it means nothing to them. Babies are very sensitive indeed to the way they are held, so that they cry with one person and rest contented with another, even when they are quite tiny. Sometimes a little girl will ask to hold a newly-arrived baby brother or sister, and this is a big event. The wise mother will remember not to give the child the whole responsibility, and will be there all the time if she lets this happen, ready to take the baby back into her own safe keeping. The wise mother will certainly not just take it for granted that an older sister is safe with the baby in her arms. This would be to deny the meaning of it all. I know people who can remember throughout their lives the awful feeling of holding the baby brother or sister, and of the nightmare of not feeling safe. In the nightmare the baby is dropped. The fear which can turn up in the nightmare as doing harm in practice makes the big sister catch hold of the baby too tightly.

All this leads on to what you do yourself quite naturally because of your devotion to your baby. You are not anxious and so are not gripping too tight. You are not afraid you will throw the baby on to the floor. You just adapt the pressure of your arms to the baby's needs, and you move slightly, and you perhaps make some sounds. The baby feels you breathing. There is warmth that comes from your breath and your skin, and the baby finds your holding to be good.

Of course there are all kinds of mothers, and there are some who are not quite so happy about the way they hold their babies. Some feel a bit doubtful; the baby seems happier in the cot. There may be something left over in such a mother of the fear which she had to deal with when she was a little girl, when her mother let her hold a newborn baby. Or she may have had a mother who was not very good at this sort of thing herself, and she is afraid of passing on to her baby some uncertainty belonging to the past. An anxious mother uses the cot as much as possible, or even hands the baby over to the care of a nurse, carefully chosen because of the natural way she handles babies. There is room for all kinds of mothers in the world, and some will be good at one thing and some good at another. Or shall I say some will be bad at one thing and some bad at another? Some are anxious holders.

It may be worth while looking even a little more closely at this business, because if you do handle your baby well I want you to be able to know that you are doing something of importance. This is a little part of the way in which you give a good foundation for the mental health of this new member of the community.

Look at it imaginatively.

Here is the infant right at the beginning (from what happens at the beginning we can see what happens, over and over again, later on). Let me describe three stages in the infant's relation to the world (represented by your arms and your breathing body), leaving out hunger and anger, and all the great upheavals. First stage: the infant is self-contained, a live creature, yet surrounded by space. The infant knows of nothing, except of self. Second stage: the infant moves an elbow, a knee, or straightens out a little. The space has been crossed. The infant has surprised the environment. Third stage: you who are holding the infant jump a little, because the door bell rang, or the kettle boiled over, and again the space has been crossed. This time the environment has surprised the infant.

First, the self-contained infant is in the space that is maintained between the child and the world, then the infant surprises the world, and thirdly, the world surprises the infant. This is so simple that I think it will appeal to you as a natural sequence, and therefore a good basis for the study of the way you hold your infant.

This is all very obvious, but the trouble is that if you do not know these things you may easily let your immense skill get wasted, because you will not see how to explain to neighbours, and to your husband, how necessary it is for you, in your turn, to have a space to yourself in which you can start your infant off with a sound basis for life.

Let me put it this way. The baby in the space becomes ready, in the course of time, for the movement that surprises the world, and the infant who has found the world in this way becomes, in time, ready to welcome the surprises that the world has in store.

The baby does not know that the space around is maintained by you. How careful you are that the world shall not impinge before the infant has found it! By a live and breathing quietness you follow the life in the infant with the life in yourself, and you wait for the gestures that come from the infant, gestures that lead to your being discovered.

If you feel heavy with sleep, and especially if you are in a depressed mood, you put the infant in a cot, because you know that your sleeping state is not alive enough to keep going the infant's idea of a space around.

If I have referred specially to tiny infants, and your management of them, this does not mean that I am not also referring to older children. Of course most of the time the older child has passed through to a much more complex state of affairs, and is not in need of the very special management which comes naturally to you when you are holding your baby who is only a few hours old. But how often it happens that the older child, just for a few minutes, or for an hour or two, needs to go back, and to go over the ground again that belongs to the earliest stages. Perhaps your child has had an accident, and comes to you crying. It may be five or ten minutes before there is a return to play. In the meantime you have had the child in your arms, and you have allowed for just this same sequence that I have been talking about. First of all, the quiet yet live holding, and then the readiness for the child to move and to find you, as the tears clear away. And at length you are able, quite naturally, to put the child down. Or a child is unwell, or sad, or tired. Whatever it is, for a little while the child is an infant, and you know that time has to be given so that there can be a natural return from essential security to ordinary conditions.

Of course I might have chosen many other examples of the way in which you have knowledge, simply because you are specialists in this particular matter of the care of your own children. I want to encourage you to keep and defend this specialist knowledge. It cannot be taught. Then you can learn things from other kinds of specialist. Only if you can keep what is natural in you is it safe for you to learn anything that doctors and nurses can teach you.

It might be thought that I have been trying to teach you now how to hold your baby. This seems to me to be far from the truth. I am trying to describe various aspects of the things you do naturally, in order that you may be able to recognise what you do, and in order that you may be able to get the feeling of your natural capacity. This is important, because unthinking people will often try to teach you how to do the things which you can *do* better than you can be *taught* to do them. If you are sure of all this, you can start to add to your value as a mother by learning the things that can be taught, for the best of our civilisation and culture offers much that is of value, if you can take it without the loss of what comes to you naturally.

1950

Note

1. Winnicott was addressing mothers here. See p. 239.

THREE

Breast-feeding as Communication

I come to this subject as a paediatrician turned psychoanalyst and as one with a long experience of the sort of case that turns up in the practice of a child psychiatrist. In order to do my work I have to have a theory of the *emotional* as well as the *physical* development of the individual child in the environment that obtains, and a theory needs to cover the whole range of what may be expected. At the same time theory needs to be flexible so that any clinical fact may if necessary modify the theoretical statement.

I am not specifically concerned with promoting and encouraging breast-feeding, although I do hope that the general trend of what I have had to say in the course of years about this matter has had exactly this effect, simply because here is something natural and it is likely that what is natural has a very good foundation.

What I want to do first is to dissociate myself from a sentimental attitude towards breast-feeding or propaganda in favour of breast-feeding. Propaganda always has another side to it which eventually turns up as a reaction to the propaganda. There is no doubt whatever that a vast number of individuals in this world today have been brought up satisfactorily without having had the experience of breast-feeding. This means that there are other ways by which an infant may experience physical intimacy with the mother. Nevertheless I myself would always be sorry if breast-feeding fails in any one case, simply because I believe that the mother or the baby or both are losing something if they lose this experience.

We are not just simply concerned with illness or with psychiatric disturbances; we are concerned with the richness of the personality and strength of character and with the capacity for happiness, as well as the capacity for revolution and revolt. It is likely that true strength belongs to the individual's experience of the developmental process along *natural* lines, and this is what we hope for in individuals. In practice this kind of strength becomes easily lost sight of because of the comparable strength that can come from fear and resentment and deprivation and the state of never having had.

If attention is given to the teachings of the paediatricians one may wonder whether breast-feeding is better than other kinds of feeding. Some paediatricians actually believe that artificial feeding if done well can be more satisfactory in terms of anatomy and physiology, which are their concerns. We need not feel that the subject is ended when the paediatrician has finished talking, especially if he seems to forget that there is more about a baby than blood and bones. From my point of view the mental health of the individual is being laid down from the very beginning by the mother who provides what I have called a facilitating environment, that is to say one in which the infant's natural growth processes and interactions with the environment can evolve according to the inherited pattern of the individual. The mother is (without knowing it) laying down the foundations of mental health of the individual.

But not only that. If we assume mental health, the mother (if she is doing well) is laying down the foundations of the individual's strength of character and richness of personality. On such a good basis the individual has a chance as time goes on to reach to the world creatively and to enjoy and use what the world has to offer, including the cultural heritage. It is unfortunately only too true that if a child is not started off well enough then the cultural heritage might just as well never have been and the beauty of the world is only a tantalising colour that cannot be enjoyed. In this way therefore there are truly the haves and the have-nots, and this has nothing to do with finance; it has to do with those who were started off well enough and those who were not started off well enough.

The matter of breast-feeding is certainly part and parcel of this vast problem, part of what we mean when we say that someone is started off by being given a good enough environmental provision. It is not the whole story, however. Psychoanalysts who are responsible for the theory of the emotional development of the individual which we use in this modern age have been responsible to some extent for putting forward the actual breast in a somewhat over-emphasized way. They were not wrong. In the course of time, however, we have come to see that a "good breast" is a jargon word, and it means satisfactory mothering and parentage in a general way. For instance, holding and handling are more vitally important as indications of management than is the actual fact of a breast-feeding experience. Also it is well known that many babies have what seems to be a satisfactory breast-feeding experience and yet they are unsatisfactory in the sense that there is already an observable defect in their developmental process and in their capacity to relate to people and to make use of objects—a defect due to poor holding and handling.

Once I have made it quite clear that the word *breast* and the idea of breast-feeding is an expression that carries with it the whole technique of being a mother to a baby then I am free to point out how important *the breast itself* can be, and I will try to do this. You will perhaps see what I am trying to get away from. I want to dissociate myself from those who try to *make* mothers breast-feed their babies. I have seen a great number of children who were given a very bad time with a mother struggling to make the breast work, which of course she is completely unable to do because it is outside conscious control. The mother suffers and the baby suffers. Sometimes great relief is experienced when at last bottle-feeding is established and at any rate something is going well in the sense that the baby is getting satisfied by taking the right quantity of suitable food. Many of these struggles could be avoided if the religion were taken out of this idea of breast-feeding. It seems to me the ultimate insult, to a woman who would *like* to breast-feed her child and who comes naturally to doing so, if some authority, a doctor or a nurse, comes along and says "You *must* breast-feed your baby." If I were a woman this would be enough to put me off. I would say: "very well then I won't." Unfortunately mothers have this terrible belief in doctors and nurses, and they think that because the doctor knows what to do if things go wrong, or should an acute surgical emergency arise, therefore the doctor knows how to get a mother and baby into relationship with each other. Usually he has no understanding whatever of this which is a matter of intimacy between mother and baby.

It is a question of getting doctors and nurses in general to understand that while they are needed, and very much needed, in case things go wrong on the physical side, they are not specialists in the matters of intimacy that are vital to both the mother and the baby. If they start to give advice about intimacy, they are on dangerous ground because neither the mother nor the baby needs advice. Instead of advice what they need is an environmental provision which fosters the mother's belief in herself. It is a very important modern development that is more and more common for the father to be able to be present when a baby is being born, and the father can bring to the situation an understanding of the importance of the first moments when the mother can take a look at her baby before taking a rest. It is the same with the establishment of breast-feeding. It is something which can become very difficult because the mother is unable to feed by the breast by deliberate effort. She has to wait for her own reactions, or on the other hand her reactions are so strong that she can hardly wait for the baby and has to be helped because of the dammed-up milk.

In regard to educating doctors and nurses in this matter, however, it must be remembered that they have so much else to learn because the demands of modern medicine and surgery are very great indeed. And doctors and nurses are quite ordinary people. It is for parents to know and to be self-conscious about their own needs at this very early stage and to insist on self-fulfillment. Just occasionally it is possible for parents to find doctors and nurses who understand what is their own function and what is the function of the parents, and then the partnership is always a very happy one. Naturally from my position I hear a very great deal from mothers about the distress caused by doctors and nurses who, while being first-rate on the physical side, cannot avoid interfering and being the opposite of helpful in the matter of the interrelationship of mother and father and baby.

There are of course mothers who have very big personal difficulties belonging to their own inner conflicts and perhaps related to their own experiences as infants. These matters can sometimes be sorted out. Where a mother has a difficulty about breast-feeding it is wrong to try to force a situation which must to some extent fail and may become a disaster. It is therefore very bad practice for those in charge to have a preconceived notion about what a mother ought to do in regard to breast-feeding. It often happens that a mother must give up early and institute another kind of feeding, and she may succeed with her second or third child and be very glad that this came to her in a natural way. Where a baby is not to be fed at the breast there are many other ways in which the mother can allow intimacy of a physical kind.

I would like to illustrate at this point the way in which these matters may be of importance at a very early stage. Here is a woman who adopted a baby at six weeks. What she found was that the baby responded well to human contact and to cuddling and to the usual holding and handling aspects of baby care. Already at six weeks, however, the mother discovered that the baby had a pattern derived from previous experience. This pattern was related only to the feeding situation. To get the baby to feed she had to put her on the floor or on a hard table, and without physical contact of any other kind hold the bottle so that the baby could respond by sucking. This abnormal feeding pattern persisted and wove itself into the texture of the child's personality and showed quite clearly to anyone watching the child's development that the very early experience of impersonal feeding had had an effect, and in this case not a good effect.

If I were to continue to give illustrative material I would only confuse the issue because the subject covers a wide range, and it is better for me to call on the experiences of those who are listening to me and to remind you that the little tiny things that happen between the mother and baby at the beginning are significant and not less so because they seem so natural and seem to be best taken for granted.

I come therefore to the positive value of breast-feeding working on the basis that breast-feeding is not absolutely essential and should not be persisted in where the mother has a personal difficulty. The obvious part of what I wish to say has to do with the tremendous richness that belongs to the feeding experience; the baby is awake and alive and the whole of the emerging personality is engaged. A great deal of the baby's waking life at first has to do with feeding. In a way, the baby is gathering stuff for dreaming, although soon there are all the other things that also become gathered in and which can reverberate in the inner reality of the sleeping child, who is of course dreaming. Doctors are so used to talking about health and disease that sometimes they forget to talk about the tremendous variations in health, variations which make it true that whereas one child's experience is weak, colourless, and even boring, another child's experience is almost too exciting, too full of colour and sensation and qualitative richness to be bearable. For some babies feeding experiences are so boring that it must be quite a relief to cry with anger and frustration, which at any rate can feel real and must involve the total personality. The first thing to do, therefore, in looking at a baby's breast-feeding experience is to think in terms of the *richness* of the experience and the involvement of the total personality. Many of the important features of the breast-feeding situation can be seen to be there when the bottle is used. For instance, the baby and the mother looking into each other's eyes, which is a feature at the early stage, does not absolutely depend on the use of the actual breast. Nevertheless one is left with a guess that on the whole the taste and smell and sensuous experience of a breast-feeding is something that is absent when the baby engages with a rubber teat. No doubt babies have ways round even this disadvantage and in some cases the overestimation in the sensuous use of rubber can be traced back to the overestimation of rubber in the bottle-feeding experience. The baby's capacity for sensuous experience can be seen in the use of what I have called transitional objects where there is all the difference in the world for the baby between silk, nylon, wool, cotton, linen, a starched apron, rubber, and a wet napkin. This is another subject, however, to which I am making reference only to remind you of the fact that in the little world of the baby tremendous things happen.

Alongside the observation of the baby's experiences which are richer when the breast is being used than with a bottle, one has to put all that the mother herself feels and experiences. I need hardly start on this big subject, attempting to describe the sense of achievement which the mother may feel when physiology and anatomy which have been rather a nuisance to her perhaps suddenly make sense and she is able to deal with the fear that the baby will eat her by finding that in fact she has something called milk with which to fob the baby off. I prefer to leave it to your imagination, but it is important to draw attention to the fact that although the feeding of a baby can be very satisfactory, however it is done, the satisfaction is of a different order altogether for the woman who is able to use a part of her own body in this way. The satisfaction links up with her own experiences when she was a baby, and the whole thing goes back to the beginning of time when human beings had scarcely moved from the position of mammalian animal life.

I now come to what I consider to be the most important observation in this field. This has to do with the fact that there is aggressiveness in the live baby. In the course of time the baby begins to kick and scream and scratch. In the feeding situation there was very powerful gum action at the beginning, action of a kind that can very easily cause cracked nipples; and some babies actually hang on with their gums and hurt quite a lot. One cannot say that they are trying to hurt, because there is not enough baby there yet for aggression to mean anything. In the course of time, however, babies have an impulse to bite. This is the beginning of something that has tremendous importance. It belongs to the whole area of ruthlessness and impulse and the use of unprotected objects. Very, very quickly babies protect the breast, and in fact even when babies have teeth they but seldom bite to do damage.

This is not because they do not have the impulse; it is because of something which corresponds to the domestication of the wolf into a dog, and a lion into a cat. With human babies, however, there is a very difficult stage which cannot be avoided. The mother can easily see the baby through this stage in which she is being sometimes destroyed by her baby if she can know about it and protect herself without becoming retaliatory and vindictive.

In other words she has one job when the baby bites and scratches and pulls her hair and kicks, and that is to survive. The baby will do the rest. If she survives, then the baby will find a new meaning to the word love, and a new thing turns up in the baby's life which is fantasy. It is as if the baby can now say to the mother: "I love you because you have survived my destruction of you. In my *dreams* and in *my fantasy* I destroy you whenever I think of you because I love you." It is this that objectifies the mother, puts her in a world that is not part of the baby, and makes her useful.

You can see that we are talking about a baby who is over six months old, and we are talking about a child of two years. We are finding a language which is important in the general description of the child's forward development in which he becomes part of the world instead of living in a protected specialised or subjective world produced by the mother's tremendous capacity to adapt to his needs. But do not let us deny the rudiments of these later things even to the newborn.

It is not our job here to go into this transition which is so important in the life of every child and enables the child to be a part of the world and to use the world and to contribute to the world. The thing that is important here is the recognition of the fact that the basis for this healthy development in the human individual is the survival of the object that has been attacked. In the case of a mother feeding a baby it is her survival not only as a live person, but also as a person who did not change at the critical moment into a vindictive person and did not retaliate. Quite soon other people, including the father, animals and toys, play the same part. It can be seen how tricky it is for the mother to separate out the weaning from the breast from this matter of the survival of the object that has just come up for destruction because of the baby's natural developmental processes. Without going into the extremely interesting complications that belong to this subject it is possible to say quite simply that the essential feature is the survival of the object against this background. It is now possible to look and see the difference between the breast and the bottle. In all cases the survival of the mother is central. Nevertheless, surely there is a difference between the survival of a part of the mother's body and the survival of a bottle. As a comment on this one can cite the extremely traumatic experience for a baby of the breaking of a bottle during the feed as when, for instance, the nursing mother drops the bottle on the floor. Sometimes it is the baby who pushes the bottle over and breaks it.

Perhaps from this observation you can come to it at your own speed and see with me that the survival of a breast which is a part of the mother has a significance which is entirely of a different order from the significance of the survival of a glass bottle. These considerations make me look at breast-feeding as another of those natural phenomena that justify themselves, even if they can, when necessary, be bypassed.

1968

FOUR

The Newborn and His Mother

This subject is so complex that I hesitate to add a new dimension. Nevertheless, it seems to me that if psychology has validity in the study of the newborn, it is only practice that it complicates.[1] In the theoretical realm, any contribution must be either wrong (in which case it leaves the problem untouched), or else has an element of truth in it, in which case it simplifies in the way that truth always does simplify.

The newborn and the mother—the Nursing Couple—is rather a wide subject, and yet I would not like the task of describing what is known about the newborn solo. It is psychology that is under discussion, and I like to assume that if we see a baby, we also see environmental provision, and behind this, we see the mother.

If I say "the mother" more often than "the father," I hope fathers will understand.

It is necessary to recognise the extreme difference that there must be between the mother's psychology and that of the infant. The mother is a sophisticated person. The baby at the beginning is the opposite of sophisticated. Many do not find it easy to ascribe anything that could be called "psychological" to an infant until some weeks or even months have passed, and it must be said that it is doctors rather than mothers who have this difficulty. Could we not say that mothers must be expected to see more than is there, and scientists must be expected to see nothing unless it is first proved?

I heard it said that it is in the newborn that physiology and psychology are one (John Davis).[2] This is a good start. Psychology is a gradual extension from physiology. There is no need for quarrelling over the date of this change. It could be variable according to events. However, the birthdate could be taken as a time when big changes occur in this field, so that the premature infant may be far better off psychologically in an incubator, whereas a postmature infant would not thrive in one but would need human arms and body contact.

It is a special thesis of mine that mothers, unless they are psychiatrically ill, do orientate to their very specialised task during the last months of pregnancy, and that they gradually recover from this in the course of weeks and months after the birth process. I have written a lot about this under the heading: "primacy maternal preoccupation." In this state mothers become able to put themselves into the infant's shoes, so to speak. That is to say, they develop an amazing capacity for identification with the baby, and this makes them able to meet the basic needs of the infant in a way that no machine can imitate, and no teaching can reach. May I take this for granted when I go on to state that the prototype of all infant care is holding? And I mean human holding. I am aware that I am stretching the meaning of the word "holding" to its limits, but I suggest that this is an economical statement, and true enough.

An infant who is held well enough is quite a different thing from one who has not been held well enough. No observation on any infant has any value for me if the quality of the holding is not expressly described. For instance we have just seen a film which had special value for me. A doctor was holding a baby who was walking, illustrating primary walking; if you watched the doctor's tongue you could see that he was being very careful and sensitive, and that the baby was not behaving in the same way that he would behave if somebody else were doing the holding. I think that paediatricians on the whole are people who are able to identify with the infant and to hold an infant, and perhaps it is this capacity to identify that draws people to paediatrics. It seems to me that it is worth mentioning this very obvious point here because sometimes great variations are described in the way an infant behaves, and I think always we should have a film of who it is that is doing the investigation, so that we can judge for ourselves whether this was someone who knew what the infant was feeling like at that time. The reason why this special property of infant care must be mentioned, even in this brief statement, is that in the early stages of emotional development, before the senses have been organised, before there is something there that could be called an autonomous ego, very severe anxieties are experienced. In fact, the word "anxiety" is of no use, the order of infant distress at this stage being of the same order as that which lies behind panic, and panic is already a defence against the agony that makes people commit suicide rather than remember. I have meant to use strong language here. You see two infants; one has been held (in my extended sense of the word) well enough, and there is nothing to prevent a rapid emotional growth, according to inborn tendencies. The other has not had the experience of being held well and growth has had to be distorted and delayed, and some degree of primitive agony has to be carried on into life and living. Let it be said that in the common experience of good-enough holding the mother has been able to supply an auxiliary ego-function, so that the infant has had an ego from an early start, a very feeble, personal ego, but one boosted by the sensitive adaptation of the mother and by her ability to identify with her infant in relation to basic needs. The infant who has not had this experience has either needed to develop premature ego functioning, or else there has developed a muddle.

I find that I must make a bare statement because it is not necessarily true that those who are experienced on the physical side will know anything much about psychological theory. In the psychology of emotional growth the individual's maturational processes, if they are to become actual, need the provision of a facilitating environment. This latter, the facilitating environment, rapidly becomes extremely complex. Only a human being can know an infant in a way that makes possible an increasing complexity of adaptation that is graded to the infant's changing needs. Maturation in the early stages, and indeed all along, is very much a matter of integration. I cannot repeat here all that has been written on details of primitive emotional development, but three main tasks come under this heading: integration of the self, the psyche dwelling in the body, and object-relating. Roughly corresponding to these are the three functions of the mother: holding, handling, and object-presenting. Here is an immense subject in itself. I have made an attempt to state this in "The First Year of Life"[3] but at the moment I am trying to keep nearer to the birthdate.

You will see that I am trying to draw attention to the fact that babies are human from the beginning, that is, assuming that they have a suitable electronic apparatus. I know that here it is not necessary for me to draw attention to the fact that babies are human. This is the common denominator of psychology which belongs to paediatrics.

It is difficult to find a way of stating the beginnings of persons. If someone is there (one could say) to collect experiences, to collate them, to feel and to distinguish between feelings, to be apprehensive at the appropriate moment and to begin to organise defences against mental pain, then I would say the infant IS, and the study of the infant from this point onwards needs to include psychology. [See Chapter 5.]

You will be familiar with various attempts that are being made to study infants by direct observation. Here I need do no more than refer to the bibliography at the end of the recent book: *Determinants of Infant Behavior, Vol. 2.*[4] I shall not be dealing specifically with this type of work, and it might be asked: Why not? since direct observation is needed to make sense to those (and there are many here) whose main line of country is physical science. But I would prefer in these few minutes to try to hand over to you a tiny little bit of my experience as a psychoanalyst and as a psychiatrist of children. I came to this a long time ago out of the practice of physical paediatrics.

How can psychoanalysis bring light to bear on the psychology of the newborn? Obviously a great deal could be said here about psychiatric quirks in the mother, or father; but to make matters manageable, I must assume some health in the parents and study the infant, and I shall also assume physical health in the infant.

Psychoanalysis came to the rescue in the first place by providing a theory of emotional development—the only theory, really. But infantile matters were only seen, in early psychoanalysis, in the symbolism of dreams, in the stuff of psychosomatic symptomatology, in imaginative play. Gradually, psychoanalysis was extended backwards in time to apply to even small children, say two and a half years. This did not give what is needed for our purpose here, however, since little children of two and a half years are a surprisingly long way away from their infancy, unless they are ill and immature.

I am suggesting that the most important development in psychoanalysis, from our point of view here, is the extension of the work of the analyst to include the study of psychotic patients. It is being found that whereas psychoneurosis takes the analyst to the patient's young childhood, schizophrenia takes the analyst to the patient's infancy, to the start, to a stage of almost absolute dependence. Briefly, failures of the facilitating environment have been experienced in these cases at a stage before the immature and dependent ego has acquired a capacity to organise defences.

To narrow down the field still further, the best patient for the research worker who studies the psychology of infancy in this way is the borderline schizophrenic, that is, one who has sufficient functioning personality to be able to come to analysis and to do the irksome work that is necessary if the very ill part of the personality is to gain relief. I can do very little more than introduce you to the way that a severely regressed patient in a steady-going analytic treatment can enrich our understanding of the infant. In effect, the infant is there on the couch, or on the floor or somewhere, and the dependence is there in full strength, the analyst's auxiliary ego function is active, the observation of the infant can be direct except that the patient is an adult who has of course a degree of sophistication. We have to allow for this sophistication which distorts the lens.

I want it to be known that I am aware of the distortions, and that nothing I say is intended to prove anything, though it may illustrate. Here are two examples of my attempt to show that I know something about the *distortions*. First, a schizophrenic boy, aged four. His mother and father are doing the nursing. He has been given very special attention, and as it is not a very severe case he is gradually recovering. In my room he is playing at being born again from his mother. He puts her legs out straight while he is on her lap, and he dives down her legs on to the floor; this is a thing he goes on doing over and over again. It is a particular game derived out of special relationship with the mother, which belongs to the fact of her having become a mental nurse of an ill child instead of a mother. Now this game involves symbolism; it joins up with all the things that ordinary, normal people like doing; and it joins up with the way being born appears in dreams. But is this a direct memory that this boy has of being born? Actually it cannot be so because he was born by caesarian section. The point I am trying to make is that any attempt to see the past in a patient has to be corrected the whole time, and I know this, yet the symbolism holds good.

Second, here is an hysterical woman "remembering" her birth. She goes on to remember it in great detail and she has anxiety dreams about it, and actually in one of the dreams there is the doctor coming, and he has a frock-coat and a top-hat on, and he has a bag, and she remembers what he said to her mother. This, of course, is a typical hysterical distortion, although it does not rule out the possibility that this woman was *also* dealing with actual birth memories. This type of dream material cannot be used in this discussion, and of course she knew about birth processes as an adult, and she had a lot of siblings born after her.

By contrast, I can give a picture of a little child of two playing the part of her new baby sister that was being born. She was trying to get through to a new relationship to the little sister. There was a specific thing that we had to do. She came in and she knew what she wanted, and she put me on the floor amongst the toys and I had to be "herself." Then she went and she got her father in to the room from the waiting-room (mother would have done, but father was there), and she sat on his lap, and now she was going to be the baby being born. To do this she jumped around on father's lap and then she went zoop down to the floor through his legs and she said: "I'm a baby!" And then she watched me and I had a specific function. I was acting her part, you see, and she told me more or less what to do, and I had to be very angry and to knock over toys and say: "I don't want a baby sister" and all that sort of thing, and this had to go on over and over again. You see how easy it was for this little girl to play the birth process by diving down, and she did it about ten times, until her father couldn't stand it any longer, and then she started getting born out of the top of his head; of course, he did not mind that so much because he is a professor and very clever in the head.

I am going to try to get down to some work now, and I would like to talk about the Moro Response. In any case you are all familiar with it, and I do not need to describe how, when the head of the baby is dropped a little, the baby reacts in a predictable way. Here is a detail of what I call *not good enough mothering*, isolated for the purpose of scientific study. This is exactly what a mother would *not* do to her infant. I mean, the reason why doctors do not get slapped in the face when they do it to the infants is because they are doctors, and mothers are frightened of doctors. Of course, one Moro Response does not upset an infant's psychology, but if you were to consider that an infant happened to be born to a mother who just had a thing about the Moro Response and every twenty minutes or so she would just take her infant up and drop the infant's head to see what would happen, this infant would not have a good enough mother. So it is exactly what a mother would not do to her infant. While a mother may have no words to describe her feelings for her baby, when she lifts him, she gathers him together.

Now I want to go over to the analytic treatment of a woman patient. This woman needed a deep and prolonged regression to dependence. Her treatment has lasted many, many years. It has provided me with a unique opportunity for watching infancy, infancy appearing in an adult. The baby who is being tested for Moro Response cannot talk about what happened. On the other hand, the woman, when she recovers from each phase of deep regression, becomes an adult with knowledge and sophistication. She can talk. Allowance has to be made for the complication that she is not only an infant but also a sophisticated person.

In the very early stage of emotional development to which this woman regressed there is a very simple idea of the self. In fact, with good enough mothering, there need be only the very beginnings of an idea of the self, or should I say, none at all. The bad holding (or the environmental failure that elicited the Moro Response) forces on the infant a premature awareness for which the infant is ill-equipped. If the baby could talk, he or she would say: "Here I was, enjoying a continuity of being. I had no thought as to the appropriate diagram for my self, but it could have been a circle." (Interrupting the baby here, it seems to me that people who make the balloons sold in the park on Easter Monday, for instance—it's the same in England—forget that what children like is a simple sphere that doesn't obey the laws of gravity. They don't want ears and noses, and writing on it, and all sorts of things like that.) "A diagram of my self could have been a circle." (This is the baby talking.) "Suddenly two terrible things happened; the continuity of my going on being, which is all I have at present of personal integration, was interrupted, and it was interrupted by my having to be in two parts, a body and a head. The new diagram that I was suddenly forced to make of myself was one of two unconnected circles instead of the one circle that I didn't even have to know about before this awful thing happened." The baby is trying to describe a personality split and also premature awareness produced by the dropping of the head.

The fact is that the infant was subjected to mental pain, and it is just this mental pain that the schizophrenic carries round as a memory and a threat, and that makes suicide a sensible alternative to living.

I have not finished with my woman patient yet. You may ask why it is that there is a drive in my patient to regress to dependence, and I first must answer this. In the so-called "borderline" case there is a drive towards progress in the emotional development that has been held up. There is no way of remembering very early experiences except by a re-experiencing of them, and as these experiences were excessively painful at the time, because they came when the ego was unorganised and the auxiliary ego of the mothering was faulty, the re-experiencing has to be done in a carefully prepared and tested situation, such as the setting provided by the psychoanalyst. Moreover, the analyst is there in person, so that when all goes well, the patient has someone to hate for the original failure of the facilitating environment which distorted the maturational processes.

In the particular case of this patient, very many details of infancy turned up and these could be discussed with her. Now it happens that with this particular patient I did a very rare thing in my practice. In the psychoanalysis of this peculiar case at one point I found myself with this patient on the couch and her head in my hand. Such actual contact is rare in psychoanalytic work and I did this very naughty thing which doesn't belong to psychoanalysis at all. I tested what it would be like to just drop her head and see if her Moro Response would show up. Of course, I knew what would happen. The patient suffered very severe mental agony. This was because of her being split into two, and from there we could go on in the end to find out what was the psychological significance of the mental agony. She was able eventually to let me know what had happened to her infant self; she taught me that the circle became two circles at that moment, and the experience was an example of a split in the personality made by a specific failure of the facilitating environment, a failure of ego-augmentation.

It is very rare that I have a chance to make a test of this kind because my job as therapist is to not make these very mistakes or failures that cause intolerable mental pain. I cannot sacrifice a patient on the altar of science. But the terrible thing is that in the course of time one makes all the mistakes simply by being human, so tests get made and we deal with the results as best we can. In this one instance I made a test deliberately.

From this one detail one can see that the Moro Response *may or may not* depend on the existence of a reflex arc. I am simply saying that it does not need to. There *need* not be a neurological background, or the response can be both neurophysiological and psychological. The one can change into the other. What I am suggesting is that it is not safe to ignore the psychology if one is in search of a complete statement.

There are only a few of these very primitive agonies. They include, for instance, falling for ever; all kinds of disintegration and things that disunite the psyche and the body. It will be readily seen that these are matters that concern forward movement in the emotional development that takes place if there is good enough mothering—forward movement of the emotional development of the infant. And at the same time, in terms of schizophrenia, there is backward movement. The schizophrenic has a drive to get into touch with the very processes which spoil the forward movement of the very early phase, which concerns the neonatal period. And this sort of way of looking at schizophrenia contributes both to the understanding of schizophrenia and to the understanding of infants.

There is a great deal of work to be done on the subject of birth memories and what the experience of birth means to the infant. I have no time to develop this theme here. But I want to give the dream of a schizophrenic girl who had a difficult birth. Before doing so, however, I must postulate a normal birth—that is, psychologically—in which psychological trauma is minimal. In a normal birth, from the infant's point of view, the infant brought about the birth because he or she was ready for it; and by squirming efforts or because of a need to breathe or something, the baby did something, so that from the point of view of the baby the birth is something "brought about by the baby." I think this is not only normal, but common. These felicitous events do not appear in our analytic treatments as much as they do in symbolism and in imaginative invention and in play. It is *the thing that has gone wrong* that comes up for treatment, and one of these things is delay which is infinite because there is no reason for the baby to expect an outcome.

Now I turn to the schizophrenic girl to whom I gave 2500 hours of my time. She had an exceptionally high I.Q.—about 180, I think. And she came for treatment asking me whether I would enable her to commit suicide for the right reason instead of for the wrong reason. In this I failed. When she had this dream she was at the point at which she was re-experiencing birth with all the distortions of a very intelligent grown woman. She had a highly neurotic mother, and there is evidence that she had been awakened to awareness, if such a thing is possible (as I believe it is), a few days before the birthdate because the mother suffered a severe shock. Then the birth was complicated by placenta praevia, not discovered early enough. This girl had started life on the wrong foot, and she never got into step.

In the middle of this new attempt on her part to encompass the effects of all this she borrowed my copy of Rank's *Trauma of Birth.* You see, another complication. These complications all have to be accepted in the kind of work I am reporting, and allowed for. The night after she read this book she had a dream which she felt was highly significant, and I think you will see that it was. For the analyst such dreams are daily bread. If you are used to dreams you will see how it includes a statement of her trust in me—the analyst—as the person holding her, that is to say, managing her case and doing her analysis. The dream also gives the picture of her permanent paranoid state, her vulnerability, her essential rawness against which she had organised every possible defence. A psychoanalyst here would draw attention to the fact that there are very many determinants of this dream which could not possibly have been as early as the birthdate. Nevertheless, I am giving it to you as an illustration. Here is her idea of having just been born:

She dreamed she was under a pile of gravel. Her whole body at the surface was extremely sensitive to a degree which it was hardly possible to imagine. Her skin was burned, which was her way of saying that it was extremely sensitive and vulnerable. She was burned all over. She knew that if anyone came and *did anything at all* to her, the pain would be just impossible to bear, both physical and mental. She knew of the danger that people would come and take the gravel off and do things to her in order to cure her, and the situation was intolerable. She emphasized that along with this were intolerable feelings comparable with those which belonged to her suicide attempt. (She had made two suicide attempts and afterwards she actually committed suicide.) She said: "You can't just bear anything any longer, the awfulness of having a body at all, and the mind that has just had too much. It was the entirety of it, the completeness of the job that made it so impossible. If only people would leave me alone; if only people wouldn't keep getting at me." However, what happened in the dream was that someone came and poured oil over the gravel, with her inside it. The oil came through and came on her skin and covered her. She was then left without any interference whatever for three weeks, at the end of which time the gravel could be removed without pain. There was, however, a little sore patch between her breasts, "a triangular area which the oil had not reached—from which there came something like a little penis or cord. This had to be attended to, and of course it was slightly painful but quite bearable. It simply didn't matter. Someone just pulled it off."

From this dream I think you can get (amongst the many other things) the idea of what it might feel like to have just been born. This was not one of those births that I call a normal birth because of the premature aware-ness that resulted from delays in the birth process.

I do know that some will find this approach unconvincing. What I have attempted to do, however, is to draw attention to work which is being done of which you might not have heard because it belongs to an alien discipline. The theory of schizophrenia as an undoing of the maturational processes of earliest infancy has much to teach the psychiatrist; also it has much, I believe, to teach the paediatrician and the neurologist and the psychologist about babies and their mothers.

1964

Notes

1. Winnicott was addressing paediatricians here. See p. 239.
2. Paediatric colleague of Winnicott at Paddington Green Children's Hospital.
3. In *The Family and Individual Development.* London: Tavistock Publications, 1965.
4. Ciba Foundation. London: Tavistock Publications, 1961.

FIVE

The Beginning of
the Individual

In a letter to *The Times* dated 3rd December 1966, Dr. Fisher[1] took up once more for discussion the question: when does the individual start? He was of course dealing with the Roman Catholic view that abortion is murder. The main thing in the letter was that surely it is the time of birth that is the obvious moment at which the individual starts. This is a point of view which could be shared by many but it seems to call for a statement of the various developmental stages which could be used in a discussion of this kind.

Here then is a statement which can be used and certainly it can be widened in scope. What seems to be needed is an acceptance of some degree of need for economy in the use of ideas along with the inclusion of reference to all the relevant physical and psychological phenomena.

(1) "Conceived of." The beginning of children is when they are conceived of. They turn up in the play of many children of any age after 2 years. It is part of the stuff of dreams and of many occupations. After marriage there comes a time when the idea of children begins to appear. Needless to say conceiving of children does not produce them, and there is a sad example of this in Charles Lamb's "Dream Child" in the *Essays of Elia*.

(2) Conception. This is a physical fact. Conception depends on the fertilization of an ovum and the firm lodging of the fertilized ovum in the endometrium of the uterus. There is no known case of parthenogenesis, except in mythology. In rare cases the conception occurs outside the uterus in the peritoneal cavity. The psychology of conception can be said to be of one kind or another, that is to say conceiving of has turned into conception or else conception is an accident. It is probable that we ought to associate the word *normal* with the idea of the child as a little accident and that it is sentimental to put too much stress on the idea that the child was conceived in relation to any conscious wish. There is indeed quite a lot to be said for the little accident theory of conception with the parents surprised at first, even annoyed because of the immense disruption of their lives which this fact entails. It is a disaster which only turns into the opposite in favourable circumstances when the parents quickly or slowly come round to the idea that this is exactly the disaster they need.

(3) The Brain as an Organ. The next stage must be an indefinite one and it could be split up into sub-stages. It would be logical to take the exact age at which it is dangerous for a mother to have German measles; in other words, the period somewhere about two to three months when there is very rapid growth at the inception of the changes which lead to there being a brain. It is a very different matter to think of a child as a human being before there is a brain and to think of the child as a human being once a brain has become anatomically established. These arguments will not of course affect those who have a tremendous emotional bias towards the idea that the human being starts at the time of the fertilization of the ovum with or without its lodgement in a suitable medium. A consideration of this stage carries with it a discussion as to whether a child who is born an encephalic is a human being, and there is infinite room for disagreement in regard to the status of children with the various degrees of mental defect based on faulty development of the individual child's computer apparatus. In practice we have no doubt that some backward children are human beings, but we may find degrees of backwardness which make us want to have a category of backwardness that puts a child outside classification as human. Tremendous emotions must be roused in any discussion on either the existence of such a borderline, or the placing of children relative to it.

(4) Quickening. Between (3) and (5) comes the evidence that the foetus is "alive and kicking." This which is of importance to the parents is not, however, part of the present series in that it is not constant. It is variable in its timing and it can occur along with any degree of failure of development of the brain tissue.

(5) Viability.   At some stage or other the unborn child can be said to be viable in the sense that if born prematurely there is a chance of survival. The chance of survival depends to a very great extent on the environmental provision. Infants have been born at six months and by very careful medical and nursing care they have been brought forward even to what appears to be a normality at the time when they should have been born. Much work has been done on the subsequent history of premature children, but for the purpose of this statement it must be taken that if one child who was born at six months has been reared to health then in theory viability is at six months, and for many this must seem to be an important stage in any discussion about the beginning of the individual.

(6) Psychology Becoming Meaningful.   At some stage or other in the development of the healthy human being there is a change which can only be described by saying that no anatomy and physiology becomes added psychology. The brain as an organ makes possible the registering of experiences and the accumulation of data and the beginnings of a sorting out of phenomena and their classification. Such words as *frustration* begin to have meaning in the sense that the infant is able to hold in the mind the idea that something was expected but the expectation was not completely fulfilled. On the basis of this kind of descriptive account one can look at the evidence for the existence of an individual person before the birth process. This must be debatable territory in any discussion, but the psychoanalyst, more than any other type of careful observer, finds himself in the position of being certain from clinical experience that the individual's psychological life is not exactly adjusted to the time of birth. The easiest way to get at this problem is to take into consideration the contrast between premature and postmature births. The psychoanalyst is forced to the conclusion that the right time for birth in the psychological sense is the full-term moment when physiologically it can also be said that the time has come for the child to leave the womb. It is even possible to formulate the idea of a normal birth, that is to say one that happens at the right moment from the infant's point of view, so that in so far as there is any mind organization at the time the infant is able to feel the whole process as natural. It would be too complicated to take into consideration here the birth traumata of various kinds, although these also throw light on this difficult problem. It is easier to make use of the very great psychological differences that can be observed between premature and postmature infants. In brief description, the premature infant finds the incubator a natural environment whereas for the postmature infant, perhaps born with a thumb in the mouth and already frustrated, an incubator existence is exactly wrong. This theme could be developed at length, but the main conclusion is that Dr. Fisher's remark about the individual starting at birth turns out to need elaboration.

(7) Birth. This is the moment chosen by Dr. Fisher in his letter, and it perhaps refers more to the change in the mother or in the parents than to the change in the infant. Physiologically the changes brought about by birth are tremendous as is well known, but it is not necessary to think that something so momentous as the beginning of the individual is exactly linked with the birth process. Possibly this notion must be abandoned in this kind of discussion. The thing in favour of including the birth process here is the immense change that takes place in the attitude of the parents. The child might have been born dead, or might have been a monster, but here is the baby, recognised by all the world as an individual.

(8) Me–Not-me. From this point on physiology can be left to take care of itself. It includes genetic factors which determine the tendency towards maturation in the individual, and it is affected by physical disease processes which may or may not supervene. It would not be disputed that a child is an individual if encephalitis, for instance, should lead to a distortion of personality growth. The discussion is therefore now in the realm of psychology, but there are two kinds of psychology. Academic psychology, as it can be called, concerns physical phenomena. The psychology that is relevant here concerns emotional factors, the establishment of the personality, and the gradual and graduated journey from absolute dependence through relative dependence towards independence. A great deal depends on the environmental provision so that it is not possible to describe an infant or a small child without including a description of the care which is only gradually becoming separate from the individual. In other words the maturational processes facilitated in an extremely complex way by the human beings who have care of the infant reach forward towards the child's repudiation of what is not-ME, and the establishment of what is ME. There comes a time when, if the infant could speak, he or she would say I AM. This stage

having been reached, further progress has to be made in the firm establishment of the stage which at first alternates with renewed contact with the more primitive stage in which everything is merged or out of which the various elements have not been properly separated from each other. There is a very definite moment here in the life of every child, although it may be diffused in terms of fixed time, when the child has realised his or her own existence and has some kind of established identity not in the mind of observers but in the mind of the child. This would be a good moment to choose for talking about the beginning of the individual, but it is of course too late in any discussion of religious practice.

(9) Objectivity. Along with these changes that belong to the growth of the individual comes the capacity of the individual child gradually to allow for the fact that whereas inner psychic reality remains personal however enriched by the perception of the environment, nevertheless there is an environment and there is a world that is external to the child that could be called actual. The difference between these two extremes is softened by the adaptation of the mother and of the parents and of the family and of those who have care of the infant and small child, but eventually the child accepts the reality principle and benefits greatly from being able to do so. All these things are a matter of growth, and they do not necessarily take place in the case of any one child who may have had a muddled environmental provision. Here again is a new stage which when reached makes for an obvious answer to the question: Is the child an individual yet?

(10) Moral Code. Interwoven with these phenomena there is the development of a personal moral code, a matter which concerns religious teachers very much. At the two extremes there are those who cannot take the risk but must plant a moral code from the beginning on the infant, and those who risk everything to enable the individual to grow a personal moral code. The up-bringing of children lies somewhere between these two extremes, but the theory of the beginning of the individual for society as well as for religious controversialists must take into account the point in time when a child feels responsible for his or her ideas and actions.

(11) Play and Cultural Experience. As a reward one might say for a satisfactory interweaving of environmental influences with the inherited maturational processes of the individual there comes about an establishment of an intermediate area which turns out to be of great importance in the individual's life. It starts with play of the intense kind that belongs only to small children and it can develop into a cultural life of infinite richness. These things, however, belong to health, and they cannot be assumed to be a fact. In so far as they exist in the case of an individual child, so they can be said to be a vitally important part of that individual.

(12) The Personal Psychic Reality.   The individual according to his or her experiences and his or her capacity to store experiences develops a capacity to believe in . . . or to trust. According to the immediate cultural provision the child will be guided towards a belief in this or that or the other, but the basis is the capacity which is based on accumulated experience both of fact and of dream. These matters although of supreme importance in a description of the individual are already too sophisticated for inclusion in a discussion on Where does the individual start? It is assumed, however, that those who are interested in the beginnings are also interested in where the individual may reach in human growth.

1966

Note

1. Then Archbishop of Canterbury.

SIX

Environmental Health in Infancy

As we consider certain problems of infancy, you[1] bring to the issues, each in a special way, an experience of the management of infants based on their growth and development and on distortions of development due to physical factors. I wish to talk about the difficulties that do not depend on physical illness. To simplify my subject I must assume that the baby is well in a physical sense. I think you will not mind my drawing attention to the nonphysical aspects of baby care since in your practice you are all the time dealing with these problems and your interest does necessarily extend outside the field of actual physical illness.

As you probably know I started off as a paediatrician and gradually changed over into being a psychoanalyst and a child psychiatrist, and the fact that I was originally a physically minded doctor has greatly influenced my work. I do happen to have a very big volume of experience which simply arises out of the fact that I have been in active practice for forty-five years and in that time one does accumulate quite a lot of data. I can do little more here than point towards the highly complex theory of the emotional development of the human individual as a person. What I must do, however, for my own sake, is to convey some of the strength of feeling which I have accumulated in these forty-five years.

It is strange but the training of doctors and nurses on the physical side undoubtedly drains away something from their interest in infants as human beings. When I myself started I was conscious of an inability in myself to carry my natural capacity for empathy with children back to include empathy with babies. I was fully aware of this as a deficiency and it was a great relief to me when gradually I became able to feel myself into the infant-mother or infant-parent relationship. I think many who are trained on the physical side do have the same sort of block that I had myself, and they have to do a great deal of work on themselves in order to become able to stand in the baby's shoes. I am aware that this is a rather funny figure of speech since babies are not born with shoes on, but I think you will understand my meaning.

It is important for the paediatrician to know about human affairs as they are at the beginning of the life of a new individual since when they talk to parents they must be able to know about the parents' important function. The doctor comes in when there is illness, but the parents have their importance all the time, apart from illness in the child. It is a terrible complication for a mother and for parents when the doctor that they call in with such confidence if the child has pneumonia is blind to all that they do in adaptation to the baby's needs when the child has not got an illness. For example, the vast majority of difficulties in infant feeding have nothing to do with infection or with the biochemical unsuitability of the milk. They have to do with the immense problem that every mother has in adapting to the needs of a new baby. She has to do this on her own because no two babies are alike and in any case no two mothers are alike and one mother is never the same with each child. The mother cannot learn to do what is needed of her either from books or from nurses or from doctors. She may have learned a great deal from having been an infant and also from watching parents with babies and from taking part in the care of siblings, and most of all she has learned a great deal of vital importance when playing at mothers and fathers at a tender age.

It is true that some mothers are able to get help of a limited kind from books, but it must be remembered that if a mother goes to a book or to someone for advice and tries to learn what she has to do we already wonder whether she is fitted for the job. She has to know about it from a deeper level and not necessarily from that part of the mind which has words for everything. The main things that a mother does with the baby cannot be done through words. This is very obvious but it is also a very easy thing to forget. In my long experience I have had a chance to know many doctors and nurses and teachers who thought they could tell mothers what to do and who spent a lot of their time giving parents instruction, and then I have watched them when they became mothers and fathers and have had long talks with them about their difficulties, and I have found that many had to forget all they thought they knew and, in fact, had been teaching.

Quite frequently they found that what they knew in this way interfered so much at the beginning that they were not able to be natural with their own first child. Gradually they managed to shed this useless layer of knowledge that is intertwined with words and settle down to involvement with this one baby.

Holding and Handling

Infant care can be described in terms of holding, especially if one allows the meaning of the term to expand as the baby grows older and the baby's world grows more complex. Eventually the term can usefully include the function of the family unit, and in a more sophisticated way the same term may be employed to describe case-work, as practised by the caring professions.

At the beginning, however, it is the physical holding of the physical frame that provides the psychology that can be good or bad. Good holding and handling facilitates the maturational processes and bad holding means repeatedly interrupting those processes because of the baby's reactions to failures of adaptation.

Facilitation, in this context, means that there is adaptation to basic need, and this happens to be something that cannot be done except by a human being. An incubator is adequate for the premature infant, but at the birthdate the baby has maturity that needs human care, even if it is valuable for the mother to be able to use a cot or a pram. The human mother can adapt to the baby's needs at this early stage because she has no other interest, for the time being.

It is the luck of most babies to be held well most of the time. On this they build confidence in a friendly world, but, more important, because of being held well enough they are able to make the grade in their very rapid emotional growth. The basis of personality is being laid down well if the baby is held well enough. Babies do not remember being held well—what they remember is the traumatic experience of not being held well enough.

Mothers know about these things and take it all for granted. They feel physically hurt when someone, maybe the doctor doing a Moro reflex, fails to protect their baby, under their eyes, from insult.

Insult is the word that conveys the effect of bad holding on the baby, and it can be said that the majority of babies come through the early weeks or months without insult. Often, I fear it is true, the insults that do occur have been given by doctors and nurses who do not happen to be at the moment concerned as the mother is with adaptation to the basic needs of the baby.

Be sure, these insults do matter. In our work with older children and with adults we find these insults add up to a sense of insecurity as well as the other thing which is that the process of development is held up by the reactions to insult which fragment the thread of continuity that is the child.

Object-Relating

When dealing with breast or bottle feeding as paediatricians you will be thinking in terms of the physiology of breast-feeding or of bottle-feeding, and your knowledge of biochemistry has special importance here. What I am drawing your attention to is the fact that when the mother and the baby come to terms with each other in the feeding situation this is initiation of a human relationship. This sets the pattern for the child's capacity for relating to objects and to the world.

My long experience has made me see that the pattern for relating to objects is laid down in babyhood and that it does matter what happens even at the beginning. It is only too easy to think in terms of reflexes. Doctors and nurses should never fall into the trap of thinking that because reflexes are a fact they are the whole story.

The baby is a human being, immature and highly dependent, and is an individual having and storing experiences. This has immense practical importance for all concerned in the management of the earliest stages. A really high proportion of mothers could establish breast-feeding if the doctors and nurses on whom they are so dependent could accept the fact that it is only the mother who can properly perform this task. She can be hindered, and she can be helped by being given support in all other respects. She cannot be taught.

There are very subtle things that the mother knows intuitively and without any intellectual appreciation of what is happening, and which she can only arrive at by being left alone and given full responsibility in this limited area. She knows, for instance, that the basis of *feeding* is *not feeding*.

It is an insult, or shall I say a kind of rape, when an exasperated nurse pushes the mother's nipple or the nipple of the bottle into the baby's mouth and starts up a reflex. No mother left on her own would do this.

A period of time is needed for many babies before they begin to search, and when they find an object they do not necessarily want immediately to make a meal of it. They want to play round with hands and mouth, and perhaps they want to hang on with their gums. There is a wide range of variation here according to infant and mother.

This is the beginning not just of feeding; it is the beginning of object-relating. The whole relationship of this new individual to the actual world has to be based on the way things start up and the pattern that gradually develops according to the experience that belongs to this human interrelationship of baby and mother.

Here again is a huge subject, one that even concerns philosophers since the paradox has to be accepted that what the baby creates was already there, and that in fact the thing that the baby creates is part of the mother which was found.

The point is that it would not have been found had the mother not been in the special state that mothers are in when they can present themselves in such a way that they are found more or less at the right moment and in the right place. This is called adaptation to need, which enables the baby to discover the world creatively.

What can we do if we are unable to teach mothers in these matters of management? What we as doctors and nurses can do is *to avoid interfering.* It is simple really. We have to know what is our speciality and we have to know just in what way mothers do need medical and nursing care. In the knowledge of this we can very easily give to the mother just that which she alone can do.

When we are treating older children and grown-up people we find that a great deal of the disturbance which we have to deal with in terms of personality distortion turns out in the end to have been avoidable; often it has been caused by doctors and nurses or by faulty medical ideas. We repeatedly find that if a doctor or a nurse or some would-be helper had not interfered with the extremely subtle natural processes which belong to the mother-infant relationship, disturbances of development could perhaps have been prevented.

Naturally, as the baby grows a little older so life becomes more and more complex. The mother's failures at adaptation are themselves an adaptation to the child's growing need to react to frustration, to be angry, and to play about with repudiation in such a way that acceptance becomes more and more significant and exciting. Mothers and fathers, on the whole, grow up with each child in a very subtle way.

Rather quickly the baby turns into a person easily recognisable as human, but really the baby has been a human from the time of birth. The sooner we all recognise this the better.

Allow me to refer to a third area of management.

Management of Excretions

At first the baby is very much concerned with intake. This includes the discovery of objects, and the recognition of them by sight and smell and the building up of the beginnings of object constancy, by which I mean that an object gains importance in itself, not simply as one of a type, or as something that can bring satisfaction.

By the process of emotional growth and development and the maturation that corresponds with developing brain tissue the baby becomes able to take a wider view of the alimentary canal and the feeding process. Let us say that the baby in the early weeks and months has known a great deal about intake, and at the same time has been excreting faeces and urine. Intake has been complicated by all sorts of outward bound activities that have had no meaning to the baby as a person.

By the age of six or seven months the baby is demonstrably able to link excretion with intake. The baby who is rapidly growing in awareness develops an interest in the inside, that is the area that exists between mouth and anus. The same is true of the mind, so that both in mind and body the baby has become a container.

From now on there are two kinds of excretion. One is felt to be harmful, and we use the word *bad* for this, and the baby needs the mother to dispose of it. The other is felt to be good, and can be material for a gift to be given in a moment of love. Along with these feelings about function there goes the corresponding development in mind and psyche.

The reason why doctors and nurses should not interfere when parents let babies find their own way of becoming what is called "clean" or "dry" is that each baby takes time to get to the sureness of a distinction between the good and the bad stuff, and to a confidence in the proper disposal of what is to be disposed of.

The mother knows in a highly sensitive way what her baby feels about these things, because, temporarily, she is attuned to these things. She helps the baby to get rid of screaming and yelling and kicking and excretory materials, and she is ready to receive the love gifts in the moments when these are ready. She meets the baby's potential in the way that the baby has potentiality at the moment, and in the exact phase of development at which the baby happens to be at the moment.

Training makes all this subtle communication between the baby and the mother much more difficult and distorts the pattern that is being laid down for appropriate giving and for constructive effort.

Worse than interference by strict training is active and specific interference by anal and urethral manipulations and by suppositories and enemas. *These are practically never necessary* and it cannot be urged too strongly that those who care for babies be left to put into practice their respect for the babies' natural functions.

Of course there are mothers and mother-figures who cannot allow natural functions to hold sway, but these are the exceptions; at any rate we must not base our attitude on what we observe that is unnatural and ill and non-maternal.

I cannot prove these matters except to those who are prepared to give me a very great deal of time. But if you can believe me then I invite you to accept that much more important than the *treatment* of psychiatric disturbance (which has been my job) is *prophylaxis;* this can be instituted immediately, not by teaching mothers how to be mothers, but by getting doctors and nurses to understand that they *must not interfere* with the delicate mechanisms that are shown to exist in the establishment of the interpersonal relationships as between baby and mother.

Note

1. Winnicott was addressing the Paediatric Section of the Royal Society of Medicine. See p. 239.

SEVEN

The Contribution of Psychoanalysis to Midwifery

It should be remembered that it is the midwife's skill, based on a scientific knowledge of the physical phenomena, that gives her patients the confidence in her that they need. Without this basic skill on the physical side she may study psychology in vain, because she will not be able to substitute psychological insight for knowing what to do when a placenta praevia complicates the birth process. However, given the requisite knowledge and skill, there is no doubt that the midwife can add greatly to her value by acquiring also an understanding of her patient as a human being.

Place of Psychoanalysis

How does psychoanalysis come into the subject of midwifery? In the first place, through its minute study of detail in long and arduous treatments of individual people. Psychoanalysis is beginning to throw light on all sorts of abnormality such as menorrhagia, repeated abortion, morning sickness, primary uterine inertia; and many other physical states can sometimes have as part of their cause a conflict in the unconscious emotional life of the patient. Much has been written about these psychosomatic disorders. Here, however, I am concerned with another aspect of the psychoanalytic contribution: I will try to indicate, in general terms, the effect of psychoanalytic theories on the relationships between the doctor, the nurse, and the patient, with reference to the situation of childbirth.

Psychoanalysis has already led to a very big change in emphasis which shows itself in the attitude of midwives today compared with those of twenty years ago. It is now accepted that the midwife wants to add to her essential basic skill some assessment of the patient as a person—a person who was born, was once an infant, has played at mothers and fathers, has been scared of the developments that come at puberty, has experimented with new-found adolescent urges, has taken the plunge and has married (perhaps), and has either by design or by accident fallen with child.

If the patient is in hospital she is concerned about the home to which she will return, and in any case there is the change which the birth of the baby will make to her personal life, to her relationship with her husband, and to the parents of both herself and her husband. Often, also, complications are to be expected in her relationship to her other children, and in the feelings of the children towards each other.

If we all become persons in our work, then the work becomes much more interesting and rewarding. We have, in this situation, four persons to consider, and four points of view. First there is *the woman,* who is in a very special state which is like an illness, except that it is normal. *The father,* to some extent, is in a similar state, and if he is left out the result is a great impoverishment. *The infant* at birth is already a person, and there is all the difference between good and bad management from the infant's point of view. And then *the midwife.* She is not only a technician, she is also human; she has feelings and moods, excitements and disappointments; perhaps she would like to be the mother, or the baby, or the father, or all in turn. Usually she is pleased and sometimes she feels frustrated to be the midwife.

Essentially Natural Process

One general idea goes right through what I have to say: that is, that there are natural processes which underlie all that is taking place; and we do good work as doctors and nurses only if we respect and facilitate these natural processes.

Mothers had babies for thousands of years before midwives appeared on the scene, and it is likely that midwives first came to deal with superstition. The modern way of dealing with superstition is the adoption of a scientific attitude, science being based on objective observation. Modern training, based on science, equips the midwife to ward off superstitious practices. What about fathers? Fathers had a definite function before doctors and the welfare state took it over: they not only felt themselves the feelings of their women, and went through some of the agony, but also they took part, warding off external and unpredictable impingements, and enabling the mother to become preoccupied, to have but one concern, the care of the baby that is there in her body or in her arms.

Change in Attitude to the Infant

There has been an evolution of attitude with regard to the infant. I suppose that throughout the ages parents have assumed that the infant was a person, seeing in the infant much more than was there—a little man or woman. Science at first rejected this, pointing out that the infant is not just a little adult, and for a long time infants were regarded by objective observers as scarcely human till they started to talk. Recently, however, it has been found that infants are indeed human, though appropriately infantile. Psychoanalysis has been gradually showing that even the birth process is not lost on the infant, and that there can be a normal or an abnormal birth from the infant's point of view. Possibly every detail of the birth (as felt by the infant) is recorded in the infant's mind, and normally this shows in the pleasure that people get in games that symbolize the various phenomena that the infant experienced—turning over, falling, sensations belonging to the change from being bathed in fluid to being on dry land, from being at one temperature to being forced to adjust to temperature change, from being supplied by pipeline to being dependent for air and food on personal effort.

The Healthy Mother

One of the difficulties that is encountered with regard to the midwife's attitude to the mother ranges round the problem of diagnosis. (Here I do not mean the diagnosis of the bodily state, which must be left to the nurse and the doctor, nor will I refer to bodily abnormality; I am concerned with the healthy and the unhealthy in the psychiatric sense.) Let us start with the normal end of the problem.

At the healthy extreme the patient is not a patient, but is a perfectly healthy and mature person, quite capable of making her own decisions on major matters, and perhaps more grown-up than the midwife who attends her. She happens to be in a dependent state because of her condition. Temporarily she puts herself in the nurse's hands, and to be able to do that in itself implies health and maturity. In this case the nurse respects the mother's independence for as long as possible, and even throughout the labour if the confinement is easy and normal. In the same way, she accepts the complete dependency of the many mothers who can go through the experience of childbirth only by handing over all control to the person in attendance.

Relationship of Mother, Doctor, and Nurse

I suggest that it is because the healthy mother is mature or adult that she cannot hand over the controls to a nurse and a doctor whom she does not know. She gets to know them first, and this is the important thing of the period leading up to the time of the confinement. She either trusts them, in which case she will forgive them even if they make a mistake; or else she does not trust them, in which case the whole experience is spoiled for her; she fears to hand over, and attempts to manage herself, or actually fears her condition; and she will blame them for whatever goes wrong whether it is their fault or not. And rightly so, if they failed to let her get to know them.

I put first and foremost this matter of the mother and the doctor and nurse getting to know each other, and of continuity of contact, if possible, throughout the pregnancy. If this cannot be achieved, then at least there must be a very definite contact with the person who is to attend the actual confinement, well before the expected date of the confinement.

A hospital set-up which does not make it possible for a woman to know in advance who will be her doctor and her nurse at the time of the confinement is no good, even if it be the most modern, well-equipped, sterile, chromium-plated clinic in the country. It is this sort of thing that makes mothers decide to have their babies at home, with the family practitioner in charge, and with hospital facilities available only in case of serious emergency. I personally think that mothers should be fully supported in their idea when they want a home confinement, and that it would be a bad thing if in the attempt to provide ideal physical care there should come a time when the home confinement would not be practicable.

A full explanation of the process of labour and childbirth should be given to the mother by the person to whom she has given her confidence, and this goes a long way towards dispelling such frightening and incorrect information as may have come her way. It is the healthy woman who most needs this and who can make best use of the true facts.

Is it not true that when a healthy and mature woman who is in a healthy relation to her husband and family reaches the moment of childbirth, she is in need of all the immense skill that the nurse has acquired? She is in need of the nurse's presence, and of her power to help in the right way and at the right moment, should something go wrong. But all the same she is in the grip of natural forces and of a process that is as automatic as ingestion, digestion, and elimination, and the more it can be left to nature to get on with it the better it is for the woman and the baby.

One of my patients, who has had two children, and who is now gradually, so it seems, coming through a very difficult treatment in which she herself had to start again—in order to free herself from the influences on her early development of her difficult mother—wrote as follows: ". . . even allowing for the woman to be fairly emotionally mature, the whole process of labour and childbirth breaks down so many controls that one wants all the care, consideration, encouragement and familiarity of the one person looking after you, as a child needs a mother to see it through (each) one of the new and big experiences encountered in its development."

Nevertheless, with reference to the natural process of childbirth one thing can seldom be forgotten, the fact that the human infant has an absurdly big head.

The Unhealthy Mother

In contrast to the healthy, mature woman who comes under the midwife's care there is the woman who is ill, that is, emotionally immature, or not orientated to the part the woman plays in nature's comic opera; or who is perhaps depressed, anxious, suspicious, or just muddled. In such cases, the nurse must be able to make a diagnosis, and here is another reason why she needs to know her patient before she gets into the special and uncomfortable state that belongs to late pregnancy. The midwife certainly needs special training in the diagnosis of psychiatrically ill adults, so that she may be free to treat as healthy those who are healthy. Naturally the immature or otherwise unhealthy mother needs help in some special way from the person who has charge of her case: where the normal woman needs instruction, the ill one needs reassurance; the ill mother may test the nurse's tolerance and make herself a positive nuisance, and perhaps she may need to be restrained if she should become maniacal. But this is rather a matter of common sense, of meeting need with appropriate action, or studied inaction.

In the case of the healthy mother and father, the ordinary case, the midwife is the employee, and she has the satisfaction of being able to give the help that she is employed to give. In the case of the mother who is in some way ill, who is unable to be fully adult, the midwife is the nurse acting with the doctor in the management of a patient—her employer is the agency, the hospital service. It would be terrible if this adaptation to ill health should ever swamp a natural procedure adapted not to illness but to life.

Of course many patients come in between the two extremes I have devised for descriptive purposes. What I wish to emphasize is that the observation that many mothers are hysterical or fussy or self-destructive should not make midwives fail to give health its due and emotional maturity its place; should not lead them to class all their patients as childish, when in fact the majority are fully capable except in the actual matters which they must be able to leave to the nurse. For the best are healthy; it is the healthy women who are the mothers and wives (and midwives) who add richness to mere efficiency, add the positive gain to the routine that is successful merely because it is without mishap.

Management of the Mother with Her Baby

Let us now consider the management of the mother after the birth, in her first relationship to the newborn baby. How is it that when we give mothers a chance to speak freely and to remember back we so often come across a comment of the following kind? (I quote from a case description given by a colleague, but time after time I myself have been told the same.)

He had a normal birth and his parents wanted him. Apparently he sucked well immediately after delivery but was not actually put to the breast for thirty-six hours. He was then difficult and sleepy, and for the next fortnight the feeding situation was most unsatisfactory. Mother felt that the nurses were unsympathetic, that they didn't leave her long enough with the baby. She says that they forced his mouth onto the breast, held his chin to make him suck, and pinched his nose to take him off the breast. When she had him at home she felt that she established normal breast-feeding without any difficulty.

I do not know whether nurses know that this is how women complain. Perhaps they are never in the position to hear their remarks, and of course mothers are not likely to complain to the nurse to whom they certainly owe much. Also, I must not believe that what mothers say to me gives an accurate picture. I must be prepared to find the imagination at work, as indeed it ought to be, since we are not just bundles of facts; and what our experiences feel like to us and the way they get interwoven with our dreams is all part of the total thing called life, and individual experience.

Sensitive Post-Natal State

In our specialized psychoanalytic work we do find that the mother who has just had a baby is in a very sensitive state, and that she is very liable for a week or two to believe in the existence of a woman who is a persecutor. I believe there is a corresponding tendency that we must allow for in the midwife, who can easily at this time slip over into becoming a dominating figure. Certainly it often happens that the two things meet: a mother who feels persecuted and a monthly nurse who drives on as if actuated by fear rather than by love.

This complex state of affairs is often resolved at home by the mother's dismissal of the nurse, a painful procedure for all concerned. Worse than that is the alternative by which the nurse wins, so to speak: the mother sinks back into hopeless compliance, and the relationship between the mother and the baby fails to establish itself.

I cannot find words to express what big forces are at work at this critical point, but I can try to explain something of what is going on. There is a most curious thing happening: the mother who is perhaps physically exhausted, and perhaps incontinent, and who is dependent on the nurse and the doctor for skilled attention in many and various ways, is at the same time the one person who can properly introduce the world to the baby in a way that makes sense to the baby. She knows how to do this, not through any training and not through being clever, but just because she is the natural mother. But her natural instincts cannot evolve if she is scared, or if she does not see her baby when it is born, or if the baby is brought to her only at stated times thought by the authorities to be suitable for feeding purposes. It just does not work that way. The mother's milk does not flow like an excretion; it is a response to a stimulus, and the stimulus is the sight and smell and feel of her baby, and the sound of the baby's cry that indicates need. It is all one thing, the mother's care of her baby and the periodic feeding that develops as if it were a means of communication between the two— a song without words.

Two Opposed Properties

Here then we have on the one hand a highly dependent person, the mother, and at the same time and in the same person, *the expert* in that delicate process, the initiation of breast-feeding, and in the whole bustle and fuss of infant care. It is difficult for some nurses to allow for these two opposed properties of the mother, and the result is that they try to bring about the feeding relationship as they would bring about a defecation in the case of loaded rectum. They are attempting the impossible. Very many feeding inhibitions are started in this way; or even when feeding by bottle is eventually instituted this remains a separate thing happening to the infant, and not properly joined up with the total process that is called infant care. In my work I am constantly trying to alter this sort of fault, which in some cases is actually started off in the first days and weeks by a nurse who did not see that though she is an expert in her job, her job does not include making an infant and a mother's breast become related to one another.

Besides, the midwife has feelings, as I have said, and she may find it difficult to stand and watch an infant wasting time at the breast. She feels like shoving the breast into the baby's mouth, or shoving the baby's mouth into the breast, and the baby responds by withdrawing.

There is another point: This is that, almost universally, the mother feels a little, or a lot, that she has stolen her baby from her own mother. This derives from her playing at mothers and fathers, and from her dreams that belong to the time when she was quite a little girl, and her father was her *beau ideal.* And so she may easily feel, and in some cases she *must* feel, that the nurse is the revengeful mother who has come to take the baby away. The nurse need not do anything about this, but it is very helpful if she avoids actually taking the infant away—depriving the mother of that contact which is natural—and, in fact, only presenting the infant to the mother, wrapped in a shawl, at feedtime. This last is not modern practice, but it was common practice till recently.

The dreams and imaginations and the playing that lie behind these problems remain even when the nurse acts in such a way that the mother has a chance to recover her sense of reality, which she naturally does within a few days or weeks. Very occasionally, then, the nurse must expect to be thought to be a persecuting figure, even when she is not so, and even when she is exceptionally understanding and tolerant. It is part of her job to tolerate this fact. In the end the mother will recover, usually, and will come to see the nurse as she is, as a nurse who tries to understand, but who is human and, therefore, not without a limit to her tolerance.

Another point is that the mother, especially if she be somewhat immature herself, or a bit of a deprived child in her own early history, finds it very hard to give up the nurse's care of her, and to be left alone to care for her infant in the very way that she herself needs to be treated. In this way the loss of the support of a good nurse can bring about very real difficulties in the next phase, when the mother leaves the nurse, or the nurse leaves her.

In these ways psychoanalysis, as I see it, brings to midwifery, and to all work involving human relationships, an increase in the respect that individuals feel for each other and for individual rights. Society needs technicians even in medical and nursing care, but where people and not machines are concerned the technician needs to study the way in which people live and imagine and grow on experience.

1957

EIGHT

Dependence in
Child Care

It is valuable to recognize the *fact* of dependence. Dependence is real. That babies and children cannot manage on their own is so obvious that the simple *facts* of dependence are easily lost.

It can be said that the story of the growing child is a story of absolute dependence moving steadily through lessening degrees of dependence, and groping towards independence. A mature child or adult has a kind of independence that is happily mixed in with all sorts of needs, and with love which becomes evident when loss brings about a state of grief.

Before birth the absolute dependence of the baby is thought of chiefly in physical or bodily terms. The last weeks of the baby's life in the womb affect the baby's bodily development and there is room for an idea of the beginnings of a sense of security (or of insecurity) according to the state of an unborn baby's mind, which of course is very restricted in its ability to function at this early stage because of lack of full development of the brain. Also there is a variable amount of awareness before birth and during the birth process according to the chance effects of the mother's state and of her ability to give herself over to the alarming, dangerous and usually rewarding agonies of the last stages of a pregnancy.

Because babies at the beginning of their lives are highly dependent creatures they are necessarily affected by everything that happens. They have no understanding such as we would have if similarly placed, but they are all the time having experiences which add up in their memory systems in a way either to give confidence in the world or alternatively to give lack of confidence and a sense of being like a cork on the ocean, a plaything of circumstance. In the extreme of environmental failure there is a sense of unpredictability.

The thing that ultimately builds up a sense of predictability in the baby is described in terms of the mother's adaptation to the baby's needs. This is a matter that is highly complex and difficult to describe in words, and in fact adaptation to a baby's needs can only be done well, or well enough, by a mother who has temporarily given herself over to the care of her baby. It cannot be done by trying hard or by a study of books. It belongs to the special state that most mothers find themselves in at the end of their nine-months' term, a state in which they are quite naturally orientated to this central thing, the baby, and they know what the baby is feeling like.

Some mothers do not get to this state with their first child, or they have reason to fail to get there with one child though they know they did get there with an earlier child. These things just can't be helped. No one must be expected to succeed always. And someone is usually available to supply what is needed—perhaps the child's father, or a grandmother or an aunt, when a mother cannot make it with any one baby. But on the whole this thing happens, if circumstances are fairly secure for the mother herself, and then the mother (perhaps after a few minutes or even hours of rejection of her baby) *knows* without the necessity of understanding everything how to adapt to her baby's needs. When she was a baby she had just these same needs. She does not remember but nothing of experience is ever lost, and somehow it happens that the mother meets the new baby's dependence, by a highly sensitive personal understanding that makes her able to adapt to real need.

A knowledge of theory is not at all necessary, and for millions of years mothers have been doing this job with pleasure and in a satisfactory way. Of course, if some theoretical understanding can be added to what is natural, so much the better, especially if the mother must defend her right to do well her own way, and (of course) to make mistakes. The willing helpers, including doctors and nurses who are needed for emergencies, cannot know as the mother knows (because of her nine-months' apprenticeship) what are the baby's immediate needs and how to adapt to such needs.

These needs take every possible form and they are not just periodic waves of hunger. It would be a pity to give examples lest this should seem to indicate that anyone but a poet could put into words that which has infinite variability. Nevertheless, a few points might help the reader to know what need looks like when a baby is in a state of dependence.

First, there are bodily needs. Perhaps a baby needs to be taken up and put to lie on the other side. Or a baby needs to be warmer, or less enclosed, so that water that exudes can be lost. Or the skin sensitivity needs a softer contact, wool for instance. Or there is a pain, colic perhaps, and for a few moments the baby needs to be carried round on the shoulder. Feeding has to be included in among these physical needs.

In this list protection from gross disturbance is taken for granted—no low-flying aircraft, the baby's cot is not blown over, the sun does not come to shine directly in the baby's eyes.

Secondly, there are needs of a very subtle kind that can only be met by human contact. Perhaps the baby needs to be involved in the mother's breathing rhythm, or even to hear or feel the adult heartbeat. Or the smell of the mother or father is needed, or there is a need for sounds that indicate liveliness and life in the environment, or colours and movement, so that the baby does not become thrown back on his or her own resources, when too young or immature to take full responsibility for life.

Behind these needs lies the fact that babies are liable to the most severe anxieties that can be imagined. If left for too long (hours, minutes) without familiar and human contact they have experiences which we can only describe by such words as:

going to pieces
falling for ever
dying and dying and dying
losing all vestige of hope of the renewal of contacts.

It is an important fact that the majority of babies go through the early stages of dependence without ever having these experiences, and they do this because of the fact that their dependence is recognized and their basic needs are met, and that the mother or mother-figure adapts her way of life to these needs.

It will be appreciated that with good care these awful feelings become good experiences, adding up to a total of confidence in people and in the world. For instance, going to pieces becomes relaxation and restfulness if a baby is in good hands; falling for ever becomes the joy in being carried and the excitement and pleasure that belong to being moved; dying and dying and dying becomes a delicious awareness of being alive; loss of hope about relationships becomes, when dependence is met by constancy, a sense of assurance that even when alone the baby has someone who cares.

Most babies get good-enough care and, what is more, they get this continuously from one person, right on until they are able to be pleased to know and to trust others who feel love in this way that makes them reliable and adaptive.

On the basis of this foundation of the experience of dependence that has been met, the baby is able to begin to respond to the demands that the mother and the environment must sooner or later be able to make on the baby.

By contrast, a certain proportion of babies have experienced environmental failure while dependence was a fact, and then, in varying degrees, there is damage done, damage that can be difficult to repair. At best the baby growing into a child and an adult carries round a buried memory of a disaster that happened to the self, and much time and energy are spent in organizing life so that such pain may not be experienced again.

At worst the child's development as a person is permanently distorted so that the personality is deformed or the character warped. There are symptoms that are probably thought of as naughty, and the child must suffer from those who feel that punishment or corrective training can cure what is really a deep-seated fact of environmental failure. Or the child as a person is so disturbed that mental illness is diagnosed, and treatment is given because of an abnormality that ought to have been prevented.

The steadying element in the consideration of these very serious matters is that in the big proportion of cases babies do not suffer in this way, and they come through without needing to spend their time and energy building a fortress around themselves to keep away an enemy that truly dwells within the fortress walls.

In the case of most babies the fact that they are wanted and loved by their mothers, and by their parents, and by the extended family, gives the setting in which each child can become an individual, not only fulfilling his or her own destiny by following the lines of hereditary endowment (in so far as external reality allows), but also happy to be able to identify with other people and with animals and things in the environment, and with society and its perpetual self-organization.

The reason why these things are usually possible is principally that dependence, absolute at first, gradually groping towards independence, was accepted as a fact and was met by human beings who adapted to the needs of the growing individual, without resentment, because of some crude sense of belonging that can conveniently be called love.

[1970]

NINE

Communication Between Infant and Mother, and Mother and Infant, Compared and Contrasted

In the first lecture of this series Dr. Sandler has been talking about the nature of psychoanalysis. In the next two lectures you will hear about unconscious communication as between parents and children and as between husband and wife. Here in this lecture I am talking about communication between infant and mother.

You will already have noted that the word *unconscious* does not appear in my title.[1] There is an obvious reason for this. The word *unconscious* would apply only to the mother. For the baby there is not yet a conscious and an unconscious in the area that I wish to examine. What is there is an armful of anatomy and physiology, and added to this a potential for development into a human personality. There is a general tendency towards physical growth, and a tendency towards development in the psychic part of the psycho-somatic partnership; there are in both the physical and the psychological areas the inherited tendencies, and these inherited tendencies on the psyche side include those that lead towards integration or the attainment of wholeness. The basis for all theories about human personality development is continuity, the line of life, which presumably starts before the baby's actual birth; continuity which carries with it the idea that nothing that has been part of an individual's experience is lost or can ever be lost to that individual, even if in various complex ways it should and does become unavailable to consciousness.

If the inherited potential is to have a chance to become actual in the sense of manifesting itself in the individual's person, then the environmental provision must be adequate. It is convenient to use a phrase like "good-enough mothering" to convey an unidealized view of the maternal function; and further, it is valuable to hold in mind the concept of absolute dependence (of baby on environment), rapidly changing to relative dependence, and always travelling towards (but never reaching) independence. Independence means autonomy, the person becomes viable, as a person as well as physically (a separate unit).

This scheme of the developing human being allows for the fact that at the beginning the baby has not separated off what is not-ME from what is ME, so that in the special context of early relationships the behaviour of the environment is as much a part of the baby as is the behaviour of the baby's inherited drives towards integration and towards autonomy and object-relating, and towards a satisfactory psychosomatic partnership.[2]

The most precarious part of the complex that is called a baby is the baby's cumulative experience of life. It really does make a difference whether I am born to a bedouin where the sand is hot, or to a political prisoner in Siberia, or to a merchant's wife in England's damp but beautiful west country. I may be conventionally suburban, or illegitimate. I may be an only child, an oldest child, or the middle one of five, or the third boy of four boys in a row. All this matters and is part of me.

Like Valdar the Oft-born, an infant is born all of various ways with the same inherited potential, but from the word Go! *experiences* and gathers experiences according to the point in time and space where he or she appears. Even being born: once it was with the mother squatting, and gravity drew the baby to the centre of the world; and another time the mother was unnaturally laid out on her back, prepared as if for an operation, and she had to shove as if at stool, because gravity only pulled the baby sideways. In one birth the mother got tired of shoving, and developed uterine inertia, and so she put everything off till tomorrow morning. So she had a good sleep, but the baby, already alerted for the high dive, had to wait for ever. This had a terrible effect, and for the whole of life that person was claustrophobic and intolerant of the uncharted interval between events.

The point is perhaps made that some kind of communication takes place powerfully from the beginning of each human individual's life, and whatever the *potential* the *actual experiential* build-up that becomes a person is precarious; development can be held up or distorted at any point, and indeed may never manifest itself; in fact, dependence is at first absolute.

It will be observed that I am taking you to a place where verbalization has no meaning. What connection can there be, then, between all this and psychoanalysis, which has been built on the process of verbal interpretations of verbalized thoughts and ideas?

Briefly, I would say that psychoanalysis had to start on a basis of verbalization, and that such a method is exactly appropriate to the treatment of a patient who is not schizoid or psychotic; that is, whose early experiences can be taken for granted. Usually we call these patients psychoneurotic, to make it clear that they do not come to analysis for correction of very early experience, or for first-time early experiences which have been missed out. Psychoneurotic patients have already come through the early experiences well enough, with the consequence that they have the privilege of suffering from personal inner conflicts and from the inconvenience of the defences they have had to set up in themselves to deal with anxiety related to the instinctual life, the chief defence being repression. These patients are bothered by the work they have to do keeping the repressed unconscious repressed, and they find relief during psychoanalytic treatment in the new simplified experiences, samples carefully chosen day by day by themselves (not deliberately of course) for confrontation in terms of the ever-shifting transference neurosis.

By contrast, in our analytic investigations, the very early phenomena come forward as primary features in two ways: firstly in the schizoid phases that any patient may pass through, or in the treatment of actually schizoid subjects (this is not my subject here and now); and secondly in the study of the actual early experiences of babies just about to be born, being born, being held after birth, being cared for and communicated with in the early weeks and months long before verbalization has come to mean anything.

What I am trying to do here, therefore, is to look at this one thing, the early life experience of every baby, with special reference to communication.

In terms of my hypothesis, at first there *is* absolute dependence, and the environment does indeed matter. Then how can it be that any baby comes through the complexities of the early developmental phases? It is certain that a baby cannot develop into a person if there is only a non-human environment; even the best machine could never provide what is needed. No, a human being is needed, and human beings are essentially human—which means imperfect—free from mechanical reliability. The baby's use of the non-human environment depends on the previous use of a human environment.

How then can we formulate a description of the next stage which concerns the baby's experience of life when in a state of absolute dependence?

We can postulate a state in the mother[3]—a psychiatric state, like withdrawal or concentration—this is something that (in health) characterizes her when she is getting towards the end of her pregnancy, and which lasts for some weeks or months after the event. (I have written about this, and I have given it a name—*Primary Maternal Preoccupation.*)[4]

We must assume that the babies of the world, past and present, have been and are born into a human environment that is good enough, that is, into one that is adaptive in just the right way, appropriately, according to the baby's needs.

Mothers (or mother-substitutes) seem to be able to reach this state, and it may help them if they can be told that it only lasts a while, that they recover from it. Many women fear this state and think it will turn them into vegetables, with the consequence that they hold on to the vestiges of a career like dear life, and never give themselves over even temporarily to a total involvement.

It is likely that in this state mothers become able in a specialized way to step into the shoes of the baby—I mean—to almost lose themselves in an identification with the baby, so that they know (generically, if not specifically) what the baby needs just at this very moment. At the same time, of course, they remain themselves, and they are aware of a need for protection while they are in this state which makes them vulnerable. They assume the vulnerability of the baby. They also assume that they will be able to withdraw from this special position in the course of a few months.

So it happens that babies usually do experience optimum conditions when absolutely dependent; but it follows that a certain proportion of babies do *not*. I am saying that these babies who do not experience good enough care in this way do not fulfill themselves, even as babies. Genes are not enough.

Without pursuing this topic I must deal with one more complication that is obstructing the evolution of my argument. It concerns the essential difference between the mother and the baby.

The mother has of course herself been a baby. It is all in her somewhere, the experiential conglomerate, with herself dependent and gradually achieving autonomy. Further, she has *played* at being a baby, as well as at mothers and fathers; she has regressed to baby ways during illnesses; she has perhaps watched her mother caring for younger siblings. She may have had instruction in baby-care, and perhaps she has read books, and she may have formed her own ideas of right and wrong in baby-management. She is of course deeply affected by local custom, complying or reacting, or striking out as an independent or a pioneer.

But the baby has never been a mother. The baby has not even been a baby before. It is all *a first experience*. There are no yardsticks. Time is not measured by clocks or by sunrise and sunset so much as by the maternal heart and breathing rates, by the rise and fall of instinct tensions, and other essentially non-mechanical devices.

In describing communication between baby and mother, then, there is this essential dichotomy—the mother can shrink to infantile modes of experience, but the baby cannot blow up to adult sophistication. In this way, the mother may or may not talk to her baby; it doesn't matter, the language is not important.

Just here you will want me to say something about the inflections that characterize speech, even at its most sophisticated. An analyst is at work, as it is called, and the patient is verbalizing and the analyst is interpreting. It is not just a matter of verbal communication. The analyst feels that a trend in the patient's material that is being presented calls for verbalization. Much depends on the way the analyst uses the words, and therefore on the attitude that is at the back of the interpretation. A patient dug her nails into the skin of my hand at a moment of intense feeling. My interpretation was: "Ow!" This scarcely involved my intellectual equipment at all, and it was quite useful because it came *immediately* (not after a pause for reflection) and because it meant to the patient that my hand was alive, that it was part of me, and that I was there to be used. Or, shall I say, I can be used if I survive.

Although psychoanalysis of suitable subjects is based on verbalization, nevertheless every analyst knows that along with the content of interpretations the attitude behind the verbalization has its own importance, and that this attitude is reflected in the nuances and in the timing and in a thousand ways that compare with the infinite variety of poetry.

For instance, the non-moralistic approach, which is basic to psychotherapy and to social work, is communicated not in words, but in the non-moralistic quality in the worker. It's the positive of the music-hall song whose refrain goes: "It's not exactly what she says, it's the nasty way she says it."

In terms of baby-care, the mother who feels like it can display a moralistic attitude long before words like "wicked" make sense to the baby. She may enjoy saying: "Damn you, you little bugger" in a nice way, so that she feels better and the baby smiles back, pleased to be burbled at. Or, more subtly still, what about: "Hushabye baby on the tree tops," which isn't very nice verbally, but forms a quite sweet lullaby?

It is even possible for a mother to show her baby, who has no language yet, that she means: "God will strike you dead if you mess youself when I've just cleaned you up," or the quite different: "You can't do that there 'ere!" which involves a direct confrontation of wills and personalities.

What then is communicated when a mother adapts to her baby's needs? I now refer to the concept of *holding*. There is a valuable economy in the use, even exploitation, of the term *holding* in description of the setting in which major communications take place at the beginning of a baby's experience of living. If I adopt this line, exploiting the concept of holding, then we have two things—the mother holding the baby, and the baby being held and rapidly going through a series of developmental phases which are of extreme importance for the establishment of the baby as a person. *The mother does not need to know what is going on in the baby.* But the baby's development cannot take place except in relation to the human reliability of the holding and the handling.[5]

We could examine the pathological or the normal, and as it is simpler to examine the normal I will adopt this one of the alternatives.

The mother's capacity to meet the changing and developing needs of this one baby enables this one baby to have a line of life, relatively unbroken; and enables this baby to experience both unintegrated or relaxed states in confidence in the holding that is actual, along with oft-repeated phases of the integration that is part of the baby's inherited growth tendency. The baby goes easily to and fro from integration to the ease of relaxed unintegration and the accumulation of these experiences becomes a pattern, and forms a basis for what the baby expects. The baby comes to believe in a reliability in the inward processes leading to integration into a unit.[6]

As development proceeds, and the baby has acquired an inside and an outside, then the environmental reliability becomes a belief, an introject based on the *experience of reliability* (human, not mechanically perfect).

Is it not true that the mother has communicated with the baby? She has said: "I am reliable—not because I am a machine, but because I know what you are needing; and I care, and I want to provide what you need. This is what I call love at this stage of your development."

But this kind of communication is silent. The baby does not hear or register the communication, only the effects of the reliability; this is registered in terms of on-going development. The baby does not know about the communication except from the effects of *failure* of reliability. This is where the difference comes in between mechanical perfection and human love. Human beings fail and fail; and in the course of ordinary care a mother is all the time mending her failures. These relative failures with immediate remedy undoubtedly add up eventually to a communication, so that the baby comes to know about success. Successful adaptation thus gives a sense of security, a feeling of having been loved. As analysts we know about this because we are all the time failing, and we expect and get anger. If we survive we get used. It is the innumerable failures followed by the sort of care that mends that build up into a communication of love, of the fact that there is a human being there who cares. Where failure is not mended within the requisite time, seconds, minutes, hours, then we use the term *deprivation*. A deprived child is one who, after knowing about failures mended, comes to experience failure unmended. It is then the lifework of the child to provoke conditions in which failures mended once more give the pattern to life.

You will understand that these thousands of relative failures of normal life are not to be compared with gross failures of adaptation—these do not produce anger because the baby is not organized yet to be angry about something—anger implies keeping in mind the ideal which has been shattered. These gross failures of holding produce in the baby *unthinkable anxiety*—the content of such anxiety is:

Going to pieces.
Falling for ever.
Complete isolation because of there being no means for communication.
Disunion of psyche and soma.

These are the fruits of *privation*, environmental failure essentially unmended.

(You will see that I have not had time to talk about communication with the intellect, even the rudimentary intellect of the baby; I must be contented with my references to the psyche half of the psycho-somatic partnership.)

It is not possible to think of *gross* adaptive failures as a form of communication. We do not need to teach a baby that things can go very wrong. If things go wrong and are not very soon mended, then the baby has been permanently affected, distorted in terms of development, and communication has broken down.

Elaboration of Theme

Perhaps I have said enough to draw attention to the silent early communications, in their basic form. I would say a little more by way of giving guidelines.

(*a*) The liveness of the intercommunication between mother and baby is maintained in special ways. There is the movement that belongs to the mother's breathing, and the warmth of her breath, indeed the smell of her which varies a great deal. There is also the sound of her heart-beat, a sound well-known to the baby, in so far as there is a person there to know anything before birth.

An illustration of this basic physical communicating is in the rocking movement, with the mother adapting her movements to those of the baby. Rocking insures against depersonalization or loss of the psycho-somatic partnership. Do not babies vary in their rocking rate? Is it not possible that a mother may find one baby's rocking rate too quick or too slow for natural as opposed to contrived adaptation? In describing this group of phenomena we can say that communication is in terms of mutuality in physical experience.

(*b*) Then there is playing. I do not mean fun and games, or jokes. The interplay of mother and baby gives an area that could be called common ground, shall I say a Tom Tiddler's ground, the no-man's-land that is each man's land, the place where the secret is, the potential space which may become a transitional object,[7] the symbol of trust and of union between baby and mother, a union which involves no interpenetration. So: not to forget playing, where affection and enjoyment in experience are born.

(c) And then there is much that could be said that has to do with the baby's use of the mother's face. It is possible to think of the mother's face as the prototype of the glass mirror. In the mother's face the baby sees him- or herself. If the mother is depressed or is preoccupied with some other ploy, then, of course, all that the baby sees is a face.[8]

(d) From here and from these silent communications we can go over to the ways in which the mother makes real just what the baby is ready to look for, so that she gives the baby the idea of what it is that the baby is just ready for. The baby says (wordlessly of course): "I just feel like . . ." and just then the mother comes along and turns the baby over, or she comes with the feeding apparatus and the baby becomes able to finish the sentence: ". . . a turn-over, a breast, nipple, milk, etc., etc." We have to say that the baby created the breast, but could not have done so had not the mother come along with the breast just at that moment. The communication to the baby is: "Come at the world creatively, create the world; it is only what you create that has meaning for you." Next comes: "the world is in your control." From this initial *experience of omnipotence* the baby is able to begin to experience frustration and even to arrive one day at the other extreme from omnipotence, that is to say, having a sense of being a mere speck in a universe, in a universe that was there before the baby was conceived of and conceived by two parents who were enjoying each other. Is it not from *being* God that human beings arrive at the humility proper to human individuality?

Finally, it may be asked, to what end is all this talk about babies and mothers? I want to say that it is *not* that we need to be able to tell mothers what to do, or what to be like. If they aren't, well we can't make them. We can of course avoid interfering. But there can be a purpose in our thinking. If we can learn from mothers and babies we can begin to know what it is that schizoid patients need of us in their peculiar kind of transference, if a treatment is in progress. And there is a feedback; from schizoid patients we may learn how to look at mothers and babies and to see more clearly what is there. But *essentially* it is *from* mothers and babies that we learn about the needs of psychotic patients, or patients in psychotic phases.

It is at these early stages of intercommunication between baby and mother that the mother is laying down the basis for the baby's future mental health, and in treating mental ill-health we necessarily come across the details of early failures of facilitation. We meet the failures, but (remember!) the successes appear in terms of the personal growth that successful environmental provision made possible. For what the mother does when she does well enough is to facilitate the baby's own developmental processes, making it possible for the baby to some extent to realize inherited potential.

All we do in successful psychoanalysis is to unhitch developmental hold-ups, and to release developmental processes and the inherited tendencies of the individual patient. In a peculiar way we can actually alter the patient's past, so that a patient whose maternal environment was not good enough can change into a person who has had a good-enough facilitating environment, and whose personal growth has therefore been able to take place, though late. When this happens the analyst gets a reward that is far removed from gratitude, and is very much like that which a parent gets when a child achieves autonomy. In the context of good-enough holding and handling the new individual now comes to realize some of his or her potential. Somehow we have silently communicated reliability and the patient has responded with the growth that might have taken place in the very early stages in the context of human care.

There remains for consideration the question whether something useful can be said about the baby's communication to the mother. I am still referring to the very early stages. Certainly there is something that happens to people when they are confronted with the helplessness that is supposed to characterize a baby. It is a terrible thing to do to plant a baby on your doorstep, because your reactions to the baby's helplessness alter your life and perhaps cut across the plans you have made. This is fairly obvious but it needs some kind of restatement in terms of dependence, because although the baby is helpless in one sense, in another sense it may be said that a baby has a tremendous potential for going on living and developing and for realizing potential. We could almost say that those who are in the position of caring for a baby are as helpless in relation to the baby's helplessness as the baby can be said to be. Perhaps there can be a battle of helplessnesses.

In making further reference to the baby's communication with the mother I suggest that this can be summed up in terms of creativeness and compliance. About this it must be said that in health the creative communication has priority over compliance. On the basis of seeing and reaching to the world creatively the baby can become able to comply without losing face. When the pattern is the other way round and compliance dominates then we think of ill-health and we see a bad basis for the development of the individual.

So in the end we can come down to the fact that the baby communicates creatively and in time becomes able to use what has been found. For most people the ultimate compliment is to be found and used, and I suppose therefore that these words could represent the communication of the baby with the mother.

I find you;
You survive what I do to you as I come to recognize you as not-me;
I use you;
I forget you;
But you remember me;
I keep forgetting you;
I lose you;
I am sad.

1968

Notes

1. See preliminary notes written for this paper, p. 240.

2. It surprises some people to be told that a baby's inherited tendencies are external factors, but they are as clearly external to the baby's person as is the mother's capacity to be a good-enough mother, or her tendency to become hampered in what she is doing because of a depressed mood.

3. When I say mother I am not excluding father, but at this stage it is the maternal aspect of the father that concerns us.

4. (1956) In *Collected Papers: Through Paediatrics to Psychoanalysis*. London: Tavistock Publications Ltd. New York: Basic Books, 1958.

5. "The Theory of Parent-Infant Relationship." (1960) In *The Maturational Process and the Facilitating Environment*. London: Hogarth Press and the Institute of Psychoanalysis, 1965.

6. "Primitive Emotional Development." (1945) In *Collected Papers: Through Paediatrics to Psychoanalysis*. London: Tavistock Publications. New York: Basic Books, 1958.

7. "Transitional Objects and Transitional Phenomena." (1951) In *Through Paediatrics to Psychoanalysis*. London: Tavistock Publications. New York: Basic Books, 1958.

8. "Mirror-role of Mother and Family in Child Development." (1967) In *Playing and Reality*. London: Tavistock Publications, 1971.

PART TWO

Talking to Parents

On Reading Winnicott

T. Berry Brazelton, M.D.

Reading these largely unpublished pieces by D. W. Winnicott is like return-
ing to a refreshing spring after a walk in the desert. Each one is an utterly
rewarding, delightful experience.

The very fact that Winnicott chose to address parents directly through
the media is of great interest. After all, his ideal "ordinary devoted mother"
is one who practices her child care unself-consciously. This broadcasting of
his child-rearing ideas could be seen as flaunting his own philosophy. But,
as is his wont, he immediately lays one's question to rest. He is not trying
to instruct parents but to help them understand what they do and then to
justify them for what they have done. A statement such as "One can only
see that one might have done the same, or one might have done worse"
illustrates his simple but powerful way of backing up parents for their
strengths, unlike the usual parenting authority who so expertly tells parents
what not to do.

I have been an admirer and a student of Donald Winnicott all my professional life. The way he combined a normative pediatric approach with
the insights of child psychiatry and psychoanalysis made him my model
long ago. His own brilliant insights are based on a deep understanding of
the parent-infant processes coupled with firm conviction that most parents
want desperately to do well by their children. These essays are sprinkled
with his positively reinforcing interpretations. Parents will feel liberated

and reassured by them, for they are delivered right from the heart, and with his deliciously quirky wit.

As he makes clear, the purpose of these talks was not to tell parents what to do, but (1) to detoxify the science of child-rearing, (2) to give them confidence in what they were doing, and (3) to free them to seek individualized help when they hit a snag in parenting their children. He continually emphasizes the parents' instinct to do the right thing, coupled with the inevitable guilt and ambivalence that makes them the sensitive parents that they are. He is never afraid of honest common sense: "A meeting of unsuccessful stepparents . . . might be fruitful. It would be composed of ordinary men and women." For being a stepparent is an unavoidably unrewarding role.

In the essay on thumb-sucking, he gives the best justification I have heard. Sucking on the thumb is the baby's first use of imagination. The real experience of sucking on his thumb has been enriched by the imagined breast or bottle. Why would anyone deprive him of this first experience in creating his own affectionate object?

These talks pare down to their essence the simple steps that lead to the parenting goals he is discussing. For example, the three stages of saying "No" start with the parents' need to assume full responsibility for the child's limits (first year), teaching him the word "no" and words associated with danger, such as "hot" (second year), and then, turning it back to him and enlarging on his choice-making experience and his ability to incorporate these limits, giving him verbal explanations (third year).

Take another question dear to the hearts of parents: "How does jealousy disappear?" In Winnicott's beautifully spare explanation we see how it is eventually defused by identifying with the person of whom one is so jealous, then by identifying with the jealously guarding mother and her feelings, using one's imagination (empathy) to take the other's perspective.

I think my favorite is the piece on "what's irksome" about being a parent. This chapter will help all parents face their negative feelings as normal and even healthy. Winnicott reminds us that what goes wrong is always irksome; when it goes right it gets ignored. So, of course, the parents' day becomes loaded with the irksome details of day-to-day living. "Children will go on being a nuisance and mothers will go on being glad they had the chance to be the victims."

This is a beautiful little volume. Winnicott distills the essential nature of being a parent. For instance, chapter 17 concludes with the provocative idea that, without guilt and ambivalence, no mother would be sensitive to her child's needs. He indeed infuses the reader with an understanding of the challenges of parenting, but he also makes his audience feel that being a "good enough mother" is one of the most gratifying roles one could seek. What a genius!

Editors' Preface to
Talking to Parents

Between 1939 and 1962 Donald Winnicott gave about fifty radio talks for the BBC, nearly all of them to parents. Transcribed, they turn out to contain some of his most lucid and compelling writing. A collection of the earlier talks, broadcast towards the end of the war, with Janet Quigley as producer, gave rise to a pamphlet entitled *Getting to Know Your Baby*. Another series, dating from 1949 to 1950, under the production of Isa Benzie, was published in a similar pamphlet called *The Ordinary Devoted Mother and Her Baby*. Both went fairly quickly out of print. Though Winnicott, because of the rules prohibiting doctors from advertising, had not put his name to the broadcasts, a following grew up, and there were many requests that the talks be reissued. It thus came about that these formed the basis of a book entitled *The Child and the Family*, edited by Janet Hardenberg and issued by Tavistock Publications in 1957[1]; a few more talks, mainly about wartime evacuation, were included in its companion volume, *The Child and the Outside World*. In 1964 Penguin Books decided to publish a selection from these two volumes under the title *The Child, the Family, and the Outside World*, which included nearly all of the broadcast talks published up to that time.

By the end of 1968, 50,000 copies of the Penguin edition had been sold, and Winnicott wrote a short speech for a party given in celebration. In it he tells of how, for some of the earlier talks, he would go to the BBC in Langham Place "driving his car over the glass and rubble of the previous night's air-raid." He goes on to say how much he was helped in the long series of talks in 1949–50 by Isa Benzie, who transmitted her enthusiasm for and confidence in his work to him and, in his words, "pulled the phrase 'the ordinary devoted mother' out of what I had talked about." He continues: "This immediately became a peg to hang things on, and it suited my need to get away from both idealisation and also from teaching and propaganda. I could get on with a description of child care as practised unselfconsciously everywhere."

Interestingly, Winnicott also makes the point that after the war he did not resume the practice of paediatrics (though he still held psychiatric clinics for children) and consequently was not so closely in touch as he had previously been with a mass of everyday material relating to mother-child interaction. For these talks he therefore found it necessary to "rekindle the clinical flame" by using material from "the regressive experiences of psycho-analytic patients, many of them adult, who were giving me a close-up of the mother-infant (or parent-infant) relationship." "At the time of these BBC broadcasts in the late forties," he wrote, "I was in a unique position, being able to see my patients in terms of both paediatrics and of a kind of psycho-analysis that was peculiarly my own. Naturally in talking over the radio I needed to keep to the language of paediatrics, though it can be seen that paediatrics for me had already become a place for the study of the infant-mother emotional tie, assuming (as one usually can do) physical health. I had moved from 'infant feeding' to 'the infant-mother mutual involvement.'"

Winnicott's book *The Child, the Family, and the Outside World* has retained its popularity up to today and still sells thousands of copies a year. It has been republished in the United States by Addison-Wesley.

Talking to Parents gathers together all the broadcast talks that were given after 1955. Only two of these have been published before: "Now They Are Five" (under the title "The Five-Year-Old") and "Security" (under the title "On Security") in Winnicott's book *The Family and Individual Development.*[2] We have included them for the sake of completeness. Also included are two papers not written for broadcasting: "Health Education through Broadcasting" is used as an introductory chapter because it states so clearly the aims that Winnicott came to see as important in giving radio talks; we have added "The Building Up of Trust" because it was written for parents (something rare for Winnicott outside broadcasting), has not yet been published, and, dating as it does from his last years, contains many of his essential ideas about children and their parents that he had spent his professional life developing. We have not been able to discover the exact audience for whom it was composed.

The collating and editing of the papers were nearly completed with the help of Clare Winnicott before her death in 1984. The editing has been kept to a minimum: hardly any editing of the radio talks themselves was necessary, as they appear to have been written by Winnicott before being broadcast; they were found in typescript among many other papers left by him. The exceptions are the two talks to stepmothers and the discussion with Claire Rayner about "Feeling Guilty." These have been transcribed from tapes, and the quality of the writing is therefore not quite the same. This also applies to the conversations between mothers that appear as part of the central series of talks ("Saying 'No,'" "Jealousy," and "What Irks?"). For these the mothers were invited to the BBC, their conversations were recorded, and Winnicott made his comments on them on a different day; but here the unrehearsed nature of what was said becomes an essential ingredient of the whole.

CHRISTOPHER BOLLAS

MADELEINE DAVIS

RAY SHEPHERD

London, 1992

Notes

1. Published in the United States by Basic Books under the title *Mother and Baby: A Primer in First Relationships*.
2. London: Tavistock, 1965; New York: Basic Books, 1965.

Acknowledgment

Madeleine Davis died while working on the last stages of preparation for *Talking to Parents*. Sadly, she has not lived to see its publication but the publishers, the editors, and all those involved with The Winnicott Trust wish to record their admiration and gratitude for her gracious and thoughtful help in preparing this and previous Winnicott works for publication.

The editors would like to thank Tavistock Publications for permission to include previously published material. Thanks are also due to the BBC, without whose foresight many of the talks on which this book is based may not have taken place, and to Claire Rayner for her thoughtful contribution to chapter 17.

TEN

Health Education
through Broadcasting

This article is written by invitation. The subject of health education through broadcasting is one that has interest for me since I have from time to time given talks over the air to parents. But it should be made clear that I am not in fact especially in favour of health education in mass form. When an audience is vast it contains many people who are not listening for the purpose of learning, but who are listening by chance or for fun, or perhaps even while they are shaving or making cakes, and so have no free hand to turn the knob. In such conditions one must surely have grave doubts as to the value of putting across anything that is important.

One may compare this with school broadcasting, where children of known ages are sitting around, suitably occupied in a mild way, but definitely expecting that for a period of time they will be receiving instruction given in an interesting way from the radio. The broadcaster who wishes to talk about health has not the advantage of a special audience.

I am referring to health education in terms of psychology and not to education in matters of physical health and in the prevention and treatment of diseases. Much of what I have to say, however, could be applied to any talks on health, because it seems to me that all health education is psychological. Those who listen to a talk on rheumatism or on blood diseases do not do so because they have a scientific interest in the subject, or because of a hunger for facts; they do it because they are morbidly interested in disease. It seems to me that in educating people in matters of health this applies, whatever the medium used, except for the complication that in broadcasting one must expect that the vast majority of people who are listening in are not interested in being taught anything at all and are merely waiting for music to restart. Perhaps I am maligning the listener, but I am at any rate expressing a doubt that I feel every time the optimistic and reassuring voice of the health doctor gives a heartening talk on the Rhesus factor, or rheumatoid arthritis, or cancer.

I do wish to make one constructive suggestion, however, with reference to broadcasting in health matters. Any kind of propaganda, or telling people what to do, is to be deplored. It is an insult to indoctrinate people, even for their own good, unless they have the chance by being present to react, to express disapproval, and to contribute.

Is there an alternative that we may allow? What one can do as an alternative is to attempt to get hold of the ordinary things that people do, and to help them to understand why they do them. The basis for this suggestion is the idea that much that people do is really sensible in the circumstances. It is astonishing how, when one listens over and over again to the descriptions mothers give of the management of a child in the home, in the end one comes down to feeling that one cannot tell these parents what to do; one can only see that one might have done the same, or one might have done worse in the circumstances.

What people do like is to be given an understanding of the problems that they are tackling, and they like to be made aware of the things that they do intuitively. They feel unsafe when left to their hunches, to the sort of things that come to them at the critical moment, when they are not thinking things out. It may be that parents gave a child a smack or a kiss or a hug or they laughed. Something appropriate happened. This was the right thing, nothing could have been better. No-one could have told these parents what to do in the circumstances, because the circumstances could not have been described in advance. Afterwards, however, the parents find themselves talking things over and wondering, and often they have no notion what they have been doing and they feel confused about the problem itself. At such a moment they tend to feel guilty, and they fly to anyone who will speak with authority, who will give orders.

Education can catch on to all these things that people do and indeed have done, and in a good way, ever since the world started to have human beings in it who were human. If one can really show people what they are doing they become less frightened, they feel more secure about themselves, so that when they are genuinely in doubt or genuinely know that they are ignorant they seek not advice but information. The reason why they seek information is that they begin to have an idea where to go for it. They begin to see that it is possible to adopt an objective approach towards matters of the mind and of feeling and of behaviour, and they become less suspicious of science, even when it encroaches on those areas which till recently have been the exclusive property of religion.

I would think that there is a very great deal to be done in this matter of taking what people feel and think and do and building upon this foundation discussion or teaching which makes for a better understanding. In this way information can be passed on without there being an undermining of the self-confidence of the listener. The difficulty is for those who do the teaching in this way to know enough and to know when they themselves are ignorant.

Sometimes a broadcast talk to parents implies: "You ought to love your child; if you don't love your child the child will suffer, will become a delinquent." "You must breast-feed your infant; you must enjoy breast-feeding your infant; this must be the most important thing in your life." "You must love your baby as soon as the baby is born; it's unnatural not to love your own baby" . . . and so on and so on. All these things are very easy to say but in fact if said they produce deplorable effects.

It would be helpful to point out to mothers that sometimes mothers do not love their babies at first, or to show why mothers often find themselves unable to feed the baby at the breast, or to explain why loving is a complex matter, and not just an instinct.

I would like to add this, that it is not possible, in talking over the wireless, to deal with gross abnormalities, either in the mother or in the child, especially abnormalities in the parents. There is no point in telling people who have difficulties that they are ill. When ill people apply for help we must take the opportunity to relieve them where we can, but we easily cause distress if we make people feel ill without being available with therapy.

Almost every bit of advice that one gives over the air gives distress somewhere. Recently I spoke about telling adopted children that they are adopted. I knew of course that I was in danger of causing distress. No doubt I did upset many, but one mother who had listened came to me from a long way away and told me exactly why it would be very dangerous *in the circumstances* to tell her adopted child that she was adopted. I had to agree, although in principle I know that it is right to tell adopted children that they are adopted, and to do so as soon as possible.

If mothers are told to do this or that or the other, they soon get into a muddle, and (what is most important of all) they lose touch with their own ability to act without knowing exactly what is right and what is wrong. Only too easily they feel incompetent. If they must look up everything in a book or listen on the wireless, they are always too late even when they do the right things, because the right things have to be done immediately. It is only possible to act at exactly the right point when the action is intuitive or by instinct, as we say. The mind can be brought to bear on the problem afterwards, and when people think things out our job is to help them. We may discuss with them the sort of problems that they are faced with, and the sort of things they do, and the sort of effect that they may expect from their actions. This need not be the same as telling them what to do.

Finally: is there a place for formal instruction over the air in child psychology? It is doubtful to me whether we are ready to give instruction of this kind. Also I am reminded of the fact that in giving instruction to groups of students (social workers, for instance, or post-graduate teachers, or doctors), one knows that such instruction cannot be given loosely, but must be given within a formal setting. Perhaps over a period of time these students are having instruction; they are given opportunity for discussing among themselves what they are told, and for reading, and they have opportunity for expressing disagreement and for contributing. Even in these favourable circumstances a proportion of those who are receiving instruction will have personal difficulties to contend with, personal difficulties brought out by the new ideas and the new approach and by the revival of difficult memories and repressed fantasies. They will have had to deal with new excitements and with a rearrangement of their philosophy of life. Instruction in psychology is not like instruction in physics or even in biology.

Instruction of parents could be done, no doubt, in a carefully controlled situation, but instruction given over the wireless is not in this category. If given it must be of an extremely restricted variety, catching up on the good things that happen to normal people. Along these lines, however, a great deal can be done, and it is to be hoped that it will remain the policy of the BBC to render social service by giving time for health education that takes into account the difficulties inherent in broadcasting.

1957

ELEVEN

For Stepparents

The Wicked Stepmother

The suggestion is sometimes made that were it not for fairy stories, ideas like that of the wicked stepmother wouldn't arise at all. I myself am sure this is wrong and that it is more true to say that no fairy story, or horror comic for that matter, can have universal appeal unless it deals with something that is inherent in each individual adult or child. What the fairy story does is to catch on to something that is true, frightening and unacceptable. Yes, all three; true, frightening and unacceptable. Little bits of the unacceptable in human nature crystallize out into the accepted myth. The question is, what crystallizes out into the stepmother myth? Whatever it is, it has to do with hate and fear as well as with love.

Each individual has a great difficulty in gathering together the aggressiveness that there is in human nature and mixing it with loving. To some extent this difficulty is overcome in earliest infancy by the fact that at first the world is felt in extremes, friendly and hostile, good and hostile, black and white; the bad is feared and hated and the good is wholly accepted. Gradually infants and children grow up out of this and reach the stage where they can tolerate having destructive ideas along with their loving impulses. They then feel guilt but they find they can do things to make good. If mother will wait the moment will come for the gesture of love that is genuine and spontaneous. The relief normally afforded in the earliest stages by the idea of the good and bad extremes is something that even mature adults cannot altogether forego. Children, and little children in particular, we easily allow some persistence of this relic of infancy, and we

99

know we can find a ready response when we read or tell stories which present the good and bad extremes.

Usually the real mother and the stepmother join up in the imagination with these extremes, and especially so because of the second thing that I want to describe which is that there are all sorts of reasons why children could hate their mothers. This idea of a hate of a mother is very difficult for everyone and some who are listening will not like to hear the word hate and mother put in the same sentence. However, it can't be helped; mothers, if they do their job properly, are the representatives of the hard, demanding world and it is they who gradually introduce reality which is so often the enemy of impulse. There is anger with mother and hatred is somewhere even when there is absolutely no doubt of love that is mixed with adoration. If there are two mothers, a real one who has died, and a stepmother, do you see how easily a child gets relief from tension by having one perfect and the other horrid? This is almost as true of the world's expectations as of a child's beliefs.

On top of all this a child comes to see or to feel eventually that mother's devotion at a very early stage has provided the essential conditions that enabled him or her to start, to start to exist as a person, with personal rights, personal impulses and a personal technique of living. In other words, there was absolute dependence in the beginning and as the child begins to be able to realize this so there develops a fear of a primeval mother who has magic powers for good and evil. How difficult it is for each one of us to see that this all-powerful primeval agency was our own mother, someone we have come to know as a lovable, but not by any means perfect or perfectly reliable, human being. How precarious it all was. And further, in the case of a girl, it is this same mother, who was at first all-powerful, who maddeningly represented hard fact, who was all the time adorable, who actually comes to stand in between the daughter and the father. Here in particular, the real mother and the stepmother start from different places; for the real mother hopes while the stepmother fears that the girl will win her father's love. Isn't this enough to show that we must not expect children to grow up all of a sudden from a tendency to split up the world in general and their two mothers in particular into good and bad, and that we must expect some persistence of these childhood ideas in adults?

We can use logical argument, we can tell ourselves over and over again that what matters is not whether people are black or white but whether they as human beings are loving and lovable. But we are left with our dreams and who would wish to be rid of fantasies? In fantasy we don't need to be grown up all the time in the way we need to be when we catch the train to the office or when we do the shopping. In fantasy the infantile, the childish and the adolescent all lie down with adult maturity. But we notice the inconvenience of fantasy when we happen to split into one or other of the black characteristics of the world's myths. I myself may have slipped into one perhaps by talking about the hate and the fear of mother that I feel has to be mixed in with the love in the fully experienced child-mother relationships. You may think I'm nuts.

The Value of the Unsuccess Story

In the study of any problem to do with human affairs we can keep super-ficial or we can go deep. If we could keep superficial we avoid a lot of unpleasantness but we also avoid deeper values. Some of the letters that came in after the recent broadcast did go beyond the obvious. For instance it was pointed out that the child who has lost the parent cannot be treated as if this had not happened and often it is preferable for a stepmother or a stepfather to allow another name so that the child keeps the name Mummy or Daddy for the parent lost. The idea of the lost parent can be kept alive and the child can be greatly helped by the attitude which makes this pos-sible. Also it was pointed out that the child taken over may be disturbed; and in this special case of a child who was not loved, the boy had had a period with the grandmother before coming to the stepmother so that he was twice deprived and consequently liable to feel hopeless about human relationships and dependabilities. If a child feels hopeless in this way then he cannot take the risk of starting up new ties and defends himself against feeling deeply and against new dependencies.

Do you know that quite a lot of mothers do not love their own infants at the time they give birth to them? They feel awful, just like the step-mother. They try to pretend they love but they just can't. How much eas-ier for them if they had been told in advance that love is a thing that may come but it cannot be turned on. Usually a mother soon comes to love, to love her infant during her pregnancy, but this is a matter for experience, not for conventional expectation. Fathers have the same problem sometimes. Perhaps this is more easily accepted, so there is less need for fathers to pretend and their love can come naturally and in its own time. Apart from not loving, mothers not infrequently hate their babies. I am speaking of ordinary women who in fact manage quite well and who see to it that someone acts for them and acts well. I know of many mothers who lived in dread lest they should find that they have harmed their own infants and they can never talk of their difficulty because of it being so unlikely that they could get understanding. There is so much in human nature that is deep and hidden and personally I would rather be the child of a mother who has all the inner conflicts of the human being than be mothered by someone for whom all is easy and smooth, who knows all the answers, and is a stranger to doubt.

Most of those who claimed success here and there could register unsuccess somewhere else, and in the right place and in the right time the unsuccess story has the very greatest value. Of course it is another matter when people go around moaning and groaning but this is certainly not what happened with our stepmother who suffered so much because she could not love her stepson. Whenever a wife or a husband takes over a stepchild there is always a lot of back history, and this back history makes all the difference. It is not just a matter of guilt feeling because of a child that is, so to speak, stolen; there is a whole story of a choice of a widow or widower, or the rescue of a person unhappily married. There are a whole host of important issues that cannot be ignored and which affect the stepparent's dream or imaginative background to the new relationship. In any one case things can be examined, and even usefully examined, but in talking generally the subject immediately becomes too vast to be covered. The woman who finds herself mothering a child who was born of a woman who is imaginatively her rival, even if dead, may easily find herself forced by her own imagination into the position of witch rather than of fairy godmother. She may indeed find no difficulty or she may, as some of the letter-writers described, like to take second place to the former wife. But many men and women are still struggling to grow up when they marry and after, and they must fight for their own rights or lose their identity and their whole feeling of being real. A woman may easily feel the presence of the other woman's child to be a reminder of the child's mother and an intolerable reminder. If this sort of thing is true and yet unconscious it can distort the picture and make impossible a natural growth of feelings towards tolerance and then love.

I have only time to mention the fact that a proportion of stepchildren are really nasty on account of the experiences they have been through. One can explain them and excuse them but the stepmother has to endure them. There is no way out for her. Fortunately most stepchildren are able to be brought round to a friendly attitude and indeed, as the letters show, in very many cases the stepchildren are just exactly like the mother's own. So often there are no difficulties or the difficulties are not big and present no threat. Many people lose sight of the perplexity of the step-situation and come to believe it is all quite simple. For people with no difficulties my sort of probing into the imaginative world must seem irksome, even dangerous. It is dangerous to their sense of security but as I have said, by losing sight of the bad dreams and even nightmares and of the depressions and suspicions that they came through they also lose sight of all that which makes sense of their achievement.

A smattering of unsuccess stories can greatly enrich our lives. Moreover, these stories can show us that there is a point in helping unsuccessful people to get together. If they get together and talk they share their burdens and sometimes lighten them. A correspondent asked for a meeting of unsuccessful stepparents. I think such a meeting might be fruitful. It would be composed of ordinary men and women.

1955

TWELVE

What Do We Know about Babies as Cloth Suckers?

There's a great deal to be got out of watching what babies do in passing the time between sleeps. But first we must get free from the idea that there is a right and a wrong; our interest arises out of the fact that from babies we can learn about babies. The speaker last week took the point of view that if a particular infant sucks his thumb or a cloth that's not where we come in to approve or to disapprove, but it's where we have a chance to get to know something about that particular infant. I agree with him and with the mothers from whose letters he quoted.

We are concerned with a wide variety of phenomena that characterise infant life. We can never know all about these because there's always a new infant, and no two infants are exactly alike either in face or in habits. We know babies not only by the line of their nose and the colour of their hair, if any, but also by their idiosyncrasies.

When mothers tell me about children I usually get them to remember what sort of things happened at the very beginning which were character-istic. They rather like reminding themselves of these things which bring up the past so vividly.

They tell me about all sorts of objects which become adopted by the infant, and which become important, and get sucked or hugged, and which tide the infant over moments of loneliness and insecurity, or provide solace, or which act as a sedative. The objects are halfway between being part of the infant and part of the world. Soon they are apt to acquire a name, like "tissie" or "nammie," which betrays their double origin. Their smell and texture are their essential elements, and you dare not wash them. Nor do you leave such an object behind when going away from home. If you are wise you let the object fade away, like the old soldier of the song who never dies; you don't destroy it or lose it or give it away.

The main thing is that you never challenge the infant: "Is this thing something you thought up, or is it part of the world that you found and took to yourself?" A little later and you will be enjoining your infant to say "ta," and so to acknowledge that that woolly dog came as a present from an aunt. But this *first* object is established as part of the furniture of the cot and pram before the word "ta" can be said or could make sense, before the infant makes a clear distinction between the me and the not-me, or while the making of this distinction is in process.

A personality is being formed and a life is being lived that has never been lived before, and this new person living this new life is what the mother and father are interested in from the moment the infant is felt to be moving in the womb. The personal life starts right away, and I shall stick to this idea even although I know that puppies and kittens also suck cloths and play, a fact which makes me say that animals, too, are more than just bundles of reflexes and appetites.

When I say that life starts right away I admit that at first life takes a very restricted form, but the personal life of the infant has certainly started by the time of birth. These odd habits of infants tell us that there is something more in infant life than sleeping and getting milk, and something more than getting instinctual gratification from a good feed taken in and kept down. These habits indicate that an infant is there already, actually living a life, building up memories, forming a personal pattern of behaviour.

To understand further I think we must reckon that there is in being from the first a crude form of what later we call the imagination. This enables us to say that the infant takes in with the hands and with the sensitive skin of the face as well as with the mouth. The *imaginative* feeding experience is much wider than the purely physical experience. The *total* experience of feeding can quickly involve a rich relationship to the mother's breast, or to the mother as gradually perceived, and what the baby does with the hands and eyes widens the scope of the feeding act. This which is normal is made more plain when we see an infant's feed being managed in a mechanical way. Such a feed, far from being an enriching experience for the infant, interrupts the infant's sense of going on being. I don't know quite how else to put it. There has been a reflex activity and no personal experience.

When you tickle an infant's toe you can produce a smile, but the infant may be feeling anything but pleased. The reflex has betrayed its owner. It almost owns the infant. It is not our job to wield the power we undoubtedly possess by eliciting reflexes, and by stimulating instinctual gratifications that do not arise as part of the rhythm of the infant's personal life.

All sorts of things an infant does while feeding seem senseless to us because they don't put on weight. I am saying that it is just these very things that reassure us that the infant is feeding, not just *being fed*, is living a life and not just responding to the stimuli we offer.

Have you ever seen an infant sucking a finger at the same time as happily breast-feeding? I have. Have you ever seen a dream walking? When an infant sucks bits of clothing, or the eiderdown or a dummy, this represents a spillover of the imagination, such as it is, imagination stimulated by the central exciting function which is feeding.

I will put it another way. Have you ever thought that the feeling round and the finger-sucking and the sucking of cloths and the clutching of the rag doll is the infant's first show of affectionate behaviour? Can anything be more important?

You perhaps take your infant's capacity for being affectionate for granted, but you soon know about it if you have a child that cannot show affection or who has lost the art. It may be possible to induce a child to eat who seems unwilling, but there is nothing you can do to make an unaffectionate child affectionate. You can shower affection on him but he turns away, either silently or with screams of protest.

These odd, off-the-mark activities that we are talking about are a sign that the infant is there as a person and, moreover, confident in the relationship to the mother. The infant is able to use objects that are symbolic, as we would say, of the mother or of some quality of the mother, and is able to *enjoy* actions that are only *playing*, and are at one or more removed from the *instinctual* act, that is to say, *feeding*.

Look at what happens if the infant begins to lose confidence. A minor deprivation may produce a compulsive element in the sucking habit, or whatever it is, so that it becomes a main line instead of a branch line. But if there should be a more severe or prolonged deprivation the infant loses all the capacity to suck the bit of cloth or to play with his mouth or to tickle his nose; the meaning goes out of these play activities.

These first play objects and these play activities exist in a world between the infant and the external world. There's a tremendous strain behind the infant's delay in distinguishing between the me and the not-me, and we allow time for this development to take place naturally. We see the infant beginning to sort things out and to know that there is a world outside and a world within, and in order to help we allow an intermediate world, one which is at the same time both personal and external, both me and not-me. This is the same as the intense play of early childhood and the day-dreaming of older children or adults, which is neither dream nor fact, yet it is both.

Come to think of it, do we *any* of us grow right up out of a need for an intermediate area between ourselves, with our personal inner world, and external or shared reality? The strain that the baby feels in sorting out the two is never altogether lost, and we allow ourselves a cultural life, something that can be shared, yet something that is personal. I refer, of course, to such things as friendship and the practice of religion. And in any case there are the senseless things we all do. For instance why do I smoke? For the answer I would have to go to an infant, who wouldn't laugh at me, I'm sure, because an infant knows better than anyone how silly it is always to be sensible.

It's strange, perhaps, but sucking a thumb or a rag doll may feel real, while a real feed may make for unreal feelings. The real feed touches off reflexes, and instincts get involved in a full-blooded way, and the infant has not yet got so far in the establishment of a self as to be able to encompass such powerful experiences. Doesn't this remind you of the riderless horse that wins the Grand National? This victory does not gain a prize for the owner because the jockey failed to keep his seat. The owner feels frustrated and the jockey may have been hurt. When you adapt yourselves to the personal needs and rhythms of your infant at the beginning you are enabling this starter in the race to keep his seat, even to ride his own horse, and to enjoy riding for riding's sake.

For the immature self of a very young child it is self-expression perhaps in the form of these odd habits like cloth-sucking that feels real to the infant, and that gives the mother and infant an opportunity for a human relatedness that is not at the mercy of the animal instincts.

1956

THIRTEEN

Saying "No"

Donald Woods Winnicott

This programme and the next two form a series. The subject is "Saying 'No'." This evening you will hear a discussion between several mothers, and I shall make a brief comment at the end. Next week and the week after I will do most of the talking, but some extracts from the discussion will be quoted, just to remind you.

I think you will enjoy the discussion, which lasts about eight minutes. It feels real to me. As you listen you can be quite sure it isn't staged. It's just the way you would discuss the same subject.

The Mothers' Conversation

Mothers

"It's very difficult to draw the happy medium, whether you tell children not to do this, not to do that all the time, or whether you let them go the whole hog. But, on the other hand, you can't have your home completely wrecked."

"I've just acquired a new home, we've had a flat for a year and we had to buy everything for it, and the new baby as well. And I've decided just to let her have the freedom of the flat, and she's a happy baby because of that."

"Yes, but she's what—twenty months?"

"Twenty-one months, and very active." (*talking together*)

"Three years! Three years of age is slightly different from twenty months." (*talking together*)

"But I've decided to maintain that attitude."

"Will your child have the same freedom when she visits other people's houses?"

"At the moment she has, because she's extremely curious, which she would be at this age."

"I think the business of children being well-behaved when they visit other people depends largely on how much freedom they do have at home. Because if they have freedom to kick around and muck around, in one way or another, then they've not . . . "

"They're not so curious."

"Then they don't want to do it anywhere else. All right, the child will when you come home from shopping take the bag of rice—if you've foolishly left it there—and scatter it all over the floor. (*laughter*) The child's not being naughty, you've been stupid. I mean, when my child does that I realise that the quicker we get over to the sandpit again, where—you know—she can scatter as much as she likes, the better we'll be." (*talking together*)

"Doesn't she ever get bored with the sandpit, and the rice is more intriguing?"

"Of course it is, but also, I mean, well, puddles for instance. I've learned this lesson from somebody else, because my child was looked after for the first year, not full time, but during the days while I was still teaching (before I had the second one I decided I wanted to go on teaching). But even in her ordinary shoes this lady would let her go into puddles, at certain times, and then say 'All right, this time you mustn't go into puddles, because you're just going out. I can't change you now.' And she wouldn't go in the puddles. And it's a very good lesson I've learned, that one. I mean, if you let the child do something when it's not going to be too much of a nuisance to you, then she won't do it when you sort of explain to her that there's a reason she shouldn't do it this time." (*talking together*)

"It doesn't get across, does it?" (*talking together*)

"It's no good just springing it, you must prepare them."

"You can make a game of the explanation: 'Let's do this,' and gently break away from whatever they're doing that's destructive, and find something else to do." (*talking together*) "Well I do . . . explain rationally. What I mean is this business of making a game of whatever the child is doing at the time, and introducing him to another game."

"Distraction?"

"Distraction, yes."

"I think it depends on not having too many things which you say 'No' about. I mean, when our first baby was very little there were two things we said 'No' about. One was some green plants we had in the living-room, we didn't want them pulled about, and the second was electrical wires, of which we had too many hanging around. We said 'No' about these; the rest—I mean if there was anything she could do damage to we put out of the way."

"The wisest thing." (*talking together*)

"These were 'No' always. And the rest weren't. So that when you said a new 'No' to something you knew for some reason she didn't understand, she didn't mind."

"I started the same with mine, with equal success."

"There are occasions when you can't avoid saying 'No.' At twenty-one months you can put things out of their reach—they probably can't climb. It does seem that plugs are things you cannot put out of the way."

"You should get proper plugs fitted—there are proper plugs for electrical appliances."

"I think you just decide that you say 'No' and stick to it. And that it's far better to be spanked by you than to give them an electric shock, or any other kind of shock."

"You can't, after all, always afford to have all the plugs moved." (*talking together*)

"I think it's not so easy as people make out to have a few 'No's' and stick to them. I think if you have a 'No' that seems important enough and interesting enough to the child it'll fascinate them just because it's the only 'No.' Take matches—they'll get a sort of thing that matches are the most interesting thing in the house because you've been so 'No' about them. I think— I think you've got to let them play with matches."

"Has anybody tried teaching them to strike matches by holding them away? . . . "

". . . but that fascinates all the more."

"I don't know, I think it's an awfully good approach, though, to show children just what does happen if they go on playing with them."

"Even to the extent of burning their fingers literally?"

"I don't know—I suppose that's a bit hard, but if they can get near enough to realise that it is hot and it could be painful and they can learn from other things what heat is."

"Yes, I was lucky; my child touched the towel rail once, and it was hot and it burnt him, and I said 'Hot'."

"My second child, he will do something and he will get hurt and he will realise, or I presume he realises, why he's been hurt; but the next day he's willing to go and do exactly the same thing again."

"It's a matter of temperament I'm sure. My first child took a mouthful of hot bacon at the age of about eighteen months, and I said 'Hot' and from then on I don't think she's ever burned herself. Because she knows what 'hot' is and she's lots of imagination and also quite frightened about it. But the second child's quite different. She's had lots and lots of mouthfuls of hot bacon."

"There are certain things they cannot do which don't exactly hurt them. Like an automatic lighting gas cooker. All my little boy has to do is lift up the lighter. Well it turns on the gas, it doesn't hurt him, it just lights up the gas and it can do a lot of damage to anything that happens to be above. He knows he shouldn't do it, and he shakes his head as he does it." (*laughter*)

"Well, isn't that where a well-timed slap comes in?"

"Isn't that surely where you have to be for rather a long time on the lookout, and the moment he gets near it you whip him away?" (*talking together*)

"It is the responsibility of the mother that a child just should not be in the kitchen, and that's that. I mean, it can only be our responsibility."

"But you're washing and cooking." (*talking together*)

"A child won't stay in its play-pen indefinitely."

"Oh no, I know, but I should have thought there was a way of getting over quite a lot of this. It's by distractions. If he goes to the gas flame, you give him something equally attractive but safe. It's the same way as with an older child, you just have to remind them all the time that they must turn the saucepan handles away, so that any younger child won't come and pull anything."

"We're rather fortunate. Our dining-room has a connecting door with the kitchen and the children have to have the dining-room as a sort of play-room, and I try to keep them in there. But I don't shut the door on them. And as long as they know that I'm just in the next room, and they can see me if they want to, they nearly always will stay in the dining-room."

"What age?"

"Oh, from the early stage, from the time they've been out of the play-pen, from about a year or so. They will come and see me round the door you know, and then they'll go back in again with all their toys and things."

"Do you think this constant being on the watch, and having to find distractions, and remind them and so on, is the most tiring thing?"

"Yes." (*talking together*)

"Added to which it's a matter of time. You're trying to do so many things at once, you're cooking, perhaps you're boiling up nappies, somebody knocks at the front door, and you suddenly turn round and find your little boy is playing with the gas taps, or he's trying to plug in an electric fire you forgot to take away the night before. That's the sort of thing that happens—you can't possibly think of everything in advance."

DWW

I expect this group of mothers went on discussing and exchanging views over a cup of tea. We have to leave them there.

This week, as I said earlier, I shall make only a brief general comment, and next week and the week after I hope to take up and develop some of the points raised. I always enjoy hearing this sort of thing, when people talk about their specialty. It's the same when farmers talk about wheat and rye and potatoes, or when any craftsman talks of his trade. For instance, these women talk of the difference between babies at twenty-four months or three years or any other age. They know what immense changes occur from month to month. At twelve months only a few words make sense to a baby as words, whereas at twenty-four months verbal explanations begin to be a good way of communicating, and an effectual method for getting co-operation when "No" is what you actually mean. We see from the discussion that there are several stages. I could sort out three. First, you are absolutely responsible all the time. Second, you begin to convey "No" to your baby because you are right in discerning the dawning of intelligence and the beginnings of your baby's ability to sort out what you allow from what you don't allow. You are not trying to deal with moral right and wrong, you are simply letting the infant know about the dangers that you protect him or her from. I think your "No's" are based on the idea of real dangers. Do you remember how two mothers talked about heat? At an appropriate moment they uttered the word "hot" and so linked up the danger with pain. But many dangers are not linked with pain in such a simple way, so "No" has to suffice until the next stage is reached. At the third stage you gain the infant's co-operation by offering an explanation. This involves language. "No" because it's hot. "No" because I say "No." "No" because I like that plant, implying that if the plant is pulled about you won't love the baby so much for a few minutes.

I have spoken about three stages, but these stages overlap. First, there is the stage at which you take full responsibility, so that if anything untoward happens you blame yourself, and this stage only very slowly becomes obsolete. In fact you continue to take responsibility, but you get some relief because of the child's growing ability to understand things. If this first stage ever becomes a thing of the past, this means your child has grown right up out of the need for family control and has become an independent member of society.

At the second stage you impose yourself and your view of the world on the infant. This stage will usually change over into the third stage of explanation, but the rate of change and the manner of it depends on the child as well as on you. Children are so different from each other in the way they develop. We can take up these points next week. Perhaps you already see that saying "No" isn't just saying "No."

⟳

Last week you heard some mothers discussing saying "No," and I made a brief comment. This week and the next I shall talk about some of the things that I found myself thinking while I was listening. But there is something I would like to say that has to do with the whole discussion. In my work I learn a great deal about the difficulties that mothers have when they are not fortunately placed. Perhaps they have big personal difficulties so that they can't fulfil themselves even when they can see the way; or they have husbands who are away or who don't give proper support, or who interfere, who are even jealous; some have no husband but they still have to bring the baby up. And then there are others who are caught up in adverse conditions, poverty, crowded dwellings, unkind neighbours. So much so that they can't see the wood for the trees. And there are also those who are caring for other people's babies.

I feel that the mothers who met here to discuss the management of their own babies are of the usual run of healthy and fortunate people, and they have the sense of security which is necessary if they are to get down to the real problems of infant care. I know that most mothers are just like these that we heard, but I like to draw attention to the fact that they are happy, partly because we lose something if we take good fortune for granted, and partly because I am thinking of all the mothers who may be listening and who are inhibited, unhappy, frustrated and not succeeding; because everyone really wants to succeed.

After saying this I remind you of three stages I sorted out for you last time. First, I said, you are caught up in a process which in effect involves you as totally responsible for the protection of the infant. Then comes a time when you can say "No," and then comes a time for explanations.

About this first stage in which you are fully responsible, I would like to say a word. You will be able to say in a few months' time that you never, not once, let your infant down, though of course you had to be a frustrating person all along because you couldn't, nor could anyone, fulfil all of an infant's needs—a good job you don't have to. There is no "No," is there, in this first stage; and I reminded you that this first stage overlaps the subsequent stages; it goes on and on and on right up to the time when your child becomes grown-up, independent of family control. You will do awful things, but I don't think you will ever really let your child down, not if you can help it.

At the next stage, what I called stage two, "No" begins to appear. You convey "No" somehow or other. Perhaps you just say "Brhhhhhhh." Or you screw up your nose or frown. Or the use of the word "No" is quite a good way unless the infant is deaf. I think if you are happy you find it easy to do this "No" business on a practical basis, establishing a way of life that fits in with yours and with the world around. Unhappy mothers, out of their own unhappiness, may tend to overdo the happy loving side of infant care, and sometimes they say "No" just because they are irritable, but that just can't be helped. And following this is stage three, which I call the stage of explanations. Some people find it a great relief when they can at last talk and hope to be understood, but I am saying that the basis of everything surely is what happens earlier.

I would like to remind you now of the part of the discussion where a mother said she introduced "No's" one at a time. I think the point is that she was clear in her own mind what she would allow and what she would not allow. If she had been in a muddle herself, the baby would have lost something valuable. Listen again to a fragment of the mothers' conversation:

Mothers

"I think it depends on not having too many things which you say 'No' about. I mean, when our first baby was very little there were two things we said 'No' about. One was some green plants we had in the living-room, we didn't want them pulled about, and the second was electrical wires, of which we had too many hanging around. We said 'No' about these; the rest—I mean if there was anything she could do damage to we put out of the way."

"The wisest thing." (*talking together*)

"These were 'No' always. And the rest weren't. So that when you said a new 'No' to something you knew for some reason she didn't understand, she didn't mind."

"I started the same with mine, with equal success."

DWW

So here we are told of a mother's capacity to adapt to the infant's need for an uncomplicated start to something which must needs become more and more complex. The infant had two "No's" at first, and then no doubt others were added, and there was no unnecessary muddle.

Then let's remind ourselves of the way a word was used before explanation could be given in words. Here in this bit the word "hot" brings us just exactly between stages two and three, as I call them.

Mothers

"Even to the extent of burning their fingers literally?"

"I don't know—I suppose that's a bit hard, but if they can get near enough to realise that it is hot and it could be painful and they can learn from other things what heat is."

"Yes, I was lucky; my child touched the towel rail once, and it was hot and it burnt him, and I said 'Hot'."

"My second child, he will do something and he will get hurt and he will realise, or I presume he realises, why he's been hurt; but the next day he's willing to go and do exactly the same thing again."

"It's a matter of temperament I'm sure. My first child took a mouthful of hot bacon at the age of about eighteen months, and I said 'Hot' and from then on I don't think she's ever burned herself. Because she knows what 'hot' is and she's lots of imagination and also quite frightened about it. But the second child's quite different. She's had lots and lots of mouthfuls of hot bacon."

"There are certain things they cannot do which don't exactly hurt them. Like an automatic lighting gas cooker. All my little boy has to do is lift up the lighter. Well it turns on the gas, it doesn't hurt him, it just lights up the gas and it can do a lot of damage to anything that happens to be above. He knows he shouldn't do it, and he shakes his head as he does it." (*laughter*)

"Well, isn't that where a well-timed slap comes in?

DWW

. . . Well, perhaps it does. You can see from the way they talk that it is in the living experience from moment to moment that all the important work is done. There are no lessons and there is no set time for learning. The lesson comes with the way the people concerned find themselves reacting.

I want to repeat, however, nothing absolves the mother of babies and small children from her task of eternal vigilance.

Mothers.

"All right, the child will when you come home from shopping take the bag of rice—if you've foolishly left if there—and scatter it all over the floor. (*laughter*) The child's not being naughty, you've been stupid. I mean, when my child does that I realise that the quicker we get over to the sandpit again, where—you know—she can scatter as much as she likes, the better we'll be."

DWW

Yes, it was her fault that the rice got spilled, wasn't it! But I guess she was annoyed though! Sometimes it's just a matter of architecture, the way rooms are arranged or a glass panel in the door between the kitchen and the child's playroom.

Mothers

"We're rather fortunate. Our dining-room has a connecting door with the kitchen and the children have to have the dining-room as a sort of play-room, and I try to keep them in there. But I don't shut the door on them. And as long as they know that I'm just in the next room, and they can see me if they want to, they nearly always will stay in the dining-room."

"What age?"

"Oh, from the early stage, from the time they've been out of the play-pen, from about a year or so. They will come and see me round the door you know, and then they'll go back in again with all their toys and things."

DWW

Yes, she was fortunate, wasn't she, in the way her rooms were arranged?

And then we hear of the strain that eternal vigilance puts on mothers. This is especially true, I think, when the woman, before she was married, had a regular job, so that she knew the satisfaction that most men know in their work, that of being able to concentrate, and then to come home and relax. Isn't the world a bit unfair to women over this? Let's hear what the group says about this.

Mothers

"Do you think this constant being on the watch, and having to find dis-tractions, and remind them and so on, is the most tiring thing?"

"Yes." (*talking together*)

"Added to which it's a matter of time. You're trying to do so many things at once, you're cooking, perhaps you're boiling up nappies, somebody knocks at the front door, and you suddenly turn round and find your little boy is playing with the gas taps, or he's trying to plug in an electric fire you forgot to take away the night before. That's the sort of thing that happens—you can't possibly think of everything in advance."

DWW

No, you certainly can't. Fortunately, eternal vigilance is not eternal, though it feels so. It only lasts for a limited time for each child. Too soon the infant is a toddler, the toddler is going to school, and vigilance is then something shared with the teachers. However, "No" remains an important word in the parents' vocabulary, and prohibiting remains a part of what mothers and fathers find themselves doing right on and until each child in his or her own way breaks out of the parental control and establishes a personal way of life and of living.

But there are some important things in this discussion which I have not yet had time to refer to, so I am glad to have the chance to continue next week.

ॐ

This week I shall go on discussing saying "No," in infant and child care. I shall do as I did before and talk about three stages, because this is a convenient way to go about developing the theme of when and how to say "No" and why. I want to describe the three stages again, but in a rather different language, so in a way it won't matter if you didn't hear last week or if you have forgotten all about it.

I did say of the three stages that they overlap. Stage one doesn't end when stage two begins, and so on. Stage one comes before you say "No"; the baby doesn't understand yet, and you are absolutely in charge, and you ought to be. You take full responsibility, and this taking of responsibility lessens but never quite ends until the child becomes grown-up, that is to say finished with the need for the controls that the family provides.

This that I call the first stage really belongs to the parental attitude, and father (if he exists and if he is around) soon takes part in the setting up and the maintaining of this parental attitude. I will go on to the next two stages later; they have to do with words and the first stage hasn't to do with words at all. So at first the mother, soon the two parents, can make it their job to see that unexpected things don't happen. They can do this deliberately, but it mainly happens in their bodies almost; it's a whole mode of behaviour that reflects a mental attitude. The baby feels secure and absorbs the mother's confidence in herself just like taking in milk. During all this time the parents are saying "No," they are saying "No" *to the world,* they say "No, keep off, keep out of our circle; in our circle is the thing we care for and we allow nothing past the barrier." If the parent becomes frightened then something has got past the barrier and the baby is hurt, just as much as if a terrible noise has got through and given the baby a sensation so acute that it's unbearable. In air-raids babies weren't afraid of bombs, but they were affected immediately when their mothers developed panic. But most infants come through the early months without ever having suffered in this way, and when eventually the world has to break through the barriers, then the growing child has begun to develop ways of dealing with the unexpected, and has even begun to be able to predict. We could talk about the various defences that the developing child acquires, but that would be another discussion altogether.

Out of this early phase in which you assume that you are responsible comes the sense of parental responsibility—the thing that distinguishes parents from children and perhaps makes nonsense of the game some people like to play whereby mother and father hope to be just pals to their children. But mothers have to be able at last to begin to let their infants know something of the dangers that they protect them from, and also to let them know what sort of behaviour would affect the mother's loving and liking. So they find themselves saying "No."

We can now see the second stage starting, when instead of saying "No" to the world around, the mother says "No" to her child. This has been referred to as introducing the reality principle, but it doesn't matter what it's called; the mother with her husband gradually introduces the infant to reality and reality to the infant. One way is by prohibition. You will be glad to hear me saying this, that saying "No" is one way, because prohibition is only one of two ways. The basis of "No" is "Yes." There are some babies who get brought up on the basis of "No." The mother perhaps feels that safety lies only in her pointing out innumerable danger situations. But it's unfortunate when the infant has to get to know the world this way. Quite a big proportion of infants can use the other method. Their expanding world has a relation to the increasing number of objects and kinds of objects about which mother is able to say "Yes." The infant's development in that case has more to do with what the mother allows than with what she prohibits. "Yes" forms the background on which "No" is added. This of course cannot entirely cover what has to be done; it's merely a matter of whether the infant is developing chiefly along one line or the other. Babies can be highly suspicious from early days, and I must remind you that there are all kinds of babies; but most of them are able to trust their mothers for a while at least. On the whole they reach out for things and for food that they have found mother approves of. Isn't it true that the whole of the first stage is one big "Yes"? It's "Yes" because you never let the baby down. You never really slip up on your over-all task. This is a great big unspoken "Yes" and it gives a firm basis for the infant's life in the world.

I know it's more complex. Soon each infant becomes aggressive and develops destructive ideas, and then naturally the baby's easy trusting of the mother is interfered with, and at times she doesn't feel friendly to the child at all, even though she remains her usual self. But we needn't deal with this sort of complication here, because we have plenty to think about when we see how complex the world quickly becomes in reality, in external reality. For instance, the mother has one set of don'ts, and the helpful grandmother has another set, or there may be a nurse. Also mothers are not all scientists; they have all sorts of beliefs which couldn't be proved. You could find a mother, for instance, who fears that anything green is poisonous, so mustn't be put to the mouth. Now how is a baby to know that a green object is poisonous and a yellow one is lovely? And what if the baby is colour-blind? I know a baby who was cared for by two people, one left-handed and the other right-handed, and this was too much. So we expect complications, but somehow infants come through; they come through to the third stage of explanation. They can then gather wisdom from the store of our knowledge; they can learn what we think we know, and the best thing is that they are now near to being able to disagree with the reasons we give.

To go over what I have said again, at first it's a matter of infant care and dependence, something rather like faith. Then it's a matter of morals; mother's version of morality has to do till the infant develops a personal morality. And then, with the explanations, there is at last a basis for understanding, and understanding is science and philosophy. Isn't it interesting to see the beginnings of big things like these already at this very early stage?

One more word about a mother's "No." Isn't this the first sign of father? In part fathers are like mothers and they can baby-sit and do all sorts of things like a woman. But as fathers, they seem to me to appear first on the infant's horizon as the hard thing in mother which enables her to say "No" and stick to it. Gradually and with luck this "No" principle becomes embodied in the man himself, Daddy, who becomes loved, and even liked, and who can administer the occasional slap without losing anything. But he has to earn the right to slap if he is going to slap, and to earn it by things like being around and by not being on the child's side against the mother. At first you may not like the idea of the embodiment of "No," but perhaps you will accept what I mean a little when I remind you that small children like being told "No." They don't want to play with soft things all the time; they like stones and sticks and the hard floor, and they like to be told where to get off as well as being cuddled.

1960

FOURTEEN

Jealousy

DWW

What do you think about jealousy? Is it good or bad? Normal or abnormal? It would be a good idea when listening to the discussion which follows, between mothers of small children, to keep in mind this question each time when some manifestation of jealousy is described. Is this what is to be expected, or is something wrong somewhere? I think the answer has to be a complex one, but there is no point in making it more complex than need be, so we first of all chose parts of the discussion which are about the sort of things that go on in every home. I don't mind saying in advance that in my opinion jealousy is normal and healthy. Jealousy arises out of the fact that children love. If they have no capacity to love, then they don't show jealousy. Later on we shall have to look at the less healthy aspects of jealousy, and especially at the hidden kind. I think you will see that in the stories that these mothers tell us, jealousy usually comes to a natural end, although it perhaps starts up again and disappears again. Eventually healthy children become able to say they are jealous, and this gives them a chance to discuss what they are jealous about, and that may help a bit. I am putting forward the idea that the first thing to be said about jealousy is that it represents an achievement in the infant's development, indicating a capacity to love.

Further achievements enable the child to tolerate being jealous. The first jealousies are usually around the arrival of a new baby, and it is well-known that jealousy is not avoided by there being only one child in the family. Anything that takes up the mother's time can bring about jealousy, just as a baby can. I really do believe that children who have met jealousy and come to terms with it are richer for the experience. This is what I think, and now I suggest that we listen to some mothers answering questions and talking about jealousy.

Mothers

"Mrs. S. you've got, I know, eight children. Have any of them been jealous of each other?"

"Two or three of them have. The first baby was fifteen months when the second one was born and I was feeding the baby when he was about three weeks old and the child was stroking his hair and saying 'ba-ba' so lovingly and I said, 'Yes, isn't he sweet?', and the next minute the voice changed and the expression changed and he cracked him over the head and said 'ba-ba' and I began to think that the child wasn't quite happy about the baby. And a week later I was getting my hat on to go out and something made me look out of the window, and the baby was just about to be thrown on the path, so I switched that around promptly by putting him back in his old place and putting the baby in the handlebar place, and I've done that with them all and I found that there is no more trouble in the pram, they don't like being put out. And that child—the first one—made scenes and cried an awful lot and stamped his feet and I think it was because of the baby."

"Is he still jealous?"

"Not at all. He has got right out of that. He is the eldest one now and he is very proud of them all, but he was for a time."

"Mrs. L., what happened with your three?"

"Well, the eldest was two when his brother was born, and three-and-a-half when his sister was born. He was an easy, happy child, and on first see-ing his brother he just took no notice at all. We tried to prepare him for the event. He just didn't understand."

"No, he was a bit young I suppose."

"Too young to understand. And his indifference lasted a week or two and then the day came when he saw the baby in the pram and he hadn't himself been in the pram for months because he was too big, but he wept bitterly."

"The baby was how old by then?"

"Oh, about three or four weeks, and he wept bitterly, and that was the beginning I think. And after that each time the baby was changed he would instantly be either wet or dirty and it took a long time for him to improve. And it was just when he was older and understood that he improved about that."

"What happened when his sister was born?"

"He always treated her with great love and affection, and so did the second boy."

"No other sort of lapses from any of them?"

"No. But later on he became aggressive when his brother began to sit up and take notice."

"You think that was a jealousy sign, do you?"

"Oh, definitely, yes. One day I found him trying to suffocate the baby in the pram, and he was most spiteful with him. And I'm afraid I used to retaliate at times on the baby's behalf, because I just couldn't bear it. But I don't think that was a good thing. It didn't improve matters at all."

DWW

These seem to me to be everyday family matters. I will remind you of the ages of the children, because the age makes such a difference. The boy who stroked the baby's hair while the baby was being fed, and then proceeded to try to throw him out onto the path, was fifteen months old when the baby was born. And then there was the two-year-old who at first seemed indifferent. He had been told what to expect, but perhaps he could not understand. It was three weeks after his brother's birth when he saw the baby in the pram that had once been his that he wept bitterly. He got over this with sympathetic help from the mother, but later when his brother began to sit up and take notice, he became aggressive and spiteful, and on one occasion he tried to suffocate the baby, in the pram. Not till he was about four did he come round to a more friendly attitude. Neither he nor his brother were jealous of the baby sister. Here is some more of the mothers' discussion:

Mothers

"Mrs. T, what about jealousies among your seven?"

"Well, the only jealousy I find has been among the girls."

"How many girls have you got?"

"There's only two, you see—there's a boy, then a girl, then four boys and then the other girl. And Jean used to ask and ask and ask, you know, 'Can we have a baby sister?' Each time it was a baby boy, and she got a bit ratty for a day or two, but it soon blew over. Well, then, she came in from school one day and I discovered she had got a baby sister, and she seemed absolutely thrilled at first. The trouble was I had the baby on the 10th, Jean's seventh birthday was on the 16th—no party, I couldn't do it. So for about a month Jean came in from school every evening, had her tea and went straight to bed crying her eyes out. We couldn't do anything with her, she wouldn't listen, but I did think she'd got over it, you know— I did think I'd got her round that. But yesterday baby was ill in bed, and I said to Jean, as innocent as you please, 'Jean would you go and get me a nightgown for Patricia?' And Jean just turned round and said, 'No, why should I? Let her go and get it herself—she's big enough now."

"She's going on being jealous?"

"Yes, it looks like it. But it's been all very peaceful since Patricia was about six weeks. Now she's gone two, and it's suddenly come out again. I can only hope that we can get rid of it again now."

"Jean isn't in any way jealous of her brothers?"

"No."

DWW

It was a week before Jean's seventh birthday that her baby sister was born, and when she had to do without her birthday party she became violently jealous. This first bout of jealousy lasted six weeks, and it all started up again when she was nine and her sister was two. Jean hadn't minded the arrival of four boy babies in the family of seven, and she had indeed always asked for a sister. I suppose the sister you actually get isn't necessarily the same as the sister you long for.

Now here is one more story:

Mothers

"Mrs. G., what about yours? Have you had any jealousies?"

"Yes, we did have. My little girl who's four-and-a-half, she was just coming up to three when the little boy was born and she was very thrilled to have a baby brother, or anyhow, to have a baby. But we found, almost from the word 'go,' that if I had the baby then she had to go and sit on my husband's knee or vice versa; she wanted me to read to her while I was feeding the baby, or at least sit beside me."

"And did that work out?"

"That did, yes. The jealousy phase blew over, faded out, and was quiet until her little brother was—what, I suppose about a year old or so, when he was up and about and in the play-pen and so on, and we had rather a lot of trouble over toys. I brought out her baby toys for him, and of course she recognised them, and 'That's mine, that's mine, that's mine.' And all this business of going back to play with baby toys, and I found I had to get some more baby toys that were exclusively his, otherwise there was no quietness about."

"She didn't want to play with those?"

"No, no, no, she wouldn't touch his, but if she saw him playing with hers, even though she hadn't touched them for about two years, she wanted them again. And that again faded out, without anything very violent happening. Now he's eighteen months, and it's come up again, this time because he's on the move and he's after her things."

". . . tugs of war over them?"

"Yes, we do, indeed. She'll get her things set up—I'm always telling her, 'Put them on the table where he can't reach,' but she'll put them down somewhere low, and she just turns her back and he'll come along and start moving them all over the place. She gets really wild—but she's very patient with him, really."

DWW

This little girl was just nearly three when her brother was born. She was thrilled about it, but she felt displaced by the baby when he was actually there on his mother's knee, and she went to her father instead. When the baby was a year old and she was four, she began to resent the baby's claim on her toys. Even toys that she had seemed to be finished with. Do you notice that she put her toys where the baby could reach them? Her mother says she is very patient with her brother much of the time, and I get the feeling that she really does like him to get at her toys, though she protests; she perhaps feels from his point of view as well as from her own.

Now that you have heard all these stories, do you feel as I do that these jealousies are part of healthy family life?

❀

I have been asking myself the question: How and when does jealousy start? And what is it that has to be there before the word jealousy or envy can begin to be used and make sense? I bring in the word envy because jealousy and envy are very closely linked, for a child who is jealous of a new baby envies the baby his or her possession of the mother's attention. I notice that those mothers who were talking about their babies did not happen to talk about jealousy in any child under fifteen months old. I wonder what you would say about this? I think that evidence of jealousy or envy might be detected earlier than at fifteen months, but not very much earlier. At nine months, for instance, a baby would be too young, too immature as a person to be jealous. At a year probably not; possibly occasionally; but at fifteen months certainly yes. Gradually as the children get older so jealousy is about more complex things, but at the beginning it is fairly obviously about a relationship that is disturbed, or about a threat to a possession which stands for a relationship. It is the relationship to the mother that is at the basis of jealousy, and this comes to include the relationship to the father as time goes on. We find that many of the earliest jealousies are obviously about mother, and they often centre round feeding. This is because for the infant at the beginning feeding is such a vital thing. For the mother feeding is only one of the many things she does for her baby, but to her too it may be very important. Here is part of the discussion between some of the mothers.

Mothers

"There's twenty-two months between them and when the second one was born—I had the second one at home—and my little boy saw him when he was a few minutes old, more or less, that was all right for a few days. Then he happened to see me feeding, and from that time on, for a couple of months, he stood and screamed every time I fed the baby, and there was nothing I could do. I tried everything to try and pacify that child and give him all the comfort I could, but it's very difficult when you're feeding a child, and he just stood and screamed. But after about two months he got over it and he seemed to get over his jealousy altogether, and then when the child—the second one began to sit up about seven or eight months—we had the same performance all over again, not the screaming but jealousy."

"Yes, mine was a bit younger; I must say I find it quite intriguing that she's not had a bottle for—oh some time—she'd forgotten how to suck. I was staggered at this because she came up and she—when I was feeding the little one and she wanted to have a go too, so I thought, good—but she didn't, she—as soon as she got near it she was sort of a bit revolted by it. I thought, all right, have a go if you want to, see what happens—and she came up several times—she's done it fairly recently, just as a sort of joke. I didn't put her off at all, I said, 'Come on, have a go,' and she didn't want it. But she has now taken to having a bottle as the baby is now on a bottle, and I give her a nasty little one, poor child, a tiny little thing, but as a token, you know."

"My elder daughter sits on my lap while the baby is feeding, and I'm breast-feeding so you can imagine it's rather a shambles. (*laughter*) She adores it you know, she pats the baby's head and strokes it . . . but then she's only seventeen months you see, so it's rather different."

"We've had jealousy with the two eldest ones, not with the second and third; but the first two, my little girl, when the second one arrived, she wanted to go on my husband's lap or she wanted to have something special or she wanted me to read to her while I was feeding the baby and that sort of thing, and then the phase went off and now the little boy is seventeen months and we do have these awful wars. Whatever one or the other has, the other wants, and the little boy now—of course there was a time when she could take anything from him, she is three years older than he is—but now he gets a jolly good hold on whatever he's got, and yells—doesn't cry but really yells fiercely at her. But they're both of them very fond of the baby in their gestures and so on, and they don't either of them seem to be jealous of the latest one."

"That isn't in fact jealousy surely when they just fight over possessions, is it . . . "

"It's because they want my attention."

"Oh, I see."

"You see, a baby toy which I will give to the little boy—something which the little girl has completely grown out of—because I've given it to him she will then immediately want it; and if I hadn't given it to the little boy, if I'd just left it lying on the table where she could have reached it if she'd wanted it, she wouldn't have taken any notice at all."

DWW

From this you can see that quite a lot has to do with the feeds. I can use the last bit of the conversation to illustrate what I want to say. I am thinking of the little girl who is often openly jealous of the second baby, which was a boy, and this wore off. And then she and the boy, who is now seventeen months old, have these awful wars over toys. But it's different the way she is jealous and the way he just hangs on and yells. One mother said: "That isn't jealousy, it's just a fight over possessions." And I agree, but it's exactly here that we can look at the way jealousy develops. I said that there is an age for jealousy. Now I want to say that after a certain age the child is jealous and before that age the child is just hanging on to a possession. First is possessing, and jealousy comes later.

I can't help being reminded of a theatre agency which advertises with the following slogan: "You want the best seats; we have them." This always makes me madly jealous so that I feel like rushing off to get the seats that I want and they have. The snag is that I have to pay for them. Using this as an illustration, I can say that up to a certain age a little boy or girl is all the time proclaiming: "I have the best mother"—only not in those words. Eventually the moment comes when the child can proclaim: "I have the best mother—you want her." This is a painful new development.

To get a clear sequence of events, we must go back a little further, though. There is a time before the baby is, so to speak, proclaiming: "I have the best mother." In this earlier stage this fact of the best mother is assumed. There is no place for advertisement. The mother, and everything that stands for her, is taken for granted by the infant. Then comes: "I have the best mother," and this marks the dawn of the baby's understanding that the mother is not just part of the baby's self, but that she comes to the baby from outside, and she might not come, and there could be other mothers. For the baby the mother now becomes a possession, and one that can be held on to or dropped. All this has to wait for development in the little child, what we call emotional growth. And then comes the second half of the slogan: "and you want her." But this is not jealousy yet, it is a matter of a defended possession. Here the child clings on tight. If the theatre did this we wouldn't be able to get to the theatre. Then at last comes the recognition that the central possession, mother, can belong to someone else. The child is now one of the people who want and is no longer one of those who have. It is somebody else who has. This is when jealousy becomes the right word to use to describe the changes that happen in a child when a new infant appears like a ghost of a past self, feeding at the breast, or sleeping peacefully in the pram.

I will repeat what I have said. I have referred to early infancy in which what is desirable is part of the self, or it makes an appearance as if created out of the infant's need. The coming and going is taken for granted by the baby. Then the thing or person who is loved becomes part of a world outside the infant, and is a possession to be held or lost. Any threat of loss of ownership leads to distress and to a fierce clinging on to the object. In the course of time and further development, the infant becomes the one who threatens, the one who hates anything new that turns up to claim the mother's attention, such as a new baby or perhaps just the book she is reading. It can now be said that jealousy has been achieved. The child envies the new baby or book, and makes every effort to regain the position lost, even if only for a time or in token form. So at the first times of jealousy it is common for us to see children trying to revert to being infants, even if only in some way or for a little while. They may even want to re-experience a breast-feed. But commonly they long to be just treated as they were treated when they had full possession, when they were the ones who had, and they knew of no-one who had not, but wanted. You may remember from the discussion in last week's programme the child who started wetting again, and you've just heard about the older one to whom the mother gave a little bottle; it was a token, she said.

When you think of all that goes on in the little child while the days and the weeks pass by, you can easily see why there is a need for a reliable environment, and this is the very thing that you can give your child better than anyone else can. You often wonder, is something right or wrong? But it is more interesting to see things in terms of the child's growth and development.

❧

The stories in the discussion show that jealousy tends to disappear, and I want to examine how this happens. What happens depends on the development that is all the time going on in the child. I think you like to know what sort of things do go on in the child, just as a matter of interest. When things go wrong, as they must do from time to time, you are at a disadvantage if you are working blind. If you know what's going on you become less sensitive to criticism and to chance remarks from passers-by.

I want to speak of three ways in which things going on in the child enable jealousy to come to an end. The first is this. Jealousy is what we see when the child is in a state of acute conflict. It might be just anxiety, except that the child knows what it is about. The jealous child is actually experiencing loving and hating, both at once, and it feels horrible. Let us think of the child. At first, perhaps, even for the child it looks rather nice to see the new baby being nursed or fed. Gradually it dawns, however, that this is not oneself but another who is there, and the love of the mother produces extreme anger, anger with the new baby, with mother, or just with everything. For a time the child only knows anger. Some of the anger gets expressed. The child screams; perhaps kicks; or hits; or makes a mess. Imaginatively everything is spoilt, broken, destroyed. Surely the thing that brings about the new development is the survival of the world, of the baby, of the mother. The new development is the child's recognition of this survival. This is just one more way in which the small child begins to sort out fantasy from fact. In the child's imagination the world was destroyed by the anger, as by an atom bomb, but it survives, and the mother's attitude is unchanged.

So it's safe, then, to imaginatively destroy, to hate. And with this new thing to help, the child becomes able to be contented with only doing a little of the screaming and hitting and kicking that would surely be appropriate.

In a few weeks the jealousy has settled down to something else, the experience of going on loving, with the love complicated by ideas of destruction. The result for us who are watching is that we see a child who is sometimes sad. It's sad to love something or someone and to dream that what one loves comes to harm.

Further relief comes from the fact that in destructive dreams the thing hurt can be something standing for the baby or the mother, perhaps a cat, or a dog, or a chair. Along with the child's sadness comes some degree of concern for the baby or whatever it was that was the object of jealousy. But mothers know they can't at first rely on the child's concern because, for a time, concern all too readily changes over to a jealous attack, and if no-one is about harm is done.

My point here is that the imaginative life begins to function, and to offer the child relief from the need for direct action, and this gives time and opportunity for the beginnings in the child of a sense of responsibility. The second way that I think jealousy can end is through the growing power of the child to absorb satisfactory experiences and make them part of the self. There grows up an accumulation of good memories in the child, memories of being cared for well; memories of nice sensations; of being bathed; of yelling; or smiling; of finding things just when and where they were expected, even better than they could have been expected. And also there is a building up of memories of satisfactions following orgies of excitement, especially feeding.

All these things could be added up and called an idea of mother or of mother and father. There is a reason why jealousy often doesn't appear at all in a child, because the child has had enough, enough at any rate to be able to spare a little.

The third thing is rather more complicated. It has to do with a child's ability to live through the experiences of others. We call this stepping into the other person's shoes. But this expression seems a bit funny when the other person is an infant feeding at the breast or being bathed or lying asleep in a cot. However do small children become able to do this? Some do take a long time, even years, before they let themselves not only see the other person's point of view but actually enjoy an extra bit of life that the other person is living. It is easy to see children—boys as well as girls—identifying themselves with their mothers. They let the mother be the actual mother while they play at being in her place, imagining them-selves into her position. Here is a bit of the discussion which illustrates this:

Mothers

"Mrs. G., what about the new baby in your family?"

"Well, neither of them—neither of the elder ones—have shown any jeal-ousy towards the new baby, but they have shown jealousy, both of them, towards each other about touching the baby or fondling the baby or hold-ing the baby."

"A sort of rivalry?"

"Yes, rivalry between them. Say I'm sitting down and I have the baby on my lap and the little girl comes over to talk to the baby. Immediately the eighteen-month-old will come charging over and try to elbow her out of the way, before she gets a look in. And from that point a sort of tug-of-war starts as to who's going to have the baby."

"What do you do?"

"Well, in that case I put a protective arm around the baby and see that they move up a few inches, to give him breathing space."

"Is that a common occurrence?"

"Yes, I think so . . . starting pulling the baby, 'It's my turn to hold the baby,' or 'It's her turn.' He's too young to leave with them, this small babe on my lap. It comes to a case of both sit down, I give it to one without letting go of it, and I count up to ten: 'Right, now the next one.' It's a good idea, but it doesn't really work."

DWW

Here is another example in which a little girl seems to identify herself with her baby brother:

Mothers

"The jealousy phase blew over, faded out, and was quiet until her little brother was—what, I suppose about a year old or so, when he was up and about and in the play-pen and so on, and we had rather a lot of trouble over toys. I brought out her baby toys for him, and of course she recognised them, and 'That's mine, that's mine, that's mine.' And all this business of going back to play with baby toys, and I found I had to get some more baby toys that were exclusively his, otherwise there was no quietness about."

"She didn't want to play with those?"

"No, no, no, she wouldn't touch his, but if she saw him playing with hers, even though she hadn't touched them for about two years, she wanted them again. And that again faded out, without anything very violent happening. Now he's eighteen months, and it's come up again, this time because he's on the move and he's after her things."

". . . tugs of war over them?"

"Yes, we do, indeed. She'll get her things set up—I'm always telling her, 'Put them on the table where he can't reach,' but she'll put them down somewhere low, and she just turns her back and he'll come along and start moving them all over the place. She gets really wild—but she's very patient with him, really."

DWW

When we used this in our first jealousy programme I said: "I get the feeling that this little girl really does like her baby brother to get at her toys, though she protests." I added: "Perhaps she feels from his point of view as well as from her own." Great enrichment comes from the ability to imaginatively live through the experience of others if this can be done without loss of the sense of what is strictly the experience of the self. Here is one of the ways that playing starts ups, and in imaginative play there is no limit to this process of identifying oneself with people and things. The child can be a vacuum cleaner or a horse; can be a queen or a prince; or can be the new baby; or the mother feeding the baby; or the father. We can't make a child able to play, but by protecting and tolerating and waiting and by hundreds of things you do without thinking you are facilitating the child's development. There is a lot more that could be said, but perhaps this is enough to show that when jealousy disappears this is because of the development that has taken place in the child made possible by consistent good care.

अ

I have talked about jealousy as a healthy, normal thing in small children, something that means that they love, and that they have already made considerable progress in their journey away from the complete immaturity that they started with. Also I have talked about some of the developments in each child which makes it possible for jealousy to stop being a feature. All the time I have made a point of saying that these developments in the infant and small child cannot take place satisfactorily without the thing that you can provide, the living relationship in which the child finds a live kind of reliability, one which depends on your being what you are.

Along with this general thing that you provide, there are some special things which you do which make a difference. For instance, you help your child to predict what is going to happen. When you know a big change must take place in the infant's life, you try to give some warning. If you add a new food, you give a taste, and then leave well alone, and probably soon the baby will want the new thing that you have ready. In the same way you try to give warning when you are fairly well on in your new pregnancy, and you feel sure you will be having a new baby. You might think it must be easier if you can use words, if you can explain, but I doubt this. Naturally if the child is already understanding language, you do explain in words and stories, and with the help of picture books. It would be funny if you didn't. But the thing that makes the difference is your attitude, and your attitude affects the issue long before language can be used. If, for instance, a new pregnancy seems to you pleasantly natural, you can gradually let your year-old child know that there is a reason why sitting on your lap isn't quite the same as it was. Your little boy or girl gets to feel that you have something in there that is important. If you happen to be someone who does not easily accept the fact of pregnancy and the changes it brings (and there are plenty of people like that), then there will grow up some mystery, and the small child whose life is about to be very much altered by the birth of a new baby will be in no way prepared when the new baby actually arrives. It is easier when the child who is affected is a bit older. Listen to this:

Mothers

"I was very anxious when I had Roger. You see, I had the two girls, fourteen and thirteen, and I wanted another child while I still could have one, and I was very perplexed about what to do about it, so I talked it over with the girls and said, how would they welcome the idea of me having another baby? And—which is an odd thing to do, isn't it, before you even conceive a child, to discuss it with your others, but I thought it wasn't a bad idea. And they were thrilled to bits, and thought it was a lovely thing, and they'd love to have a child, a baby. And so we all decided it would be a boy. And Susan, my younger daughter, then thirteen—Roger was premature and I told the midwife that I'd started labour—would she let Susan know, and if she'd like to come in and watch labour, she could do so. And she came bouncing in before school, and I was in the throes, you see, so I said, 'Well'—taking a deep breath and thinking I could ruin this child for life— 'Well, this is a labour pain, and this is how you go on about it.' And she gave me a hearty smack on the back and said, 'Well, I expect you've got hours of it yet.' You know. 'See you after school,' and off she went. So she's now going to have her own baby next month, and I think she's thoroughly enjoying it. Well prepared, I should think."

DWW

That girl was thirteen, and of course the mother talked to her, but I think it was the mother's attitude that counted. What about younger children? Children of one or two years are a long way from understanding why there are twenty-nine days in February this year, and yet it is quite possible for them, isn't it, at one or two, to feel themselves a little bit into the position of being the mother of a baby? I am talking about feelings rather than about the child's mind. Most children by one year have some object that is very special to them, and which they sometimes nurse in a crude sort of way, and quite soon they are obviously playing at mothers and babies.

I said that you help you child to predict. There are other things you do; for instance, you try to be fair, and this is very difficult; you can only try. And you can hope that you haven't got a big favourite; except, of course, the new baby at the beginning who needs to feel that he has all of you. You and the child's father share your responsibility in all sorts of ways. And it is to the father that the child naturally turns when dissatisfied with mother and her new preoccupation. Most fathers would like to be a help, and they hate to be so much out at work that they are of no practical use.

And then again, on the whole you do not find yourself giving the precious objects of other children to the new baby, but you let each baby start afresh collecting objects and specialising. So although the main developments which are going on in the child are made possible because the child can rely on you, there are also many things that you do to meet special moments of stress.

You do know, I expect, that tremendous feelings are involved, and that in fact little children don't feel things less than we do. I wonder whether they don't feel things more. We grown-up people count ourselves lucky if we have found ways of keeping in touch with some of the intensity of experience that belongs to early childhood. Small children not only feel things with the utmost intensity, but also they can't be distracted from the actual thing that's bothering them. They haven't yet had time to organise personal methods for dealing with or for warding off feelings that are too painful, so that's why they yell; and that's why it makes so much difference when you can help your small child to predict anything that is going to happen that is out of the ordinary.

In the period of waiting for a predicted event, some arrangement of defences can become set up within the child's personality. Rather like what you see on your table when your children are playing soldiers and are arranging armies to defend or to attack a fort. The idea that the feelings of little children are very intense, and that anxieties and conflicts are so painful for them that they have to organise within themselves defences leads me on to the last thing that I want to say in this talk about jealousy. This has to do with abnormal jealousy. It often happens that things go wrong. Either jealousy doesn't cease, and continues as open jealousy, or else it goes under the counter, so to speak, and distorts the child's personality.

In the bringing up of children there is no point in aiming at perfection. Much that goes wrong mends in time; or mends well enough so that it doesn't show. But some does not mend. When I said and repeated several times that jealousy is normal and healthy, I was talking about young children. In the growth and development of the personality, there comes about in each boy or girl an ability to tolerate feeling jealous, to keep quiet about it, and to use it as a spur for action. If your friend has got something better than you have, you can fairly easily wait; perhaps you will catch up with her later, or perhaps you will be glad you bought something else instead. You weigh things up. I expect there are plenty of things about you that other people envy. It's all part of life and of people living together.

You grew up to manage these things fairly easily, but you started as I did with but little ability to bide your time. But we must admit that in some people there is a permanent distortion of the personality. People like that manage, usually without knowing what they are doing, to provoke their immediate environment to act in just such a way that it makes them jealous. These people are unhappy, and are uncomfortable to live with, and I would not mean that this kind of jealousy is healthy.

In the discussion there was one mother who was particularly honest in talking about herself, and the way her jealousy of her brother persisted:

Mother

"Well, I was an only child . . . at three my mother presented me with a baby brother. I didn't think it was very funny. I was jealous as a schoolchild, and I used to bite him, I did. . . . He never used to know that I'd done it, mind, and I never admitted I'd done it . . . but even now—I'm twenty-nine, my brother's twenty-six—and Mum will say, 'Well, it's like this. I've just bought William so-and-so,' and I say, 'Oh, did you?' You see? Sort of 'I don't care.' She says, 'All right, all right, what shall I buy you?' And she'll tell me exactly what she paid for William and make sure that I get exactly the same. She bought him a signet ring. . . . I know it's silly, I know it's catty, I mean, I'm married and he isn't married, but if she buys a signet ring for him I promptly come back and say, 'Can't he afford to buy his own?' You see? I got a birthstone ring the next week."

DWW

In people with really jealous temperaments we can be sure that for them there was once, in their early days, a good cause for jealousy. The unfortunate thing for really jealous people is that they had no clear chance to be angry and jealous and aggressive at the time when this would have been sensible and manageable. If they had had such a chance they would probably have got through the jealous phase and come out of it as most children do. Instead the jealousy went right inside and the real reason for it got lost, and so wrong reasons for jealousy are constantly being brought forward now and the claim made that they are justifiable in the present. The way to prevent such distortion is for you to give your small children the sort of early care which enables them to be jealous at the appropriate moment. I suppose that in health jealousy changes into rivalry and ambition.

1960

FIFTEEN

What Irks?

DWW

There are some people who are rather shocked if they find they can have other than loving feelings towards small children. If you listen to the following conversation you will find that these mothers happen to be people who are pretty certain about loving; they take it for granted, and they are not shy to talk about the seamy side of home life. These mothers were definitely asked to talk about what they felt was irksome to them, and they found no difficulty apparently in responding to the invitation. Here is the beginning:

Mothers

"Well, I wanted you to come here this afternoon to tell me what you find irksome about being a mother. Mrs. W., how many children have you got, first of all?"

"I have seven children, ages from twenty to three."

"Do you, in fact, find it rather an irksome job, being a mother?"

"Well, yes I do, I think, on the whole, if I'm quite truthful. I think the difficulty really in a family is the little annoying things like the constant untidiness and always chasing about to try and get them to bed—those sort of things I find irksome."

"Mrs. A.?"

"Well, I've got only two children—one a toddler and one a baby, and of course it's the poor toddler that irritates me. Like Mrs. W. it is the little things and also lack of time to cope with the children—it always seems to be a rush and my young son always wants to go and do something else when we have about two winks in which to get ready to go out."

"Mrs. S.?"

"Yes, I have two girls, one three and one just a year and I think I agree with the other two—that the time is a big thing, that there is never quite enough time to do all that I'd like to do."

"Do you mean there are other things than looking after the children that you'd like to be doing and you aren't—things for yourself?"

"Well, yes, I think there are. I do love looking after the children and—on the whole I find it's a pretty rewarding but a hurried business. I think that when I get tired it's particularly difficult. I do get tired at times. I do my best not to but it's not very easy. . . . "

"What do you think causes the tiredness among mothers? Do you think it's that you have too many jobs to do in a limited time, or is it a kind of fighting against the situation?"

"No, I think it's too many jobs to do in a limited time. At say six o'clock bedtime, one has had tea with the children, the tea things have to be washed up, the other child has to be fed and supper has to be prepared for your husband—all to be done in about an hour." (*laughter*)

DWW

Here's a good start. With several children your home can't look tidy, and it's impossible to keep a tidy mind. It's always a rush, because you have to keep an eye on the clock and all that sort of thing. And children—the smaller ones at any rate—haven't got to the age at which it can be fun to conform and to copy the grownups. The world was made for them and they act on this assumption. Then there is this matter of tiredness which is always important. When you are tired things that are usually interesting can become irksome, and if you haven't had enough sleep you are fighting a need for sleep, and this leaves less of you for the enjoyment of all the very interesting things the children are doing, which are signs every day of their development.

You will have noticed that this time I am talking about mothers and their feelings rather than about the children they are looking after. It's only too easy to idealise a mother's job. We know well that every job has its frustrations and its boring routines and its times of being the last thing anyone would choose to do. Well, why shouldn't the care of babies and children be thought of that way too? I think these mothers won't remember exactly what they felt like in a few years' time and they would be very interested to play over this recording at a time when they had reached the calm waters of a grandmotherly status.

Mothers

". . . all to be done in about an hour."

"We have complete chaos every night from half-past-five until half-past-seven . . . when we really don't know if we're coming or going. Things are supposed to happen at certain times but they never do because something else dreadful happens—somebody spills their milk, or something dreadful—or even—the cat gets on somebody's bed and they can't go to sleep because the cat is there or isn't there, and they come down six times to see what I'm doing, and there is complete chaos." (*laughter*)

DWW

I like that bit about the cat, which either is there or isn't there! It's not a matter of your doing things rightly or wrongly. What's wrong is just the way things are, which makes it look as if the other way round would be right, but of course it wouldn't be. Or perhaps you don't notice all the things that go well, but everything that goes wrong a little bit becomes an awful issue resulting in screams and yells.

In the next bit a mother refers to something that must be very common, the feeling that some special skill is getting rusty in her, or something that it would be fun for her to learn has to be postponed almost indefinitely.

Mothers

"Do you find that there are things for yourself that you would like to be doing, like writing a novel or baking a special cake or anything peculiar to yourself that the children prevent you from doing?"

"Well, I am very interested in social work and all those kinds of things. I would like to do things I have been told I could do or offered a part in even if I've not been able to because I haven't had the time, and I have found it very frustrating not to be able to do any of these things because I have to be at home."

"Yes, I did a sewing class last year which I thoroughly enjoyed, but when the second child came along I just found I couldn't get ready in time and then by about eight o'clock I thought, 'Oh dear, I really can't be bothered to go out to it.'"

"Are there things that you would like to be doing?"

"Yes, I'm very fond of sewing and that's a very irritating job when children . . . (laughter) . . . I really like it and I get frightfully immersed in it and let time slip by rather and that leads to trouble and I'm not a good timekeeper either. I like to forget about time very much."

"I find one very irritating thing is to have to stop whatever I'm doing in the morning and prepare a meal—a midday meal which I would get by with on something like a boiled egg, but . . . I have a husband as well so I have to . . . " (talking together)

DWW

Here are husbands coming in along with the children, expecting things and completely destroying any effort the wife—mother—may be making to preserve a personal interest of her own, one that demands concentration. It's just here that the wife may easily find herself wishing she were like a man, with a nice tidy job, office hours, or trade union rules and regulations protecting him from the very things that she finds irksome. I think that at this stage she can't possibly understand how it is that some men can envy women—envy them because they are at home, and because they are cluttered up with chores and in a most gorgeous mess of babies and children. So here we go back to the mess and the untidiness.

Mothers

"I think the untidiness I find a dreadful problem because I have domestic help and when I've gone all over the house and tidied it all up within twenty-five minutes you would think I hadn't touched it for two or three years, because it's full of toys which they must have and little bits of paper which they must cut up. I shouldn't complain about it—they must do it of course, and it's a great frustration not to make any fuss about it, but you let them do it."

"Well, I find that when mine are little, up to the age of about four, school age we'll say, going to first school, they want to be where I am, and if I'm cooking in the kitchen, well, that means they are also cooking in the kitchen, and if I'm doing things upstairs, they are also upstairs. They don't go away from me, they follow me about, which is intensely irksome, I think, at times."

DWW

So what about keeping the mess in one place?

Mothers

"Do you find it easier to let them roam at will anywhere in the house or do you try and confine them to their own quarters?"

"No, I have one room which I hope and pray they will not make an awful mess in, but they invariably do make an awful mess in every room in the house—they do go everywhere."

"Do you think it's possible to confine them?"

"Well, I don't know if I've been lucky, but Christopher seems to realise that he is supposed to play in the nursery."

"How old?"

"Two years—over two."

"Can he see you from the nursery?"

"No, no, it's away from the kitchen, but it's a flat so we're all on the same level so he can just come along—he'll come and play in the kitchen as well. Which, of course, a lot of people think is wrong. I didn't think of putting up a barrier until it was too late. In the sitting-room and the dining-room we have old-fashioned door handles and he can't quite get his hand around them, so they, so far, have been kept tidy."

DWW

There's nothing for it; it has to be accepted that mothers with several small children do tend to live in a shoe. For the time being they don't know what to do. Perhaps as the children grow older peace returns to the fold, but perhaps not.

Mothers

"We have one extraordinary battle every night over the question of the dogs' dinner—who is going to give the dogs their dinner. There's a rota, you see, for giving the dogs their dinner, but there's always some reason why the person whose turn it is shouldn't do it. (*laughter*) And it will take a good twenty-five minutes when you have your dogs lined up, you see, before the dogs get any dinners at all because this frightful arguing which I—suddenly I find very irksome—the arguing that goes on in big families. Not only about dogs' dinners but when you sit down to a meal somebody will say something and before you know it there you are—everybody is shouting everybody else down because it's all a matter of principle, you see—and we've frightful arguments on all kinds of subjects."

DWW

All these examples illustrate in how many ways the care of small children can be irksome, and this is true however much the children are loved and wanted. The problem is one for the mother whose privacy is being invaded. Surely somewhere there is a little bit of herself that is sacrosanct, that can't be got at even by her own child? Shall she defend herself or surrender? The awful thing is that if the mother has something hidden away somewhere, that is exactly what the small child wants. If there is no more than a secret, then it is the secret that must be found and turned inside out. Her handbag knows all about this. Next week I would like to develop this theme of the strain on the mother.

⟡

At the end of last week, after the mothers of small children had been talking about things that are irksome for mothers, I took up one idea and gave it special emphasis: the way mothers have their privacy invaded and turned inside-out. I want to develop this idea because I think it has a lot to do with what can be irksome for parents, and for mothers especially.

You will remember that these are mothers who like being married and having children, and they are fond of their children, and they wouldn't have it differently; but when they were definitely asked to refer to what annoyed them, they responded with gusto.

There will be some who will not have had the same kind of experiences. Some, at one extreme, had a worse time, got completely distracted and muddled, and had to get help. Here the muddle won, and so the mother became irritable or in some other way she was unable to go on being herself as she would like to be. Others at the other extreme will have had no feeling of disorder and invasion; they were able to keep the parlour neat and clean and somehow their infants and small children fitted into a set pattern, and there was peace most of the time. Here the mother and her essentially rigid system of rights and wrongs dominated the scene, and the infants and children had to adapt, whether ready to adapt or not. There is, of course, a lot to be said for peace and order, *if* it can be got without too much stunting of the children's spontaneity.

It is always necessary for us to remember that there are all kinds of parents and all kinds of children, and on this basis we can discuss the variations without saying that one kind is good and another kind is bad. But don't you think that extremes, one way or another, are usually signs of there being something wrong somewhere?

Often parents will say that in Victorian days it was easy, children were relegated to the nursery and nobody thought, whenever they did or didn't do something, that they were all the time building up or breaking down a child's mental health. But even in the Victorian era the vast majority of people brought up children all on the floor and round their feet, and making a mess and a noise just here, there and everywhere, and without the help of nurses with starched aprons. Every age has its customs, but I think something has stayed the same always, this awful tendency of the small child to get right into the centre where mothers keep their secrets. The question is: can a mother defend herself successfully and keep her secrets without at the same time depriving the child of an essential element—the feeling that the mother is accessible? At the beginning the child was in possession, and between possession and independence there must surely be a half-way house of accessibility.

The onlooker can easily remember that it is only for a limited time that this mother is free-house to her children. She had her secrets once and she will have them again. And she will count herself lucky that for a while she was infinitely bothered by the infinite claims of her own children.

For the mother who is right in it there is no past and no future. For her there is only the present experience of having no unexplored area, no North or South Pole but some intrepid explorer finds it, and warms it up; no Everest but a climber reaches to the summit and eats it. The bottom of her ocean is bathyscoped, and should she have one mystery, the back of the moon, then even this is reached, photographed, and reduced from mystery to scientifically proven fact. Nothing of her is sacred.

Who would be a mother? Who indeed, but the actual mother of children! And some rather special people; those children's nurses who find a way of working in with the actual parents.

You may ask, what is the use of trying to put into words what's irksome about being a mother? I think mothers are helped by being able to voice their agonies at the time that they are experiencing them. Bottled up resentment spoils the loving which is there at the back of it all. I suppose that's why we swear. A word at the right moment gathers together all the resentment and publicises it, after which we settle down to a new period of getting on with whatever we are doing. In practice I find that mothers are helped by being brought into touch with their bitter resentments. Incidentally most of them don't need help, but for the benefit of those who do need help I once wrote down a list of a dozen or so main reasons why mothers might find they hate their children.[1] You'll understand that I am talking about mothers who do love their children, and who are not afraid to look at their other feelings. For instance, this particular baby is not the baby the mother conceived of; not exactly the idea of a baby that she had in her mind. In a way a picture she painted might seem more her own creation than the baby who has become so real a thing in her life. The real baby certainly didn't come by magic. This actual boy or girl came by a laborious process, one which involved the mother in danger both during the pregnancy and during the birth. This actual baby that is now hers hurts her when suckling even although the process of feeding can be very satisfactory. Gradually the mother discovers that the child treats her like an unpaid servant and demands attention, and at the beginning is not concerned for her welfare. Eventually the baby bites her and it is all in love. The mother is expected to love this baby wholeheartedly at the beginning, lock, stock and barrel, the nasty bits as well as the nice bits and the mess included. Before long the baby begins to get disillusioned about the mother and shows it, refusing good food which is offered so that the mother becomes doubtful about herself. And the baby's excited love is cupboard love and after satisfaction has been obtained the mother gets thrown away like orange peel. Shall I go on with this list of reasons why a mother might hate her baby?

In these early stages the baby has no knowledge at all about what the mother is doing well, and what sacrifices she makes in order to do it well, but if things go wrong complaints appear in the form of yells. After experiencing an awful morning of screaming and temper tantrums, the mother goes out shopping with her baby and the baby smiles at a stranger who says: "Isn't he sweet!" or "Isn't she a nice friendly little creature!" The mother has a shrewd idea all the time that if she fails her baby at the start there will be a long period of paying for it, whereas if she succeeds she has no reason whatsoever to expect gratitude. You can easily think up a dozen or so reasons of your own. Probably you won't find anything worse than the one I am picking out for discussion, the way children invade your inmost reserve. If possible I would like to make some sense of this for you.

At the very beginning there is no difficulty, because the baby is in you and part of you. Although only a lodger, so to speak, the baby in the womb joins up with all the ideas of babies you ever had, and at the beginning the baby actually is the secret. The secret becomes the baby.

You have plenty of time in nine months to develop a special relationship to this phenomenon, secret turned baby, and by the time you are a few months gone you are able to identify yourself with the baby that is in you. To reach this state of affairs you have to have a rather calm state of mind, and you are immensely helped if your husband is absolutely in it with you, and is dealing with the world for both of you.

It seems to me that this special relationship to the baby comes to an end, but not at exactly the time of the birth of the baby. I think this special state of affairs lasts a few weeks after the birth, unless there are special circumstances unfortunately bringing you down to earth, like having to leave the maternity ward, or having to dismiss an unsuitable nurse, or your husband getting ill, or something.

If you are lucky and there are no awkward complications, the special state can start to end gradually. Then you start on a process of re-establishing yourself as a grown-up person in the world, and this takes several months. Your baby needs you to be able to do this, although the process brings pain for the baby. There now starts a tremendous struggle—the baby, no longer being the secret—makes a claim on all your secrets. Although fighting a losing battle your baby stakes claim after claim in a perpetual gold rush, but the gold is never enough; a new claim must be staked. And in any case you are recovering your own individual separate status, and your gold mines become ever more and more inaccessible. You don't quite recover, however. If you did, it would mean you had finished with being a parent. And of course if you have several children the same process starts up again and again, and you are forty-five years old before you can look around and see where you yourself stand in the world.

This is a big subject that I have started up, and I only have time to say one more thing. I do believe from talking to innumerable mothers and from watching their children grow, that the mothers who come off best are the ones who can surrender at the beginning. They lose everything. What they gain is that in the course of time, they can recover, because their children gradually give over this perpetual staking of claims and are glad that their mothers are individuals in their own right, as indeed they themselves quickly become.

You perhaps know that children who are deprived of certain essential elements of home life (in fact the sort of things we've been talking about) tend to have a permanent feeling of resentment; they bear a grudge against something, but as they don't know what that something is, society has to take the strain and the children are then called antisocial.

So I feel rather hopeful about these mothers who describe their battle on behalf of the clock against the invading hordes of their children. In the end this battlefield is not strewn with corpses, but with individual children who are not deprived children, who are not problem children, or delinquent. Instead the children are adolescents, each able to stand up in his or her own right. And it's when your children exist in their own right that you can afford to do so too. You can afford to be yourself, with your secrets, which brings you back (although with a difference) to where you were before you were invaded by your children.

Last week I did all the talking, and I chose one aspect of the problem of these mothers because I thought it could be important. I never forget that mothers of small children are usually tired and are often lacking sleep, but I chose to talk about the mother's loss of her privacy. This week I would like to get back to the discussion. In the extract which follows you will hear about struggles that go on between the children in a family, what might be called internecine feuds, and their effects on the mother's nerves.

Mothers

"I find they quarrel so much. I really do wonder why. You'd think they were bitter enemies instead of loving brothers and sisters—they fight and shout—they are, I think, very fond of each other underneath it all. If an outsider comes in they will all band together and stand up for each other, or if anybody is sick they will run down to bring home a little something, but they quarrel from morning till night and I think it gets on my nerves to come in and hear, 'You did.' 'No I didn't.' 'Yes you did.' 'Yes I shall.' 'No I shan't.' 'Yes you will.' 'I hate you.' And doors bang and they start bashing each other about you see, and I'm rushing to tear them apart. They do quarrel dreadfully."

"I suppose it's a way of working off energy—nervous and otherwise."

"I expect so, but it's very irritating."

"It's terrible on a mother's nerves. Yes, I can remember that happening too. My younger sister and I used to bicker . . . and I used to get my mother down."

"This is just wear and tear on mothers. It's nothing really big. Well, the big things I think you can always cope with them because they're rather unusual . . . it's a crisis that someone can rise to. . . . (*talking together*) . . . It's the little everyday constant sort of things, like a drip on stone, isn't it—drip, drip, drip."

DWW

Yes, drip drip drip! and to what purpose? There is a purpose, you know. Last week I said that in my opinion each child goes right in and claims whatever is there, and now I want to add that if anything is found there the children use it, and use it up. There is no quarter given, no mercy shown, no half-measures. The mother gets rough usage. Her source of energy is reached and tapped, and with boring repetition drained. Her main job is survival. Boring repetition is a thing that comes into the next bit.

Mothers

"We have 'good night' stories which I do find rather irksome, because I've told them every night without fail—and if ever we're going out, of course they sense it, don't they—children . . . "

"Oh, yes, they do."

"You can't cut short a line, you can't even say . . . which would normally do—it has to be done every single night if you're sick or well or dead or dying—two dreadful stories have to be read and I do think that sometimes is . . . " (*talking together*)

"Yes, I could just take that little book and tear it up."

DWW

". . . and tear it up." There might be quite a few listening who will be glad to hear those words just once uttered. Yet the stories will go on being repeated, and accurately repeated, and children will go on needing these limited territories which they know in detail and in which there are no surprises. It's this certainty that there will be no surprises that makes for restfulness and prepares the way for a slipping over into sleep.

The next quotation from the discussion deals with the unrewarding stages, the times when a child who is developing well for one reason or another has to go back or becomes unresponsive or definitely defiant. Here a little girl deals with her jealousy of the baby by losing her own achievement and becoming like a baby.

Mothers

"My older daughter has been able to dress herself now for—oh, nine months, and she suddenly decided she's not going to dress herself any more. She's perfectly capable. She can't do zips and buttons up behind, but she can do the ones up in front, but she says 'No,' she's going to be a baby and she sprawls on my lap like the little one—so there we are, I now have to dress them both in the morning and undress them both at night."

"Well, I can foresee this business of letting them dress themselves. I don't have to do it yet because he isn't capable yet, but I can see that this is going to be an irritating point to me—watching him slowly putting things on the wrong way round. . . . (*talking together*) . . . because I can't—I like to do things quickly."

DWW

This is another thing that can be irksome, adapting to each child's rhythm. By temperament some children are slower than their mothers and some quicker. It's a big problem for a mother to adapt to each child's needs in this matter of quickness and slowness. Especially irksome is the task of a quick mother adapting to a rather backward child. Yet if the child and the mother get out of touch with each other on this matter of timing, the child loses the ability to act, becomes stupid, and leaves more and more to the mother or nurse. For the child, it's just as bad when the child is quick and the mother is slow, as you will readily imagine. The mother may be slow, perhaps, because she is in a depressed mood, but the child doesn't know about reasons why, and can't allow for them. No doubt a certain amount can be done by planning, but young children tend to upset the best plans, simply because they can't see any need for looking ahead. They live in the present. In the next bit, we hear about planning.

Mothers

"Well, part of this lack of time is this business of organising oneself in order to go out—planning one's afternoon to fit in a feed at two o'clock and get back for a feed at six o'clock. The shopping I think is the main thing because I go down to a market about four miles away which is very cheap and it's quite a performance getting both children, one fed by bottle and one fed by spoon, both dressed and ready to go out—and one of them has a sleep anyway which makes it even later—and then rushing madly around trying to get back in time to feed the other one with the bottle again. Then there are other things like going out to tea sometimes . . . this afternoon for instance getting us organised. It takes about an hour to get the three of us ready."

"It's a terrible job."

"By the time you've got yourself ready and the other two, I mean . . . "

"Yes, the other two seem to have—they've got a bit scruffy."

"It's the planning of it—the thinking out the best times to go."

"The small examples like that are probably the most irksome of all—I think they're the most irritating, yes."

"After all, I mean, I love my two children. I don't find them irritating all the time, it's just the little things."

"Something that does annoy me a little bit is the next meal—what they're going to have—what they're all going to have."

"Do you plan meals very far ahead?"

"No, no. I'm not a planner. Something sort of—you know—as we get nearer the meal . . . (*laughter*) . . . something materialises. . . . Mind you, I shop—I do one shop a week so I have enough in the house for the following week, but when and where it's to be used, it's not decided until a fairly late hour."

"Well, I'm amazingly lucky about lunch, because Christopher's favourite meal is mince. I'm fed up with mince." (*laughter*)

"They've got a very limited taste haven't they sometimes. Makes it easy . . ."

"Yes, very easy."

DWW

A bit of hope creeping in. But a mother plans, and she does as much organising as possible, but somehow she can't bring together the needs of each child and the dictatorship of the clock, the relative distance between home and shop, and the fact of her own limited strength. In the end we return to the picture of a mother struggling to cope at one and the same time with the children's individual needs and with the world as she knows it.

Mothers

". . . But another great irritation is having to interrupt my household jobs—my vacuum-cleaning or something—I feel that I can get the room done in ten minutes if only I'm allowed to, but to have somebody come up behind me and 'I need to do potty'—he's sitting on the potty and you've got to be there—you've got to be there and . . . "

"Yes, you can't go away and do something else."

"And he makes it into a game." (*laughter*)

"And then something boils over on the stove, and you've left the vacuum-cleaner on because you think you'll only be a minute . . . "

"Oh, I find constant interruptions very irritating—I suddenly hear a scream from somewhere and have to put everything down whether it's cooking—floury hands and everything—and rush out to find out what's happened."

"Well, if I have floury hands I say, 'Look, you don't want me to do anything with my hands like this, do you?'"

"And that works?"

"Yes. 'I'll do it later.' I'm afraid I do that a lot, and also when we've—when irritating things crop up like 'Oh dear, we've left such and such behind,' Elizabeth says, you know, we'll be going out somewhere and she was going to take a doll, or she was going to take a shopping basket—I say, 'Oh well, you'll have to bring it next time.' It's like a dream at the moment."

DWW

There is a limit, and all the time as each child grows there is a more and more clearly defined limit to the demands that a small child has a right to make on the mother. And who shall set this limit? To some extent, the mother finds she can gradually defend herself.

Mothers

"Lots depends on what sort of night you had as well." (*laughter*)

"I'd had a dreadful night and I really was cross with him that day and if he showed any signs of being annoying, I'm afraid I just sort of blew up."

"And does it make him worse?"

"No, I think he senses that I've really come to the end of things and he'd better be quiet. And he surprisingly is."

DWW

But I expect in the end it's the father who has to come in and defend his wife. He has his rights too. Not only does he want to see his wife restored to an independent existence, but also he wants to be able to have his wife to himself, even if at certain times this means the exclusion of the children. So in the course of time the father puts his foot down, which brings me back to my talk of several weeks ago on "Saying 'No'." In one of those programmes I suggested that particularly when the father puts his foot down that he becomes significant for the small child, provided he has first earned the right to take a firm line by being around in a friendly sort of way.

Irksome indeed the care of small children can be, but the alternative, the regimentation of the very young child, is the most awful idea a mother can think of. So I suppose children will go on being a nuisance and mothers will go on being glad they had the chance to be the victims.

1960

Note

1. D. W. Winnicott, "Hate in the Countertransference," in *Through Paediatrics to Psycho-Analysis* (London: Hogarth, 1975; New York: Basic Books, 1958).

SIXTEEN

Security

Whenever an attempt is made to state the basic needs of infants and of children, we hear the words "what children need is security." Sometimes we may feel this is sensible and at other times we may feel doubtful. It may be asked, what does the word *security* mean? Certainly parents who are overprotective cause distress in their children just as parents who can't be reliable make their children muddled and frightened. Evidently then it is possible for parents to give too much security, and yet we know that children do need to feel secure. How can we sort this out?

Parents who can manage to keep a home together do in fact provide something that is immensely important to their children, and naturally when a home breaks up there are casualties among the children. But if we are just simply told that children need security, you would feel that something must be missing in this statement. Children find in security a sort of challenge, a challenge to them to prove that they can break out. The extreme of the idea that security is good would be that a happy place to grow up in would be a prison. This would be absurd. Of course there can be freedom of the spirit anywhere, even in a prison. The poet Lovelace wrote:

Stone walls do not a prison make,
Nor iron bars a cage

implying that there is more to be thought of than the actual fact of being held fast. But people must live freely in order to live imaginatively. Freedom is an essential element, something that brings out the best in people.

Nevertheless we have to admit that there are some who can't live in freedom because they fear both themselves and the world.

To sort out these ideas, I think we must consider the developing infant, child, adolescent, adult, and trace the evolution not only of individual persons but also of what is needed of the environment by these individuals as they evolve. Certainly it is a sign of healthy growth when children begin to be able to enjoy the freedom that can increasingly be given to them. What are we aiming at in bringing up children? We hope that each child will gradually acquire a sense of security. There must build up inside each child a belief in something; not only something that is good but also something that is reliable and durable or that recovers after having been hurt or after being allowed to perish. The question is, how does this building up of a sense of security take place? What leads to this satisfactory state of affairs, in which the child has confidence in the people around and in things? What brings out the quality we call self-confidence? Is the important thing an innate or personal factor or is it moral teaching? Must there be an example that is to be copied? Is an external environmental provision necessary to produce the desired effect?

We could review the stages of emotional development through which every child must pass in order to become a healthy and eventually an adult person. This would take a long time but it could be done. In the course of this review we could talk of the innate processes of growth in the individual and the way (necessarily very complex) in which human beings become persons in their own right. Here, however, I want to refer to the environmental provision, the part we play and the part that society plays in relation to us. It is the surroundings that make it possible for each child to grow, and without adequate environmental reliability the personal growth of a child can't take place, or such growth must be distorted. And as no two children are exactly alike, we are required to adapt specifically to each child's needs. This means that whoever is caring for a child must know that child and must work on the basis of a personal living relationship with that child, not on the basis of something learnt and applied mechanically. Being reliably present and consistent to ourselves we provide the stability which is not rigid but which is alive and human, and this makes the infant feel secure. It is this in relation to which the infant can grow and which the infant can absorb and copy.

When we offer security we do two things at once. On the one hand because of our help the child is safe from the unexpected, from innumerable unwelcome intrusions and from a world that is not yet known or understood. And also, on the other hand, the child is protected by us from his or her own impulses and from the effects that these impulses might produce. I need hardly remind you that very young infants need care absolutely and can't get on on their own. They need to be held, to be moved, to be cleaned up, to be fed, and to be kept at the right temperature and to be protected from draughts and bangs. They need their impulses to be met and they need us to make sense of their spontaneity. There is not much difficulty at this early stage because in most cases each infant has a mother, and the mother at this time concerns herself almost entirely with her infant's needs. At this stage the infant is secure. When a mother succeeds in this thing that she does at the beginning the result is a child whose difficulties really do belong not to the impingements of the world but to life and to the conflict that goes with live feelings. In the most satisfactory circumstances, then, in the security of infant care that is good enough, the infant starts living a personal and individual life.

Very soon infants begin to be able to defend themselves against insecurity, but in the first weeks and months they are but feebly established as persons and so if unsupported they become distorted in their development when untoward things happen. The infant that has known security at this early stage begins to carry around an expectation that he or she won't be let down. Frustrations—well, yes, these are inevitable; but being let down,—well, no! All this is pretty straightforward.

The question we are concerned with here is, what happens when a sense of security becomes established in the child? I want to say this. There then follows one long struggle *against* security, that is to say, security that is provided in the environment. The mother, after the initial period of protection, gradually lets the world in, and the individual small child now pounces on every new opportunity for free expression and for impulsive action. This war against security and controls continues throughout childhood; yet the controls go on being necessary. The parents continue to be ready with a disciplinary framework, with the stone walls and iron bars, but insofar as they know what each child is like, and insofar as they are concerned with the evolution of their children as persons, they welcome defiance. They continue to function as custodians of the peace but they expect lawlessness and even revolution. Fortunately in most cases relief is obtained both for the children and for the parents through the life of imagination and play, and by cultural experiences. In time and in health children become able to retain a sense of security in the face of manifest insecurity, as for instance when a parent is ill or dies or when someone misbehaves or when a home for some reason or other breaks up.

Children need to go on finding out whether they still can rely on their parents, and this testing may continue till the children are themselves ready to provide secure conditions for their own children and after. Adolescents quite characteristically make tests of all security measures and of all rules and regulations and disciplines. So it usually happens that children do accept security as a basic assumption. They believe in good early mothering and fathering because they've had it. They carry with them a sense of security and this is constantly being reinforced by their tests of their parents and of their family and of their school teachers and of their friends and of all sorts of people they meet. Having found the locks and bolts securely fastened, they proceed to unlock them, and to break them open; they burst out. And again and again they burst out. Or else they curl up in bed and play blue jazz records and feel futile.

Why do adolescents especially make such tests? Don't you think it's because they're meeting frighteningly new and strong feelings in themselves, and they wish to know that the external controls are still there? But at the same time they must prove that they can break through these controls and establish themselves as themselves. Healthy children do need people to go on being in control, but the disciplines must be provided by persons who can be loved and hated, defied and depended on; mechanical controls are of no use, nor can fear be a good motive for compliance. It's always a living relationship between persons that gives the necessary elbow room which true growth needs. True growth carries the child or adolescent on to an adult sense of responsibility, especially a responsibility for the provision of secure conditions for the small children of a new generation. Isn't it possible to see all this going on in the works of creative artists of all kinds? They do something very valuable for us, because they are constantly creating new forms and breaking through these forms only to create new ones. Artists enable us to keep alive, when the experiences of real life often threaten to destroy our sense of being really alive and real in a living way.

Artists of all people best remind us that the struggle between our impulses and the sense of security (both of which are vital to us) is an eternal struggle and one that goes on inside each one of us as long as our life lasts.

In health then children develop enough belief in themselves and in other people to hate external controls of all kinds; controls have changed over into self-control. In self-control the conflict has been worked through within the person in advance. So I see it this way: good conditions in the early stages lead to a sense of security, and a sense of security leads on to self-control, and when self-control is a fact, then security that is imposed is an insult.

1960

SEVENTEEN

Feeling Guilty

Claire Rayner[1]: When my daughter was just a few weeks old, a relative of mine telephoned in quite a disguised voice and said she was an official of the NSPCC. Now oddly enough, although in the past I'd always spotted these jokes when she played them on me, this time I fell for it and I got a terrific uprush of guilty fear. I mean I was afraid, what had I done to cause this. I found this a very interesting reaction. It took me some time to get over it; in fact the whole day. I still had this nasty sick feeling inside that I'd done something I shouldn't.

DWW: Mm, I should think so. But apart from feeling guilty, isn't there here something just to do with the fact that a sudden thing had come in, just at a time when you were not really back in the world? I mean I was thinking that just before you have a baby and just afterwards, you're in rather a protected position in the world and you don't expect these sorts of things. Wouldn't something, even a big noise or anything unexpected, make you feel awful just at that time?

CR: Well, yes, I agree there, but this was so specifically a feeling of guilt. You know there are so many fears, aren't there? You hear a loud noise and you get one sort of fear, and you get the fear—the anticipatory fear something nasty is going to happen—you're going to the dentist and you've got that sort of fear. But this was a guilty fear. I had done something wrong and

I was going to be caught out, you know; this was the way I felt. That I'd been discovered in a crime.

DWW: Yes, well, I do see what you mean, and I like the idea of discussing this with you because there's something that's interested me very much, and that is that in talking as observer and psychologist and all that sort of thing, talking to mothers, and fathers, about their children, I find that however careful one is, one tends to make them feel guilty. I've taken a lot of trouble to try and put things in such a way that it's not critical and that it's trying to explain things rather than to say this is wrong and all that. And yet people constantly come to me and say, every time you talk, or every time I read something you write, I feel so wicked; so I'm rather interested in this problem.

CR: Well, that's one sort of guilt, isn't it? Someone reads an article or a book that says you should do this and they immediately feel guilty because they haven't. But there are other thoughts. I know one young women who I don't think had ever done any reading of articles of this sort who as soon as her baby arrived developed a cleaning compulsion. I mean she'd been an ordinary average sort of housewife before, but once the baby turned up she—she scrubbed everything that he—he came in contact with to within an inch of its life. She changed his clothes three or four times a day, couldn't bear it if he had a mark on him, if he was at all dirty, and as he grew older, this extended itself. You see when he was tiny it was his pram, his cot, his own room. Now he's beginning to crawl around and this—this cleaning thing—has extended itself to the other rooms that he crawls in. Her living room carpet, she scrubs it every week, shampoos it, but this seems to me an odd sort of thing to do, I can't help feeling that she feels guilty about something, to behave in this way. I don't know if you agree with me?

DWW: Well, I think that it's a rather useful sort of extreme example really, because it introduces the idea that somebody can feel guilty without knowing it, because in that extreme, it seems to me that most observers would be able to tell that this mother has a fear that she's—that some harm is going to come to the child and that she has to do everything she can, but

I don't suppose she knows that at all. She feels simply just that she feels awful if she isn't cleaning everything up and she probably feels awful even when she is cleaning everything up. So I think that there must be a lot of different ways in which we could see, when we are looking on, that somebody is probably operating under a sense of guilt and they probably don't know it. But still there is the other end of the problem where there's a general latent sense of guilt which is, I think, mainly what's interesting us.

CR: Yes I thought about this a good bit. I can't help wondering how often it can stem from jealousy between a mother and her child. If I can be a bore and quote my own case again. When my small daughter was born I discovered—I'd got her home when this happened—that I was jealous of her in relation to my husband. I was afraid, I think—looking back at it, I didn't realise it at the time but now I do—that she would steal some of his regard from me. I didn't feel there was room for her in our relationship then. Once I'd recognised this, this quite real jealousy, it went. As soon as I admitted it was a jealousy it just disappeared, which is interesting I think. But I wonder how many other mothers feel a jealousy. If they have a daughter, what about the discrepancy in their ages? There's so much emphasis these days in magazines and so on about women being young and beautiful, is it not possible that a woman with a little girl is suddenly made very much aware of the fact that she is no longer as young as she was, no longer as young as this child is, that her life in part is over? That here is this young thing whose life is just starting. Can she feel jealous of this? Guilty about the jealousy? Do you think that's a possibility?

DWW: Well, I think that by being very frank about yourself you are describing one of ever so many different ways in which different people, various people might feel guilty because they've had ideas about their children which they weren't expecting. In your case you said you might feel jealous because you had a little girl and you're interested in your husband's reactions to the little girl and so on; well, then, if you'd had a boy that would have been different. So somebody else has a boy but they're anxious and feeling wicked because they're surprised to find that they didn't want a boy, or for some reason or another they didn't start off loving the baby as they thought they ought to. Everybody's got a pre-conceived notion of some sort of ideal state in which everything goes well and mothers and babies just love each other, and so I think that what you're drawing attention to is just one example of a whole group of reasons why any particular mother might have an unexpected emotion about her baby and feel guilty, thinking that she oughtn't to have it. And for instance it might be that she found she loved her baby perfectly naturally and this made her feel awful because she didn't feel that her mother had loved her in the same way, and then she felt she was . . . presenting her mother with an example. I mean I remember seeing a little girl sitting on the floor being awfully nice to a doll and one could tell that she was telling her mother what a rotten mother she thought her mother was to her just at that moment. I feel that in other words there's a tremendous variation of different kinds of reasons why various people can have unexpected feelings and emotions about their newborn baby. (*CR*: Yes.) But I still think there are some rather more inherent things which must be absolutely universal, if we could only get at them.

CR: Yes, you know I was just remembering when I was a pupil midwife I noticed that so often the mother's first question about the baby was not "What is it?" but "Is it all right?", "Is it normal?" I was interested in this then; I'm far more interested in it now. I can't help wondering why a mother should be afraid that there should be something wrong with the baby, it's a very common fear, isn't it? That you're going to produce a (*DWW*: Yes . . .) monster or something that has something wrong with it.

DWW: I think it's not only common but it's rather normal, you see. I mean there are some people—of course there are all kinds of people, there have to be and it's a good thing—but some people really separate off the having of babies from the rest of their lives to a remarkable degree. But one can't say it's necessarily normal to do so. With most people—if they have children—there's the whole fantasy of having children joined up with just actually having one. There's the whole fantasy which would have turned up in their playing at fathers and mothers when they were children, and in their ideas. There's a very variable amount of love and hate and . . . aggression mixed up with kindness and everything in it all, and so it seems to me that there is something inherent that we could find in absolutely everybody really. When they have a baby they can understand perfectly well with their minds where the baby came from, but still in their fantasies their baby is something they produced and they don't feel that they could have produced something perfect. And they're right. I mean if they tried to paint a painting, or to produce any other kind of work of art or even to cook a dinner, they can't be certain that the thing's going to be absolutely perfect. And yet they can produce a perfect baby.

CR: Would this mean then that when the mother asks this question and the answer is that the baby is normal, it's all right, perfectly normal, that her guilt, the guilt that prompted this question is gone—it's washed away?

DWW: Yes, that's what I mean really, that then the baby returns to being a baby and all the fantasies are fantasies. But if on the other hand there's just something doubtful about the baby, or the nurse even just says it's all right, only delays a little while, the mother then has time just to join up all the fantasies and the fears and the doubts with her idea of the baby and fails to get the full reassurance. And if there's really something wrong, then she has to deal with a very bad period in which she feels responsible for that, because she's had this tie-up with the idea of the baby with the actual pregnancy. (*CR*: Yes.) With the baby inside her. Two quite separate things really but they so easily don't get separated out if the baby doesn't turn out to be quite normal.

CR: Yes, I see.

DWW: And I'd say on the other hand that if the baby turns out to be quite normal, then the baby isn't as good as one of the fantasies that she had about the baby.

CR: Yes. I can't help wondering though if these feelings of guilt are so common. They must have a certain value. Guilt in itself isn't a bad thing, is it? Would it not encourage a mother's sense of responsibility towards her child in a way?

DWW: Yes. Well I think it's awfully like—if you take cooking. If somebody really had no feelings at all of doubt I don't think they'd be very interesting cooks really. The thing is that before a party for instance nearly everybody feels a bit worked up because a thing might go wrong, and of course they probably put on too much food in case there isn't enough and all that sort of thing; all these things are practically universal. But the fact is that people come to the party and enjoy it and then they eat up—even the amount that's too much. It seems to me that what you're saying is that it's really necessary for people to doubt themselves in order to feel fully responsible.

CR: Yes, yes I feel this. If you didn't feel guilty a bit about your child, you wouldn't want to protect him quite so much, would you? I mean if you just felt that everything was going to be all right and normal all the time and nothing could possibly go wrong, and the child suddenly shot a temperature, you'd say, "Oh well, nothing can go wrong; why bother? Why go to the doctor? There's no need, nothing can possibly go wrong this way . . . "

DWW: Yes, from my point of view it's a very practical matter because I spend a lot of my time seeing mothers who bring their children to hospital, and I feel that they come to me worried about their children, they're worried in terms of their child, and if they weren't, they wouldn't notice when the child was ill. (CR: Yes.) They often come when the child's quite well. A mother might say to me that the child fell yesterday and hurt his head, and "I'm just—I'm not quite sure whether he's as well as he was and is it all right?" Well, that's quite right that she should come, and my job is probably to say, "Yes, I've examined the child and the child's all right." And then I feel I'm dealing with the mother's sense of guilt about her child, which is all right—it stops once she's done her bit, she's had the thing checked up; or perhaps if she didn't have to come to the doctor she could just watch and think and see that things are all right after all. But it is the sense of guilt that makes her sensitive I think (CR: Yes), and have doubt about herself. Because I do find that there are parents who haven't got this capacity for a sense of guilt and who don't even notice when their children are ill.

CR: Yes, it must be rather pleasant, if I can put it that way, for the child. I mean for a little child the world and its responsibilities are enormous, overwhelming, aren't they? And a mother who is willing to accept to herself the blame for the things that happen, to blame herself and protect him in this way, it must be very pleasant for the child; mother's guilt becomes a cushion, doesn't it? Against the world at large.

DWW: Yes. I think on the whole if you could choose your parents, which of course is one thing we can't do, we would rather have a mother who felt a sense of guilt—at any rate who felt responsible, and felt that if things went wrong it was probably her fault—we'd rather have that than a mother who immediately turned to an outside thing to explain everything, and said it was due to the thunderstorm last night or some quite outside phenomenon and didn't take responsibility for anything. I think of the two, certainly of the two extremes, we'd rather have the mother who felt very responsible.

1961

Note

1. Claire Rayner, who trained as a nurse, is a writer and well-known radio and television broadcaster. She is the author of many books on child care and health.

EIGHTEEN

The Development of a Child's Sense of Right and Wrong

Some people think that ideas of right and wrong grow in the child like walking and talking, though some people think you have to implant them. My own view is that there is room for something in between these two extremes, there's room for the idea that the sense of good and bad, like much else, comes naturally to each infant and child, provided certain conditions of environmental care can be taken for granted. These essential conditions can't be described in a few words, but in the main it is this; that the environment should be predictable and at first highly adapted to the infant's needs. Most infants and small children do in fact get these essentials.

I do want to just say that the basis of morality is the baby's fundamental experience of being his or her own true self, of going on being; reacting to the unpredictable breaks up this going on being, and interferes with the development of a self. But this is going back too far for this discussion. I must go on to the next phase in development.

As each infant begins to collect a vast experience of going on being in his or her own sweet way and to feel that a self exists, a self that could be independent of the mother, then fears begin to dominate the scene. These fears are primitive in nature, and are based on the infant's expectation of crude retaliations. The infant gets excited, with aggressive or destructive impulses or ideas, showing as screaming or wanting to bite, and immediately the world feels to be full of biting mouths and hostile teeth and claws and all kinds of threats. In this way the infant's world would be a terrifying place were it not for the mother's general protective role which hides these very great fears that belong to the infant's early experience of living. The mother (and I'm not forgetting the father) alters the quality of the small child's fears by being a human being. Gradually she becomes recognised, by the infant, as a human being. So instead of a world of magical retaliations the infant acquires a mother who understands, and who reacts to the infant's impulses. But the mother can be hurt or become angry. When I put it this way, you will see immediately that it makes an immense difference to the infant if the retaliatory forces become humanised. For one thing, the mother knows the difference between actual destruction, and the intention to destroy. She says "Ow!" when she gets bitten. But she is not disturbed at all by recognising that the baby wants to eat her. In fact, she feels that this is a compliment, the only way the baby can show excited love. And of course, she is not so easy to eat. She says "Ow!" but that only means that she felt some pain. A baby can hurt the breast, and especially so if teeth unfortunately appear early. But mothers do survive, and babies have a chance to gain reassurance from her survival. Moreover, you do give babies something hard, don't you, something which has good survival value, like a rattle or a bone ring? Because you know that it is a relief for the baby to be able to bite all out, on to something.

In these ways, the infant has a chance to develop the use of fantasy alongside actual impulsive action, and this important step results from the mother's consistent attitude and general reliability. Also this environmental reliability provides a setting in which the next movement forward in development can take place. This next stage is one that depends on the contribution that the infant can make to the parents' happiness. The mother is there at the right moment, and she will receive the impulsive gestures that the infant makes towards her, and which mean so much to her, because they really are a part of the infant and not just reactions. There is the reactive smile that means little or nothing, but there is also the smile that eventually turns up that means that the infant feels loving, and feels loving at that moment towards the mother. Later, the infant splashes her in the bath or pulls her hair or bites the lobes of her ear or gives her a hug, and all that sort of thing. Or the infant produces an excretion in a special way that implies that the excretion has gift meaning. And that it has value. The mother feels immensely built-up by these tiny things if they are spontaneous. On account of this, the infant is able to make a new development and integration, to accept in a new and a fuller way responsibility for all the nastiness and destructiveness felt in the moments of excitement—that is to say in the experience of the instincts.

The most important instinct for the infant is that roused in feeding, and this becomes joined up with the fact of loving and liking, with affectionate play. And the fantasies of eating the mother and father become all mixed in with the reality of eating which is displaced onto the eating of food. The infant is able to start to accept full responsibility for all this ruthless destruction because of knowing about the gestures which also turn up and which indicate an impulse to give, and also because of knowing from experience that the mother will be there at the moment at which true loving impulses appear. In this way, there becomes a measure of control over what feels good and what feels bad, and so by a complex process and because of growing powers that make the infant able to hold together various experiences—what we call integration—the infant gradually becomes able to tolerate feeling anxious about the destructive elements in the instinctual experiences, knowing that there will be opportunity for repairing and rebuilding. We give this toleration of anxiety a name. We call it a sense of guilt. We can see the sense of guilt developing along with the establishment of the infant's confidence in the reliability of the environment, and we also see the capacity for a sense of guilt disappearing, along with the loss of confidence and the reliability of the environment, as when a mother has to be away from her infant, or when she is ill or perhaps just preoccupied.

Once the infant has begun to be able to have guilt feelings, that is to say to relate constructive behaviour with anxiety about destruction, then the infant is in the position to sort out what feels to be good and what feels to be bad. It is not a direct take-over from the parents' moral sense, but a new moral sense, starting up as it should in the case of each new individual. The feeling that something is right certainly links up with the infant's idea of the mother's or the parents' expectations, but more deeply rooted is the meaning of good and bad that is linked with this sense of guilt—the balance between anxiety about the destructive impulses and the capacity and opportunity for mending and for building. What lessens the guilt feelings feels good for the infant, and what increases the guilt feelings feels bad. In fact, the innate morality of the infant, as it develops out of crude fears, is much more fierce than the morality of the mother and father. Only what is true and real counts for the infant. You have quite a job teaching your child to say "Ta!" out of good manners and not from gratitude.

You will see that according to the theory I use in my work, you are making it possible for your infant to develop a sense of right and wrong by your being a reliable person in this formative early phase of your infant's living experiences. Insofar as each child has found his or her own guilt sense, so far, and only so far, does it make sense for you to introduce your ideas of good and bad.

If you can't succeed with your infant in this way (and you will be better with one infant than with another) you'll have to make the best of being a strict human being, though you know that better things could be happening in the infant's natural development process. If you fail altogether, then you must try to implant ideas of right and wrong by teaching and by drill. But this is a substitute for the real thing, and is an admission of failure, and you will hate it; and in any case this method only works as long as you, or someone acting for you, are there to enforce your will. On the other hand, if you can start your infant off so that through your reliability he or she develops a personal sense of right and wrong in place of crude and primitive fears of retaliation, then you will find later you can reinforce the child's ideas, and enrich these ideas by your own. For as children grow they like to copy their parents, or to defy them, which is just as good in the end.

1962

NINETEEN

Now They Are Five

In a very recent court case a learned judge is reported to have said, in reference to the case of a child of nearly five whose parents had split up: "Children of that age are notoriously resilient." I have no wish to criticize the judgment given in this case, but it is open to us to discuss the question: Are children of five years notoriously resilient? Resilience, it would seem to me, comes only with growth and maturity, and we may hold the view that there is no time in the development of a child at which it could be said that the child is resilient. Resilience would imply that we could expect compliance on the part of the child without danger to the growth of the child's personality and the establishment of the child's character.

It might indeed be argued that there are some special features of this five-year stage which would make you especially careful not to relax your watch on environmental reliability. Tonight I'm trying to look at these special features.

You watch your children grow, and you are astonished. It's all so slow, and yet at the same time it all happens in a flash. That's the funny thing about it. A few weeks ago you had a baby. And then he was a toddler, and today he's five, and tomorrow he will be at school—or she, whichever applies. And in a few weeks he will have practically started going to work.

There is a contradiction here which is interesting. The time passed both slowly and quickly. Or, I could say, when you were feeling things from the point of view of your child time practically stood still. Or it started off still, and only gradually began to move. The idea of infinity comes from the memory traces in each one of us in our infancy before time started. But when you jump across to having your own grown-up experiences, you realise that five years is almost nothing.

This has a curious effect on the relationship between what you remember and what the child remembers. You yourself remember clearly what happened a month ago, and now suddenly you find your five-year-old is not remembering his aunt's visit or the arrival of the new puppy. He remembers some things, even early things, especially if they have been talked about, and he uses the family saga which he learns almost as if it were about someone else, or as if it referred to characters in a book. He has become more aware of himself and of the present time, and along with this he has come to forget.

He now has a past, and in his mind a hint of half-forgotten things. His teddy bear is at the back of the bottom drawer, or he has forgotten how important it once was, except when he suddenly feels a need for it again.

We could say that he is emerging from an enclosure; the walls of the enclosure began to have gaps, and the fences became uneven in thickness; and lo and behold, he's outside. It's not easy for him to get back inside again or to feel he's back inside, except if he's tired or ill, when you reassemble this enclosure for his benefit.

The enclosure was provided by you, his mother and father, and by the family, and by the house and the courtyard, and by the familiar sights and noises and smells. It also belongs to his own stage of immaturity and to his reliance on your reliability, and to the subjective nature of the infant world. This enclosure was a natural development from your arms that you put round him when he was an infant. You adapted in an intimate way to your infant's needs, and then you gradually de-adapted, according to the rate at which he became able to enjoy meeting the unexpected and the new. So, since children are not really like each other much, you find you've made an enclosure in which each child lives, one for each child; and it's out of this enclosure that your son or daughter now emerges—ready for a different kind of group, a new kind of enclosure, at least for a few hours a day. In other words, your child will go to school.

Wordsworth referred to this change in his "Ode: Intimations of Immortality from Recollections of Early Childhood":

Heaven lies about us in our infancy,

Shades of the prison-house begin to close
Upon the growing boy . . .

Here surely, the poet felt the child's consciousness of the new enclosure, in contrast with the baby's unawareness of dependence.

Of course, you've already started up the process by using a nursery school if a very good one happens to be near where you live. In a good nursery school a small group of toddlers can be given opportunity for play, and can be provided with suitable toys and perhaps a better floor than you yourself own, and someone is always present to supervise your child's first experiments in social life, such as bashing the next child on the head with a spade.

But the nursery school is not much unlike home, it's still a specialised provision. The school we are now considering is different. The primary school may be good or not so good, but it will not be adaptive like the nursery school, not specialised except perhaps at the very beginning. In other words, your child will have to do the adapting, will have to fit in with what is expected of the pupils at the school. I do hope he's ready for this because if he is there is a great deal to be got out of the new experience.

You've given a lot of thought to the management of this big change in your child's life. You've already talked about school, and the child has played at schools and has looked forward to the idea of experiencing an extension of the bit of teaching you and others have already put in.

Difficulties do arise at this stage because environmental changes have to be fitted onto changes that are happening in the child because of growth. I've had quite a lot to do with difficulties of children at this age, and I would say this, that in the vast majority of cases of difficulty there is no deep-seated trouble at all, no real illness. The strain has to do with the need for one child to be quick, for another to be slow. A few months make a lot of difference. You may feel that your child whose birthday is in November is champing the bit waiting to be admitted, whereas your child whose birthday is in August gets packed off to school a month or two early. In any case, one child eagerly goes on to the deeper waters, while another tends to lie shivering on the brink and fears to launch away. And by the way, some of the brave pushers-on suddenly shrink back after putting a toe in and go back inside you and refuse to re-emerge from the enclosure for days or weeks or longer. You get to know what sort of a child you have, and so you talk to the school teachers, who are quite used to all this, and they just wait, and play the fish on a long line. The thing is to understand that coming out of the enclosure is very exciting and very frightening; and that once out, it's awful for the child not being able to get back, and that life is a long series of coming out of enclosures and taking new risks and meeting new and exciting challenges.

Some children have personal difficulties that make them unable to take new steps, and you may need help if the passing of time does not cure, or if you have other indications that a particular child is ill.

But there may be something wrong with you, the perfectly good mother, when your child shrinks back. If this can be so then I think you would not wish me to leave it out. I'll tell you what I mean.

Some mothers operate in two layers. At one layer (shall I call it the top layer?) they only want one thing, they want their child to grow up, to get out of enclosure, to go to school, to meet the world. At another layer, deeper I suppose, and not really conscious, they cannot conceive of letting their child go. In this deeper layer where logic is not very important the mother cannot give up this most precious thing, her maternal function— she feels she is maternal more easily when her baby is dependent on her than when, by growth, he comes to enjoy being separate and independent and defiant.

The child senses this only too easily. Although happy at school, he comes panting home, he screams rather than go into the school door each morning. He's sorry for you because he knows you can't stand losing him, and that you haven't got it in you to turn him out because of your nature. It's easier for him if you can be glad to be rid of him, and glad to have him back.

You see, a lot of people, including the best, are a bit depressed part of the time or almost all the time. They have a vague sense of guilt about something and they worry about their responsibilities. The liveliness of the child in the home has been a perpetual tonic. Always the child's noises, even his cries, have been a sign of life, and have just given the right reassurance. For depressed people all the time feel they may have let something die, something precious and essential. The time comes when their child is due to go to school and then the mother fears the emptiness of her home and of herself, the threat of a sense of internal personal failure which may drive her to find an alternative preoccupation. When the child comes back from school, if a new preoccupation has come about, there will be no place for him, or he'll have to fight his way back into the mother's centre. This fighting his way back becomes more important to him than school.

The common result is that the child becomes a case of school refusal. All the time he's longing to be at school, and his mother longs for him to be just like other children.

I knew a boy who at this stage developed a passion for joining things together with string. He was always tying the cushions to the mantelpiece and the chairs to the tables, so that it was precarious moving about in the house at all. He was very fond of his mother, but always uncertain of getting back to her centre because she quickly became depressed when he left her, and in no time she had replaced him with something else she was worried about or doubtful about.

If you're a bit like this you may perhaps be helped by understanding that these things often happen. You may be glad that your child is sensitive to his mother's and other people's feelings, but sorry that your unexpressed and even unconscious anxiety should make the child sorry for you. He's unable to get out of the enclosure.

You may have had an experience of this difficulty he's in at an earlier date. You may, for instance, have found it difficult to wean him. You may have come to recognise a pattern in his reluctance to take any new step, or to explore the unknown. At each of these stages you were under threat of losing your child's dependence on you. You were in the process of acquiring a child with independence and a personal slant on life, and although you could see the advantages to be gained by this you couldn't get the necessary release of feeling. There's a very close relationship between this vaguely depressive state of mind—this preoccupation with undefined anxieties—and the capacity of a woman to give a child her full attention. I can't really talk about one without referring to the other. Most women live, I suppose, just on the borderline.

Mothers have all sorts of agonies to go through, and it's rather good when the babies and the children don't have to get caught up in them. They have plenty of agonies of their own. Actually they rather like having their own agonies, just as they like new skills and a widening vision, and happiness.

What is this that Wordsworth calls the "Shades of the prison-house"? In my language it's the changeover from the small child's living in a subjective world to the older child's living in a world of shared reality. One infant starts off in magical control of the environment—if you give good enough care—and creates the world anew, even you and the door-knob. By the age of five the child has become able to perceive you more as you are, to acknowledge a world of door-knobs and other objects that existed before his conception, and to recognise the fact of dependence just at the time when he's becoming truly independent. It's all a matter of timing, and I believe you are managing it beautifully. Somehow or other people usually do. There are plenty of other ways in which life can affect your child at this age. I mentioned the child's teddy bear. Your child may well be addicted to some special object. This special object that was once a blanket or a napkin or one of your scarves or a rag doll first became important for him or her before or after the first birthday, and especially at times of transition, as from waking to sleeping life. It's immensely important; it gets treated abominably; it even smells. You are lucky that the child uses this object and not you yourself, or the lobe of your ear, or your hair.

This object joins the child to external or shared reality. It's a part both of the child and of you, the mother. One of your children with such an object has no use for it in the day, but another takes it everywhere. At five the need for this thing may not have ceased, but many other things can take its place—the child looks at comics, has a great variety of toys, both hard and soft, and there is the whole cultural life waiting to enrich the child's experience of living. But you may have trouble when the child goes to school, and you will need the teacher to go slow, and not to ban this object absolutely from the classroom just at first. This problem nearly always resolves itself within a few weeks.

I would say that the child is taking to school a bit of the relationship to you that dates right back to infantile dependence, and to early infancy, to the time when he was only beginning to recognise you and the world as separate from the self.

If the anxieties about going to school resolve themselves then the boy will be able to give up taking this object along with him, and instead will have a truck or an engine along with the string and liquorice in his pockets, and the girl will somehow manage by screwing up her handkerchief, or perhaps she'll have a secret baby in a matchbox. In any case children can always suck their thumbs or bite their nails if hard put to it. As they gain confidence they usually give up these things. You learn to expect children to show anxiety about all moves away from being part and parcel of you and of home, moves towards citizenship of the wide, wide world. And anxiety may show as a return to infantile patterns which mercifully remain to provide reassurance. These patterns become a sort of built-in psychotherapy which retains its effectiveness because you are alive and available, and because you are all the time providing a link between the present and the child's infancy experiences of which their infantile patterns are relics.

One other thing. Children tend to feel disloyal if they enjoy school and if they enjoy forgetting you for a few hours. So they vaguely feel anxious as they get near home, or they delay their return without knowing why. If you have reason to be angry with your child please don't choose the moment of his or her return from school to express it. You too may be annoyed that you were forgotten, so look out for your own reactions to the new developments. It would be better not to be cross about that ink on the tablecloth until you and the child have re-established contact.

These things present no great difficulty if you know what's happening. Growing up is not all honey for the child, and for the mother it's often bitter aloes.

1962

TWENTY

The Building Up of Trust

It should be easy to write about stress that belongs to the early ages, simply because everyone knows that very young children need continuous and reliable care, else they do not develop properly. At the next stage of individual development we expect children to have gathered into themselves innumerable samples of good care, and they go forward with a measure of belief, belief in people and in the world, so that it takes quite a big thing to knock them sideways. At the earlier age, however, this belief in things and this trust in people are in process of being built up.

This is the main thing that we notice about the very young, that although they trust us their faith can easily be shattered. For this reason we are especially careful to be reliable in essentials.

It will be understood that we do not do this by deliberate effort or by the study of books or by listening to lectures, but we do it because little children draw the best out of us, so that for a while we behave quite well. We do not even quarrel in public—that is to say, in front of the children, and we allow ourselves to seem to be drawn together by the very fact of the children's existence.

Some people are too much taken up with managing their own lives and their own difficult temperaments, so that they cannot do for the children what the children need, but children can understand a great deal so long as a home exists, and the parents are seen together, and if there is warmth even in a cold climate, and food that can be expected and enjoyed, and an absence of the sudden unpredictable noise that hurts physically and cannot be explained away. With physical conditions that can be known and, so to speak, caught hold of, children can stand some strain in the relationship between the parents, since it is, for them, a good thing that at any rate the parents are there, are alive, and have feelings. At the same time it is true that the growth of young children is more easily accomplished if they have the parents in an easy relationship the one with the other. Indeed it is the interpersonal world of the parents that is symbolised for the child by the stability of the house and the liveliness of the street, and not nearly so true the other way round, that the house and the street find symbolism in the parents' relationship with each other.

Not Idealism

I must be careful. So easily in describing what very young children need I can seem to be wanting parents to be selfless angels, and expecting the world to be ideal, like a suburban garden in summer with father cutting the grass, and mother preparing the Sunday dinner, and the dog barking at an alien dog over the garden fence. Of children, even of babies, it can be said that they do not do well on mechanical perfection. They need human beings around them who both succeed and fail.

I like to use the words "good enough." Good enough parents can be used by babies and young children, and good enough means you and me. In order to be consistent, and so to be predictable for our children, we must be *ourselves*. If we are ourselves our children can get to know us. Certainly if we are acting a part we shall be found out when we get caught without our make-up.

Danger of Teaching

My problem is to find a way of giving instruction without instructing. There is a limit to the value of being taught. Indeed it is important for parents who start looking into books for advice that they know that they do not have to know everything. Most of what goes on in the developing individual baby or child happens whether you understand it or not, simply because the child has an inherited tendency towards development. No-one has to make a child hungry, angry, happy, sad, affectionate, good or naughty. These things just happen. You have already finished that part of your responsibility and have laid down the details of your child's inherited tendencies when you chose your partner, and when the one spermatozoon penetrated the one egg. At that fateful moment the book on heredity was closed, and things started to work themselves out in terms of the body and mind and personality and character of your child. This is a matter of physiology and anatomy. The way these things work themselves out is extremely complicated, and if you wish to do so you can spend your life on an interesting research project connected with human development; such work will not, however, help you with your own child, who needs you indeed.

What to Know

What is it, then, that parents can usefully know? I would suggest that there are two main things to know, one of which has to do with the process of growth, which belongs to the child, and the other has to do with the environmental provisions, which is very much your responsibility.

The Process of Growth

Once it has been pointed out to you it is surely quite obvious that your baby has a tendency to live and breathe and to eat and drink, and to grow. You will be wise if you assume these matters to be true from the very beginning.

It helps a lot to know that you do not have to make your baby into a child, to make your child grow, to make your growing child good or clean, to make your good child generous, to make your generous child clever at choosing the right presents for the right people.

If you stand back and watch you soon see the developmental process at work, and you get a sense of relief. You have started up something that has its own built-in dynamo. You will be looking for the brakes.

Every comment I make must be modified by the other observation, which is that no two children are alike, so that you may find yourself bothered by one child's lifelessness and by another child's dynamism. But the main principle holds in all cases, that it is the child's own developmental processes that make the changes you are looking for.

So the first useful principle has to do with the innate tendencies that belong to each young child.

The Environment

The second useful principle has to do with your special place as the environment and as the provider of environment. No-one has to prove to you that a baby needs gentle handling and warmth after being born. You know it to be true. If someone doubts this it is for him or her to prove that what you know is wrong.

After all, you have been a baby yourself, and you have memories to guide you, apart from all you may have learned when watching and participating in the care of babies.

The environment you provide is primarily yourself, your person, your nature, your distinguishing features that help you to know you are yourself. This includes of course all that you collect around yourself, your aroma, the atmosphere that goes with you, and it includes the man who will turn out to be the baby's father, and it may include other children if you have them, as well as grandparents and aunts and uncles. In other words, I am doing no more than describe the family as the baby gradually discovers it, including the features of the home that make your home not quite like any other home.

Interaction

So here there are two distinct things, the inborn tendencies of the baby, and the home that you provide. Life consists in the interaction of these two things. At first the interacting goes on under your very nose, and later it goes on outside the area of your immediate surroundings—at school, or in friendships, or away at a holiday camp, and of course *within* the mind or in the personal living of your boy or girl.

You could if you wished spend your time comparing your child's behaviour with some standard you have set up, based on your own family pattern, or the pattern handed out to you by someone you admired. But you may get a much richer and a much more profitable experience by comparing the child's personal struggle towards independence with the dependence which you made possible because your child had trust in you and in the general set-up of your home.

Two Kinds of Stress

I have outlined the child's development in this way in order to simplify my task of describing stress. It is possible to say that stress comes from one of two directions; although in practice we must expect to find mixtures.

The Internal Process

The first has to do with the fact that the developmental process in the human individual is extremely complicated, and things can go wrong from within. This is what psychoanalysis is all about. There is no need whatever for parents or those who care for young children to know what are the strains and stresses which are inherent in the establishment of the individual personality and character and the gradual ability of the baby and child to make a relationship to the family and to the community, to become part of society without too great a loss of personal impulse and creativity.

Parents and others who have to do with children may find these to be matters of extreme interest; but the important thing is to be able to get there imaginatively rather than to be able to understand.

Your child playing under the table stands up and the table hits his head. He rushes to you and prepares for a good cry. You make appropriate noises and put your hand where the head got hurt, and perhaps you mend it with a kiss. After a few minutes all is well, and play under the table is resumed. What would have been the gain if you had been able to write a thesis on various aspects of this event?

1. This is the way children learn while they are playing. They must look before they leap. . . .
2. The table did not really hit the child's head, but at that age the first assumption will be of that kind, and one child is more likely than another to cling on to the "persecution" theory of trauma; this has to do with a difficulty in accepting the fact of one's own aggression, and perhaps with rage that became lost because of its painfulness

as an experience for a baby or small child who is not yet sure of keeping integrated when powerful emotion is roused. . . .

3. Would this be a good moment for giving a lecture: "You see, if you move about like that without thinking you will hurt yourself, and one day. . . . "

No, I think it is better when the whole matter is sealed off with a healing kiss, simply because you know what you would be feeling like if you were that little child who has been hit on the head by a nasty hard vindictive table. This is called empathy and if you have not got it you cannot learn it anywhere.

But of course, you might be a lonely person, and this bang on the head could become a heaven-sent chance for you to make contact with someone, so you kiss and hug, and put the child to lie down, and you become sentimental; perhaps you call in the doctor first to make sure there has been no internal damage!

In this case the child has triggered off something in you that has to do with your own problems, and for the child the result is bewilderment. This is outside the child's understanding, and in looking at the episode we have got away from the inherent processes in the child's living and developing. Lucky is the child who, on the whole, is left free to get on with experiencing day by day the new things that come within his or her ever-increasing capacity.

A great deal happens in the dark interstices of your aspidistra, if you have one, and you may be completely ignorant of biology; yet you may be famous in your street for your aspidistra and its clean green leaves, with no brown edges.

There is no more fascinating study than that of the way a baby becomes a child and an adolescent and an adult, but a study of what is known is not part of what children need of their parents. Perhaps for teachers and those who are rather more detached from the child than parents are in everyday living experiences there is more to be said for a study of what is known and what is not known of the developmental processes. Certainly those who have care of the abnormal and those who set out to do treatment of children who are ill in terms of emotional development and in terms of personality and character, these persons do need to make a deep study of this very subject.

It is tempting to start describing the difficulties that are inherent. Let two examples suffice. One is the universal problem of ambivalence, loving and hating the same person or thing at one and the same time. Another is the experience that each child must go through to a greater or lesser extent of feeling at one with the instinctual drives as they manifest themselves in the bodily organs, or alternatively feeling more at home with the sex opposite to that of the child's body.

There are many other conflicts that we see our children suffering from and trying to solve, and we know that many children become ill because they cannot find a work solution. But it is not the job of the parent to turn psycho-therapist.

The Environmental Provision

Contrasting with the workings of the internal process in the child is the environmental provision. This is you, and it is me, and it is the school and it is society, and here we become interested in a new way because we are responsible.

For babies and young children the environmental provision either gives a chance for the internal process of growth to take place or else it prevents this very thing.

The key word could be "predictability." Parents, and especially the mother at the start, are taking a lot of trouble to shield the child from that which is unpredictable.

It will be seen that at a quick or slow pace this or that child is becoming able to put two and two together and to defeat unpredictability. There is an amazing variation here, according to the small child's capacity to defeat unpredictability. But there remains the need for mother. An aeroplane flies low overhead. This can be hurtful even to an adult. No explanation is valuable for the child. What is valuable is that you hold the child close to yourself, and the child uses the fact that you are not scared beyond recovery, and is soon off and away, playing again. Had you not been there the child could have been hurt beyond repair.

This is a crude example, but I am showing that by this way of looking at child care, stress can be described in terms of failure of environmental provision, just where reliability is needed.

It is the same thing when a mother must leave a little child in a hospital for a few days, as has been emphasized by Bowlby, and also by James and Joyce Robertson in their poignant film "A Two-Year-Old Goes to Hospital." By this age the child has really come to know the mother as a person, and it is herself that he must have, not just her care and protection. Stress at this age comes from the fact that the mother is absent over a period of time that is longer than that over which the child can keep alive the mental image of the mother, or can feel her live presence in the imaginative world of dream and play, sometimes called "inner psychic reality." Doctors and nurses are busy doing their job of body-care, and they often do not know or have no time to consider the fact that as a result of too long a separation a child's personality can be altered completely through environmental interference, and the basis can be laid down for a character disorder that we cannot mend.

It is always the same: there was good enough environmental provision in terms of predictability, according to the child's ability to predict, and then there was an unreliability that automatically broke up the continuity of the child's developmental process. After this the child has a gap in the line between now and the roots of the past. There has to be a new start. Too many of these new starts result in a failure in the child of the feeling *I am, this is me, I exist, it is I who love and hate, it is me that people see and that I see in mother's face when she comes, or in the mirror.* Growth processes become distorted because the child's integrity has broken up.

It happens that a large proportion of children, especially of the unsophisticated and the uneducated of the world, do in fact go through early childhood without having experienced this break in the continuity of life that is so disastrous. Such children have had the opportunity to develop (at any rate in the early stages) according to their own inborn tendencies towards development. They are the privileged ones.

Unfortunately a proportion of children, especially in sophisticated cultures, do have to carry round with them for life some degree of distortion of personal development caused by environmental unpredictability and the intrusion of the unpredictable, and they lose a clear sense of *I am, I am me, I exist here and now, on this basis I can enter into the lives of others, and without a sense of threat to my own basis for being myself.*

Study of Environmental Factors

I rather tended to pour cold water over the idea that parents should study the developmental processes inherent in individual growth, and based on hereditary tendencies. It is not so clear to me that a study of the environmental provision is useless. Surely, if mothers know that what they do is vitally important for their babies and small children they will be in a stronger position to fight for their rights when it is lightly suggested that mothers and babies, or mothers and young children, should be parted. This so often means that the baby is to be cared for impersonally.

The world has much to learn in this respect, especially doctors and nurses who are primarily concerned with health and disease in bodily terms. Mothers and fathers must fight their own cause here, because no-one else will fight for them. No-one else really minds as the parents mind.

This brings me to the last point, which is that even this matter of environmental provision, reliability, adaptation to infant needs, does not need to be learnt. There is something about having a baby (even preparing for adopting a baby) that alters the parents. They become orientated to the special task. I wanted to give it a name so I called it "primary maternal preoccupation," but what's in a name?

This orientation to the needs of the baby depends on many things, one of which is that the mother and the father do really carry round with them hidden memories of having been babies themselves, and of having been cared for in terms of reliability, of shielding from unpredictability, and of opportunity to get on with the highly individual matter of personal growth.

So somehow nature has provided for this very acute or even absolute need of babies and small children by making it natural for parents to narrow down their world temporarily, just for a few months, so that the world is there in the middle and not all round outside.

Summary

Stress can be looked at therefore in two ways. One way takes us to a study of the internal stresses and strains inherent in emotional growth. The other way has more practical significance (unless we are psycho-analysts) in that here stress results from relative or gross failure in the environmental provision. These failures can be described in terms of unreliability, destruction of trust, the letting in of unpredictability, and a once and for all or a repeat pattern of the breakup of the continuity of the individual child's line of life.

On the whole those who care for children are found by careful selection, not taught in class.

Babies are quite good at selecting their own mothers, at any rate in respect of this matter of primary maternal preoccupation. Beyond that, I doubt whether I would rate them so highly. But they have to make use of what they find they have as parents.

1969

PART THREE

The Child in the Family

Introduction

by Stanley I. Greenspan, M.D.

Winnicott is one of those rare pioneers into the mental life of children who provided insights both to psychoanalysts on the one hand and practically-minded, concerned parents on the other hand. Remarkably, his insights and contributions ring as true today as they did many years ago. He anticipated many of the modern concepts that have evolved through systematic studies of infants' and young children's emotional development.

In these essays, Winnicott focuses his attention on the child in the family. First, he cautions caregivers to be modest in the way in which they intervene in a complex, dynamic process. It's easy to want to give advice regarding child rearing, but, as Winnicott points out, giving such advice is tampering with a complex web of relationships and dynamics that will often be opaque to the advice-giver. In this way, Winnicott anticipated dynamic systems theory—a currently prominent way of thinking about individuals, families, cultures, and societies. Dynamic systems theory emphasizes the complex interplay of many factors—the role of feedback in an interconnected system.

But Winnicott does not leave advice-givers or helpers with their hands tied. He also shows the benefits of exploring the dynamics of family relationships, if those doing it can listen and take in the feelings and the history without overstepping their boundaries.

He points out the value of offering help when conducted with a respect for the complexity of family roles, awareness of the limitations of one's own role, and with the goal of understanding and encouraging the natural course of adaptation, rather than overly simplistic advice-giving. In other words, Winnicott was one of the first to grasp and put into words the processes by which human beings grow emotionally. This growth can be helped along by someone offering help with understanding and reflection. A supportive, reflective relationship that doesn't oversimplify or intrude is a much more powerful ally in the process of growth than might ordinarily be recognized.

In these informative essays, Winnicott emphasizes the importance of the mother and the family, and shows how basic strengths, such as the capacity for "concern" develop within this setting. Winnicott also shows how the basic lessons of life, such as loyalty versus disloyalty and indeed all children's learning develops within a nurturing, dynamic system.

Winnicott's essays provide both insights and guidance for the modern family and for the many kinds of professionals who work with children and families today. In his concepts, I can see the roots of many of the principles that led to the development of my own thinking about children. As I read Winnicott now, I see how his thinking influenced many of my teachers, who in turn conveyed these wonderful principles to their students. For example, when I write about the ways a child' mind grows through nurturing interactions I feel the influence of Winnicott. My concept and philosophy of "floor time" as a way parents can nurture their children's attention, engagement, emotional signaling, problem-solving, creative and imaginative use of ideas, and logical-reflective thinking, has roots in Winnicott's understanding of the critical role of parent-child relationships. Much of our current thinking about strengthening families and early intervention, which recognizes multiple factors interacting together, including individual differences in the child, relationships between children and caregivers and between families and the larger culture owe much to Winnicott's insightful observations.

In Winnicott's delightful essays we see the origins of many of the fundamental concepts that guide enlightened care of children today. They offer insights not only into the history of these concepts but also into useful, current applications.

TWENTY-ONE

Advising Parents

The title of this section is perhaps rather misleading. All my professional life I have avoided giving advice, and, if I succeed in my purpose here, the result will be not that other workers will know better how to advise parents, but rather that they will feel less inclined than they may do now to give advice at all.

However, I have no wish to carry this attitude to absurd lengths. If a doctor is asked: "What shall I do with my child whose illness has been diagnosed as rheumatic fever?" he will advise the parents to put the child to bed and to keep him there until the doctor feels that the danger of heart disease is over. Or if a nurse finds nits in a child's hair she gives instructions which may lead to a satisfactory disinfestation. In other words, in the case of physical illness, doctors and nurses sometimes know the answer because of their special training, and they fail if they do not act accordingly.

But many children who are not physically ill nevertheless come under out care; for instance in maternity cases the work is not curative, because mother and baby are usually healthy. Health is much more difficult to deal with than disease. It is interesting that doctors and nurses may feel bewildered when they are faced with problems that do not relate to physical disease or deformity; they have had no training in healthiness that is comparable to their training in ill health or definite disease.

My observations on the subject of giving advice fall into three categories:

1. The difference between treatment of disease and advice about life.
2. The need to contain the problem in oneself rather than to offer a solution.
3. The professional interview.

Treatment of Disease and Advice about Life

As doctors and nurses today become increasingly concerned with psychology, or the emotional or feeling side of life, they need to learn one thing, which is that they are not experts in psychology. In other words, they must adopt quite a different technique with parents as soon as they arrive at the border between the two territories, those of physical disease and of living processes. Let me give a crude example:

A paediatrician sees a child because of some condition of the glands in the child's neck. He makes his diagnosis, and informs the mother, giving her the diagnosis and the outline of the proposed treatment. The mother and the child like this paediatrician because he is kind and sympathetic and because he handled the child well during the physical examination. The doctor, being up to date, gives the mother time to talk a little about herself and her home. The mother remarks that the boy is not really happy at school, and tends to get bullied; she is wondering whether to change the boy's school. All is well up to this point, but now the doctor, accustomed to giving advice in his own field, says to the mother: "Yes, I think it would be good the change the school."

At this point the doctor has stepped outside his domain, but he has carried with him his authoritarian attitude. The mother does not know it, but he advised a change of school only because he had recently changed the school of one of his own children who had been getting bullied, and so the idea was fresh in his mind. Another kind of personal experience would have made him advise against a change of school. In fact, the doctor was not in a position to give advice. While he was listening to the mother's story he was performing a useful function, without knowing it, and then he behaved in an irresponsible way and advised, and quite unnecessarily too, since he had not been asked.

This sort of thing happens all the time, in medical and nursing practice, and it can be stopped if only doctors and nurses understand that they do not have to settle problems of *living* for their clients, men and women who are often more mature persons than the doctor or nurse who is advising.

The following example illustrates an alternative method:

Two young parents came to see a doctor about their second infant, aged eight months. The baby "would not wean." There was no illness. In the course of an hour it emerged that the mother's mother had sent her to the doctor. In fact the grandmother had had difficulty in weaning the infant's mother. There was a depressed mood in the background, both in the grandmother and in the mother. As all this emerged the mother was surprised to find herself crying copious tears.

The resolution of this problem was brought about by the mother's recognition that the problem lay in her relation to her own mother—after this she could get on with the practical problems of the weaning, which necessitated her being able to be unkind to her infant as well as to love her. Advice would not have helped much, because the problem was one of an emotional readjustment.

In contrast, this next incident concerns a girl whom I saw when she was ten years old:

The trouble was that she, an only child, had been giving her parents a bad time, though she was very fond of them. A careful history-taking showed that the difficulties started when the child was weaned at eight months. She had done very well, but never became able to enjoy food after leaving the breast. At three she was taken to a doctor, who unfortunately failed to see that the child was in need of personal help. She was already restless, unable to persevere in play, and all the time a nuisance. The doctor said: "Cheer up, mother, she'll soon be four!"

In another instance, the parents had a consultation with a paediatrician at the time that they were experiencing a weaning difficulty:

This doctor examined and found nothing wrong, and quite rightly told the parents so. But he went further. He told the mother to complete the weaning immediately, which she did.

This advice was neither good nor bad, it was just simply out of place. It cut right across the mother's unconscious conflict about weaning the child, the only one she was likely to have (she was thirty-eight). Of course she took the specialist's advice; what else could she do?—but he ought never to have given it. He should have stuck to his limited job and should have handed over the understanding of the weaning difficulty to someone who could stretch out and around this much wider problem of living and of relationships.

This kind of thing is not, unfortunately, rare; it is a matter of everyday medical practice. I give another example, at rather greater length:

I was rung up by a woman who said that she was involved with a children's hospital, but wanted to talk about her baby in a different way. An appointment was made and she came with her baby, who was nearly seven months old. The young mother sat in the chair with her baby on her lap, and I was very easily able to establish the conditions which I need for observing a baby of this age. I mean that I was able to talk to the mother and yet to deal with the baby without her help or her interference. It quickly became apparent that she was a rather normal sort of person with a feeling for her baby which was easy. There was no jigging up and down of the baby on her knee and nothing false.

The birth of the baby had been straightforward. The baby was "born sleepy"; it was very difficult to get her to take; in fact she would not wake. The mother described how an attempt was made in the maternity ward to force the infant to take. She wanted to feed her baby by breast and felt that she could do so. She expressed the breast milk, which was given by bottle for a week. The sister was determined to make the child take, and tried incessantly pushing the teat of the bottle in and out of the child's mouth, tickling the child's toes, and jigging the child up and down. All these procedures had no effect and the pattern persisted, so that, even much later on, the mother found that whenever she did anything active in regard to the feeding of the infant this sent the child to sleep. At the end of one week an attempt was made at breast-feeding, but the mother was not allowed to use her intuitive understanding of the infant's needs. It was extremely painful to her. She felt that no one really wanted it to succeed. She had to sit up and take no part while the sister did all she could to make the infant feed. The sister, ordinarily kind and skilled, grasped the child's head and pushed it against the breast and so on. After a little of this, which only produced deeper sleep, breast-feeding was given up and there was a noticeable deterioration following this distorted attempt.

Rather suddenly, at two and a half weeks, there was an improvement. At a month the baby was 6 lb 6 oz (6 lb 9¾ oz at birth) and went home with the mother. The mother was told to feed the baby with a spoon.

The mother had on her own discovered that she could feed her baby perfectly well, although by this time the breast had ceased to function. She was feeding the baby for one and a half hours at a time, and then she switched over to being ready to give multiple small feeds. But by this time a children's hospital had become concerned with the child because of certain physical abnormalities, and advice was given in the hospital outpatient department. This advice seemed to be based on the idea that the mother must be fed up, whereas in fact she was enjoying feeding her baby, and did not mind at all that it was a difficult art. She had to defy the doctors who gave her advice. (Her comment at this point was: "Definitely the next time I am not having my baby in hospital.") Innumerable investigations were carried out at the hospital in spite of the mother's protests, but naturally she felt that she must leave the physical side to the doctors. There was a shortening of the left forearm, and a cleft palate involving the soft tissues only.

On account of the physical abnormalities the mother felt it necessary to keep under the children's hospital, but this meant that she had to stand being given advice about the feeding of the baby, advice which was usually based on a misunderstanding of her own attitude. She was told to give solids at three months to save herself the trouble of the long feeds or the frequent feeds. This was of no use, and she left over the matter of the introduction of solids. The baby at seven months had begun to want solids, as a result of sitting propped up while the parents ate. She was allowed an occasional tidbit and so gradually had the idea that there was another kind of food. Meanwhile she had been fed on milk and chocolate pudding, and weighed 14 lb 4 oz.

Why did the mother come to see me? She found that she wanted support for her own idea of her infant. First, the infant was fully developed for her age, that is to say, not in any way backward, whereas there had been vague suggestions at the hospital that the child might be backward. Second, she was quite willing to accept the deformity of the forearm but not to accept having innumerable investigations, and especially she refused to have the child's arm in a splint. It is evident that the mother felt about her infant's needs in a more sensitive way than the doctors and nurses could hope to feel. For instance, she had been alarmed when the hospital asked to have the baby in for one night simply to have a blood test done. This she disallowed, and the hospital carried out the investigations in the outpatient department without the further complication of having the baby in the ward.

The problem therefore with this mother was that she recognized very clearly her dependence on the hospital on the physical side, and she was engaged in trying to deal with the fact that the physically-minded specialists had not come round to the idea that the baby was yet a human being. At one point when she protested against the splinting of the arm during the early weeks of the child's life she was definitely told that this baby was not yet able to be affected by things happening to it, although she felt quite certain that the baby was in fact adversely affected by the compilation of the splint; she could see, in fact, that the infant would be left-handed, and that the splint must hamper the left hand at a vitally important stage, in which reaching out and grasping are creating the world.

Here is a picture of the baby (nearly seven months) at the consultation:

As I came into the room the baby fixed me with her eyes. As soon as she felt I was in communication with her she smiled and clearly felt as if she were communicating with a person. I took an unsharpened pencil and held it in front of her. Still looking at me, and smiling and watching me, she took the pencil with her right hand and without hesitation put it to her mouth where she enjoyed it. In a few moments she used her left hand to help, and then she held it in her left hand instead of in the right hand while mouthing it. Saliva was flowing. All this continued in one way and another until, after five minutes, in the usual way she dropped the pencil by mistake. I returned the pencil and the game re-started. After another few minutes the pencil dropped again, less obviously by mistake. She was now not entirely concerned with putting it in her mouth and at one stage put it between her legs. She was dressed, since I had not thought it necessary to undress her. The third time she dropped the pencil deliberately and watched it go. The fourth time she put it down near her mother's breast and dropped it between the mother and the arm of the chair.

By this time we were near the end of the consultation, which lasted half an hour. When the pencil play had come to an end the baby had had enough and began to whimper, and there were necessarily an awkward few minutes at the end with the baby feeling that it would be natural to go but the mother not quite ready to do so. There was no difficulty, and the mother and baby went out of the room fully contented with each other.

While all this was going on I was talking to the mother and only once did I have to ask her not to translate what we were talking about in terms of moving the baby; for instance, when I asked about the wrist she naturally went to turn up the sleeve.

The consultation achieved no great purpose except in so far as the mother got support where she needed it. She needed support in regard to her very real understanding of her own infant, which had to be defended on account of the inability of the physical doctors to recognize the boundary of their speciality.

A more general criticism is expressed by a nurse who wrote:

I have worked for long periods at a famous private maternity home. I have seen babies herded together, cots touching, shut up in a stifling airless room all night, no attention being paid to their cries. I have seen mothers, their babies just brought to them for their feeds, all trussed up with nappies round their necks, and their arms pinned down, the baby's mouth held to the mother's breast by the nurse, trying to make it feed, sometimes for an hour, until the mother is exhausted and in tears. Many mothers had never seen their own babies' toes. Mothers with their own 'special' nurses fared equally badly. I have seen many cases of definite cruelty to the baby by the nurse. In most cases any doctor's orders are ignored.

The fact is that in health we are constantly engaged in keeping time with natural processes; hurry or delay is interference. Moreover, if we can adjust ourselves to these natural processes we can leave most of the complex mechanisms to nature, while we sit back and watch and learn.

The Problem Contained within Oneself

I have already introduced this theme in my illustrations. It can be stated in this way. Those who have been trained in physical medicine have their own special skills. The question is, should they or should they not go outside their special skill and enter the field of psychology, that is to say, of life and living? My answer is this. Yes, if they can gather into themselves and contain the personal, family, or social problems that they meet, and so allow a solution to arrive of its own accord. This will mean suffering. It is a matter of enduring the worry or even the agony of a case history, of conflict within the individual, of inhibitions and frustrations, of family discord, of economic hardship, and it is not necessary to be a psychology student to be useful. One hands back what one has temporarily held, and then one has done the best that can be done to help. If, on the other hand, it is in a person's temperament to act, to advise, to interfere, to bring about the sort of changes he or she feels would be good, then the answer is: no, this person should not step outside his or her speciality, which concerns physical disease.

I have a friend who does marriage counselling. She has not had much training except as a teacher, but she has a temperament which allows her to accept, during the counselling hour, the problem as it is given her. She does not need to probe to see if the facts are correct and whether the problem is being presented in a one-sided way; she simply takes over whatever comes, and suffers it all. And then the client goes away home somehow feeling different, and often even finding a solution to a problem that had seemed hopeless. Her work is better than that of many who have been given special training. She practically never gives advice, because she does not know what advice to give, and she is not that kind of a person.

In other words, those who find themselves stepping outside the area of their special skill can perform a valuable function if they can immediately stop giving advice.

The Professional Interview

Psychology if practised at all must be done within a framework. An interview must be arranged in a proper setting, and a time limit must be set. Within this framework we can be reliable, much more reliable than we are in our daily lives. Being reliable in all respects is the chief quality we need. This means not only that we respect the client's person and his or her right to time and concern. We have our sense of values, and so we are able to leave the client's sense of right and wrong as we find it. Moral judgement, if expressed, destroys the professional relationship absolutely and irrevocably. The time limit of the professional interview is for our own use; the prospect of the end of the session deals in advance with our own resentment, which would otherwise creep in and spoil the operation of our genuine concern.

Those who practise psychology in this way, accepting limits, and suffering for limited periods of time the agonies of the case, need not know much. But they will learn; they will be taught by their clients. It is my belief that the more they learn in this way the richer they will become, and the less they will feel inclined to give advice.

TWENTY-TWO

The Mother's
Contribution to Society

I suppose that everyone has a paramount interest, a deep, driving propulsion towards something. If one's life lasts long enough, so that looking back becomes allowable, one discerns an urgent tendency that has integrated all the various and varied activities of one's private life and one's professional career.

As for me, I can already see what a big part has been played in my work by the urge to find and to appreciate the ordinary good mother. Fathers, I know, are just as important, and indeed an interest in mothering includes an interest in fathers, and in the vital part they play in child care. But for me it has been to mothers that I have so deeply needed to speak.

It seems to me that there is something missing in human society. Children grow up and become in their turn fathers and mothers, but, on the whole, they do not grow up to know and acknowledge just what their mothers did for them at the start. The reason is that the part the mother plays has only recently begun to be perceived. But here I must make something clear; there are certain things I do not mean.

I do not mean that children should thank their parents for conceiving them. Surely they may hope that the original coming together was a matter of mutual pleasure and satisfaction. Parents certainly cannot expect thanks for the fact of a child's existence. Babies do not ask to be born.

There are other things I do not mean. For instance, I do not mean that children are under any obligation to their fathers and mothers at all on account of their cooperation in home-building and family affairs, even though gratitude may eventually develop. Ordinary good parents do build a home and stick together, thus providing the basic ration of child care and thus maintaining a setting in which each child can gradually find the self and the world, and a working relationship between the two. But parents do not want gratitude for this; they get their rewards, and rather than be thanked they prefer to see their children growing up and themselves becoming parents and home-builders. This can be put the other way round. Boys and girls can legitimately blame parents when, after bringing about their existence, they do not furnish them with that start in life which is their due.

In the last half century there has been a great increase in awareness of the value of the home. (It cannot be helped if this awareness came first out of an understanding of the effect of the bad home.) We know something of the reasons why this long and exacting task, the parents' job of seeing their children through, is a job worth doing; and, in fact, we believe that it provides the only real basis for society, and the only factory for the democratic tendency in a country's social system.

But the home is the parents', not the child's, responsibility. I want to be very clear that I am not asking any one to be expressing gratitude. What particularly concerns me neither goes back so far as conception nor is it as far forward as home-building. I am concerned with the mother's relation to her baby just before the birth and in the first weeks and months after the birth. I am trying to draw attention to the immense contribution to the individual and to society that the ordinary good mother with her husband in support makes at the beginning, and which she does simply through being devoted to her infant.

Is not this contribution of the devoted mother unrecognized precisely because it is immense? If this contribution is accepted, it follows that every man or woman who is sane, every man or woman who has the feeling of being a person in the world, and for whom the world means something, every happy person, is in infinite debt to a woman. At the time when as an infant (male or female) this person knew nothing about dependence, there was absolute dependence.

Once again, let me emphasize, the result of such recognition when it comes will not be gratitude or even praise. The result will be a lessening in ourselves of a fear. If our society delays making full acknowledgement of this dependence, which is a historical fact in the initial stage of development of every individual, there must remain a block both to progress and to regression, a block that is based on fear. If there is no true recognition of the mother's part, then there must remain a vague fear of dependence. This fear will sometimes take the form of a fear of WOMAN, or fear of a woman, and at other times will take less easily recognized forms, always including the fear of domination.

Unfortunately, the fear of domination does not lead groups of people to avoid being dominated; on the contrary, it draws them towards a specific or chosen domination. Indeed, were the psychology of the dictator studied, one would expect to find that, amongst other things, he in his own personal struggle is trying to control the woman whose domination he unconsciously fears, trying to control her by encompassing her, acting for her, and in turn demanding total subjection and "love."

Many students of social history have thought that fear of WOMAN is a powerful cause of the seemingly illogical behaviour of human beings in groups, but this fear is seldom traced to its root. Traced to its root in the history of each individual, this fear of WOMAN turns out to be a fear of recognizing the fact of dependence. There are therefore good social reasons for instigating research into the very early stages of the infant-mother relationship.

For my part, I happen to have been drawn towards finding out all I can about the meaning of the word "devotion," and towards being able, if possible, to make a fully informed and fully felt acknowledgement to my own mother. Here a man is in a more difficult position than a woman; he obviously cannot come to terms with his mother by becoming a mother, in turn, and in due course. He has no alternative but to go as far as he can towards a consciousness of the mother's achievement. The development of motherliness as a quality in his character does not get far enough, and femininity in a man proves to be a side-track to the main issues.

One solution for a man caught up in this problem is to take part in an objective study of the mother's part, especially the part she plays at the beginning.

At present, the importance of the mother at the start is often denied, and instead it is said that in the early months it is only a technique of bodily care that is needed, and that therefore a good nurse will do just as well. We even find mothers (not, I hope, in this country) being told that they *must mother* their infants, this being the most extreme degree of denial that "mothering" grows naturally out of being a mother. It often happens that just before an understanding of some matter, there is a stage of denial, or blindness, or deliberate not seeing, just as the sea withdraws from the sands before throwing forward the thundering wave.

Administrative tidiness, the dictates of hygiene, a laudable urge towards the promotion of bodily health—these and all sorts of other things get between the mother and her baby, and it is unlikely that mothers themselves will rise up in concerted effort to protest against interference. Someone must act for the young mothers who are having their first and second babies, and who are necessarily themselves in a dependent state. It can be assumed that no mother of a newborn baby will ever go on strike against doctors and nurses, however much frustration exists, because she is otherwise engaged.

Though many of my broadcast talks are directed to mothers, the young mothers who are chiefly concerned are unlikely to read them. I have no wish to alter this. I cannot assume that young mothers will ever want to know what it is that they do when they find that they enjoy minding their own infants. They naturally fear lest instruction shall spoil their enjoyment and their creative experience, which is the essential element leading to satisfaction and growth. The young mother needs protection and information, and she needs the best that medical science can offer in the way of bodily care, and prevention of avoidable accidents. She needs a doctor and a nurse whom she knows, and in whom she has confidence. She also needs the devotion of a husband, and satisfying sexual experiences. No, the young mother is not usually a learner from books. Nevertheless, in preparing broadcasts for publication I have kept to the form of direct talk with young mothers for the reason that this provides a discipline. A writer on human nature needs to be constantly drawn towards simple English and away from the jargon of the psychologist, valuable as this jargon may be in contributions to scientific journals.

Probably some who have already been through the mothering experience, and who therefore can afford to have a look round, will be interested to read what is said in this way, and they may be able to help to do what is so much needed at the present time, that is to say, to give moral support to the ordinary good mother, educated or uneducated, clever or limited, rich or poor, and to protect her from everyone and everything that gets between her baby and herself. We all join forces in enabling the emotional relationship between the mother and her new baby to start and to develop naturally. This collective task is an extension of the job of the father, of the father's job at the beginning, at the time when his wife is carrying, bearing and suckling his infant; in the period before the infant can make use of him in other ways.

TWENTY-THREE

The Family and
Emotional Maturity

The psychology with which I am concerned takes maturity to be synonymous with health. The child of ten who is healthy is mature for the child of ten; the healthy three-year-old is mature for the child of three; the adolescent is a mature adolescent and is not prematurely adult. The adult who is healthy is mature as an adult, and by this we mean that he or she has passed through all the immature stages, all the stages of maturity at the younger ages. The healthy adult has all the immaturities to fall back upon either for fun or in time of need, or in secret auto-erotic experience or in dreaming. To do justice to this concept of "maturity at age" one would need to re-state the whole theory of emotional development, but I assume in my readers some knowledge of dynamic psychology and of the theory by which the psycho-analyst works.

Given this concept of maturity, then, my subject is the role of the family in the establishment of individual health. And this prompts the following question for consideration: can the individual achieve emotional maturity except in the setting of the family?

There are two ways of approaching the subject of individual development if we divide dynamic psychology into two parts. First there is the development of the instinctual life, the pregenital instinctual functions and fantasies building up into full sexuality, this being reached, as is well known, before the beginning of the latency period. Along this line of thought we arrive at the idea of adolescence at a time at which the puberty changes dominate the scene, and the defences against anxiety that were organized in the first years reappear or tend to reappear in the growing individual. All this is very familiar ground. By contrast, I want to take the other way of looking at things whereby each individual starts with almost absolute dependence, reaches to the lesser degrees of dependence, and so begins to achieve autonomy.

It may be profitable to think in this second way rather than in the first way. If we do so we need not be too much concerned with the age of a child or adolescent or adult. What we are concerned with is the environmental provision which is well adapted to the needs of the individual at any one particular moment. In other words, this is the same subject as that of maternal care, which changes according to the age of the infant, and which meets the early dependence of the infant and also the infant's reaching out towards independence. This second way of looking at life may be particularly suited to the study of healthy development, and our aim at the present moment is to study health.

Maternal care becomes parental care, the two parents together taking responsibility for their infant, and for the relationship between their infants and their children. Moreover, the parents are there to receive the "contributing in" which comes from the healthy children in the family. Parental care evolves into the family, and the word family begins to extend itself further to include grandparents and cousins, and the people who become like relations because of their neighbourliness, or because they have some special significance—for instance, godparents.

When we examine this developing phenomenon, which starts with maternal care and goes right on to the persisting interest that the family has in the adolescent boy and girl, we cannot fail to be impressed by the human need for a steadily widening circle for the care of the individual, and also by the need the individual has for a place into which a contribution can be made from time to time when the individual has the urge to be creative, or to be generous. All these ever-widening circles are the mother's lap and her arms and her concern.

I have made much in my writings of the very delicate adaptation that mothers make to the needs of their infants, needs which vary from minute to minute. Who but the infant's mother troubles to know and feel the infant's needs? I should like to follow up this theme here and to say that it is only the child's own family that is likely to be able to continue this task started by the mother and continued by the mother and father, the task of meeting the individual's needs. These needs include dependence and the individual's striving towards independence. The task includes meeting the

changing needs of the growing individual, not only in the sense of satisfying instincts, but also in the sense of being present to receive the contributing in that is a vital feature of human life. And this task further
includes acceptance of the breaking out in defiance and also of the return
to dependence that alternates with defiance.

Immediately it is evident that in referring to defiance and dependence I
am discussing something which appears quite typically in adolescence and
can be well observed there; in fact it constitutes a main problem of management: how to be there waiting when the adolescent becomes infantile
and dependent, and takes everything for granted, and at the same time be
able to meet the adolescent's need to strike out defiantly to establish a personal independence? It is likely to be the individual's own family that is
best able and willing to meet such a claim, the simultaneous claim on the
parents' tolerance of even violent defiance, and on their time, money and
concern. The adolescent who runs away has by no means lost the need for
home and family, as is well known.

At this point I should like to recapitulate: the individual in the course of
emotional growth is going from dependence to independence, and in
health retains the capacity for shifting to and fro, from one to the other.
This process is not achieved quietly and easily. It is complicated by the
alternatives of defiance and of return from defiance to dependence. In defiance the individual breaks through whatever is immediately around him or
her, giving security. In order that this breaking through shall be profitable,
two things are necessary. The individual needs to find a wider circle ready
to take over, and this is almost the same as saying that what is needed is the
capacity to return to the situation that has been broken up. In a practical
sense the little child needs to break away from the mother's arms and lap,
but not to go into space; the breaking away has to be to a wider area of control; something that is symbolical of the lap from which the child has broken away. A slightly older child runs away from home, but at the bottom
of the garden has finished running away. The garden fence is now symbolical of the narrower aspect of holding which has just been broken up, shall
we say the house. Later, the child works out all these things in going to
school and in relation to other groups that are outside the home. In each
case these outside groups represent a getting away from the home, and yet
at the same time they are symbolical of the home that has been broken
away from and in fantasy broken up.

When these things go well, the child is able to come back home in spite of the defiance inherent in the going away. We would describe this in terms of the child's inner economy, in terms of the organization of the personal psychic reality. But to a large extent success in the discovery of a personal solution depends on the existence of the family and on the parental management. Put the other way round, it is very difficult for a child to work out the conflicts of loyalties in moving out and in without satisfactory family management. Understanding management is usually available because usually there is a family, and there exist parents who feel responsible and who like to take responsibility. In the vast majority of cases the home and the family do exist and do remain intact and do provide the individual with an opportunity for personal development in this important respect. A surprising number of people can look back and say that whatever mistakes were made their family *never really let them down,* any more than their mother let them down in the matter of maternal care during the first days, weeks, and months.

Within the home itself, when there are other children the individual child gains immeasurable relief from having opportunity for sharing problems. This is another big subject, but the point that I would make here is that when the family is intact and the brothers and sisters are true siblings, then each individual has the best opportunity for beginning to lead a social life. The main reason is that at the centre of everything is the relationship to the actual father and mother, and however much this separates the children because it makes them hate each other, its main effect is to bind them, and to create a situation in which it is safe to hate.

All this is only too easily taken for granted when there is an intact family, and we see the children growing up and presenting symptoms which are often symptoms of healthy development even though they are awkward and disturbing. It is when the family is not intact, or threatens to break, that we notice how important the intact family is. It is true that a threat of breakdown of the family structure does not necessarily lead to clinical illness in the children, because in some cases it leads to a premature emotional growth and to a precocious independence and sense of responsibility; but this is not what we are calling maturity at age, and it is not health, even if it has healthy features.

Let me enunciate a general principle. It would seem to me to be valuable to understand that as long as the family is intact then everything relates ultimately to the individual's actual father and mother. In the conscious life and fantasy the child may have got away from the father and mother, and may have gained great relief from doing so. Nevertheless, the way back to the father and mother is always retained in the unconscious. In the unconscious fantasy of the child it is always on his or her own father and mother that a claim is made fundamentally. The child gradually comes to lose much or nearly all of the direct claim on the actual father and mother, but this is conscious fantasy. What has happened is that gradually displacement has taken place from the actual parents outwards. The family exists as something which is cemented by this fact, that for each individual member of the family the actual father and mother are alive in the inner psychic reality.

In this way we see two tendencies. The first is the tendency in the individual to get away from the mother and away from the father and mother and away from the family, each step giving increased freedom of ideas and of functioning. The other tendency works in the opposite direction and it is the need to retain or to be able to regain the relationship with the actual father and mother. It is this second tendency which makes the first tendency a part of growth instead of a disruption of the individual's personality. It is not a question of recognizing intellectually that the ever-widening area of relationships retains symbolically the idea of the father and the mother. What I am referring to is the individual's ability actually to get back to the parents and to the mother, back to the centre or back to the beginning, at any appropriate moment, perhaps in the flash of a dream or in the form of a poem or in a joke. The origin of all the displacements is in the parents and in the mother, and this needs to be retained. This is something which has a wide area of application: we can think, for example, of the emigrant, who finds a way of life in the antipodes and eventually comes back to make sure that Piccadilly Circus is as it was. I hope by this to have shown that if the unconscious fantasy is taken into account, which of course it must be, the child's constant exploration of wider areas and the child's constant search for groups outside the family and the child's defiant destruction of all rigid forms are the same thing as the child's need to retain the primary relationship to the actual parents.

In the healthy development of the individual, at whatever stage, what is needed is a steady progression, that is to say, a well-graduated series of defiant iconoclastic actions, each in the series being compatible with the retention of an unconscious bond with the central figures or figure, the parents or the mother. If families are observed it will be seen that immense trouble is taken in the natural course of events by parents to maintain this series and to organize the graduation so that the sequence of the individual's development is not broken.

A special case is provided in the sexual development, both in the establishment of a personal sexual life and in the search for a mate. In marriage there is expected a coincidental breaking out and away from the actual parents and the family, and at the same time a carry-through of the idea of family-building.

In practice these violent episodes are often hidden by the process of identification, especially identification of the boy with the father and of the girl with the mother. A life solution in terms of identification is not satisfactory, however, except in so far as the individual boy or girl has reached the dream of violent overthrow. In relation to this theme of the repeated breakthrough which is characteristic of the lives of growing individuals, the Oedipus complex comes as a relief, since in the triangular situation the boy can retain the love of the mother with the idea of the father in the way, and similarly the girl with the mother in the way can retain the longing for the father. Where only the child and the mother are concerned, there are only two alternatives, to be swallowed up or to break free.

The more we examine these matters the more we see how difficult it is for any group to take all the trouble that is required to keep these things going well unless that group is the family to which the child belongs.

It is hardly necessary for me to add that the opposite cannot be assumed; that is to say, if the family does its best for a child in all these respects, this does not mean that the child will therefore develop to full maturity. There are many hazards in the internal economy of each individual, and personal psychotherapy is mainly directed towards the clearing up of these internal strains and stresses. To follow up this theme would be to go over to the other way of looking at individual growth that I referred to at the beginning of this section.

It is useful to remember, when considering the role of the family, the contributions that have been made by social psychology and anthropology on this subject. In regard to social psychology, Willmott and Young's recent study, *Family and Kinship in East London*,[1] may be mentioned. In regard to anthropology, we are familiar with the ways in which various aspects of the family vary from locality to locality and from time to time; how sometimes it is the uncles and aunts who bring up the children, and the actual paternity may be lost as far as consciousness is concerned, but there is always evidence of unconscious knowledge of true parenthood.

To return to the concept of maturity as health. It is only too easy for individuals to jump forward a stage or two, to become mature in advance of their age, to become very well established as individuals where they ought to be less well established and more dependent. It is necessary to keep this in mind when we study the emotional maturity or immaturity of individuals who have been brought up away from their own families. These individuals may develop in such a way that at first we feel like making the comment: how established and how independent he or she is, and what a good thing it must be to have to fend for oneself early in life! I do not accept this, however, as a final statement, because I feel that for maturity it is necessary the individuals shall not mature early, not become established as individuals when in their age group they should be relatively dependent.

When I now look back, and consider the question that I raised tentatively at the outset, my conclusion is that if one accepts the idea of health as maturity at age, the emotional maturity of the individual cannot be achieved except in a setting in which the family has provided the bridge leading out of parental care (or maternal care) right across into the social provision. And it must be remembered that social provision is very much an extension of the family. If we examine the ways in which people provide for young children and for older children, and if we look at the political institutions of adult life, we find displacements from the home setting and the family. We find, for instance, the provision of opportunity for children who break away from their own homes to find a home from which they can once more break away if necessary. The home and the family are still the models on which is based any sort of social provision which is likely to work.

There are two main features, then, which (in the language that I have chosen to use here) the family contributes to the emotional maturity of the individual: one is the continued existence of the opportunity for dependence of a high degree; the other is the provision of the opportunity for the individual to break away from the parents to the family, from the family to the social unit just outside the family, and from that social unit to another, and perhaps to another and another. These ever-widening circles, which eventually become political or religious or cultural groupings in society, and perhaps nationalism[2] itself, are the end-product of something that starts off with maternal care, or parental care, and then continues as the family. It is the family that seems to be especially designed to carry the unconscious dependence on the father and mother, the actual father and mother, and this dependence covers the growing child's need defiantly to break out.

This way of reasoning uses the concept of adult maturity equated with psychiatric health. It could be said that the mature adult is able to identify himself or herself with environmental groupings or institutions, and to do so without loss of a sense of personal going-on-being, and without too great a sacrifice of spontaneous impulse, this being at the root of creativity. If we examined the area covered by the term "environmental groupings," then the highest marks would go to the widest meaning of the term, and to the most comprehensive area of society with which the individual feels identified. An important feature is the individual's capacity, after each example of iconoclastic acting out, to rediscover in the broken-up forms the original maternal care and parental provision and family stability, all of that on which the individual was dependent in the early stages. It is the family's function to provide a practice ground for this essential feature of personal growth.

Here are two sayings come surprisingly together:

1. Things ain't wot they was!
2. *Plus ça change, plus c'est la même chose.*

Mature adults bring vitality to that which is ancient, old, and orthodox by re-creating it after destroying it. And so the parents move up a step, and move down a step, and become grandparents.

Notes

1. Young, M., and Willmott, P. (1957). London: Routledge and Kegan Paul.
2. However much we long for a grouping that is international, we cannot afford to slur over the idea of nationalism as a stage in development.

TWENTY-FOUR

The Development of the Capacity for Concern

The origin of the capacity to be concerned presents a complex problem. Concern is an important feature in social life. Psychoanalysts usually seek origins in the emotional development of the individual. We want to know the aetiology of concern, and the place where concern appears in the child's development. We also are interested in the failure of the establishment of an individual's capacity for concern, and in the loss of concern that has to some extent been established.

The word "concern" is used to cover in a positive way a phenomenon that is covered in a negative way by the word "guilt." A sense of guilt is anxiety linked with the concept of ambivalence, and implies a degree of integration in the individual ego that allows for the retention of good object-imago along with the idea of a destruction of it. Concern implies further integration, and further growth, and relates in a positive way to the individual's sense of responsibility, especially in respect of relationships into which the instinctual drives have entered.

Concern refers to the fact that the individual *cares*, or *minds*, and both feels and accepts responsibility. At the genital level in the statement of the theory of development, concern could be said to be the basis of the family, where both partners in intercourse—beyond their pleasure—take responsibility for the result. But in the total imaginative life of the individual, the subject of concern raises even wider issues, and a capacity for concern is at the back of all constructive play and work. It belongs to normal, healthy living, and deserves the attention of the psychoanalyst.

There is much reason to believe that concern—with its positive sense—emerges in the earlier emotional development of the child at a period before the period of the classical Oedipus complex, which involves a relationship between three persons, each felt to be a whole person by the child. But there is no need to be precise about timing, and indeed most of the processes that start up in early infancy are never fully established, and continue to be strengthened by the growth that continues in later childhood, and indeed in adult life, even in old age.

It is usual to describe the origin of the capacity for concern in terms of the infant-mother relationship, when already the infant is an established unit, and when the infant feels the mother, or mother-figure, to be a whole person. It is a development belonging essentially to the period of a two-body relationship.

In any statement of child-development, certain principles are taken for granted. Here I wish to say that the maturation processes form the basis of infant- and child-development, in psychology as in anatomy and physiology. Nevertheless, in emotional development it is clear that certain external conditions are necessary if maturation potentials are to become actual. That is, development depends on a good-enough environment, and the earlier we go back in our study of the baby, the more true it is that without good-enough mothering the early stages of development cannot take place.

A great deal has happened in the development of the baby before we begin to be able to refer to concern. The capacity to be concerned is a matter of health, a capacity which, once established, presupposes a complex ego-organization which cannot be thought of in any way but as an achievement, both an achievement of an infant- and child-care and an achievement in terms of the internal growth-processes in the baby and child. I shall take for granted a good-enough environment in the early stages, in order to simplify the matter that I wish to examine. What I have to say, then, follows on complex maturational processes dependent for their becoming realized on good-enough infant- and child-care.

Of the many stages that have been described by Freud and the psychoanalysts who have followed him, I must single out one stage which has to involve the use of the word "fusion." This is the achievement of emotional development in which the baby experiences erotic and aggressive drives toward the same object at the same time. On the erotic side there is both satisfaction-seeking, and on the aggressive side, there is a complex of anger employing muscle erotism, and of hate, which involves the retention of a good object-imago for comparison. Also in the whole aggressive-destructive impulse is contained a primitive type of object relationship in which love involves destruction. Some of this is necessarily obscure, and I do not need to know all about the origin of aggression in order to follow my argument, because I am taking it for granted that the baby has become able to combine erotic and aggressive experience, and in relation to one object. Ambivalence has been reached.

By the time that this becomes a fact in the development of a child, the infant has become able to experience ambivalence in fantasy, as well as in body-function of which the fantasy is originally an elaboration. Also, the infant is beginning to relate himself to objects that are less and less subjective phenomena, and more and more objectively perceived "not-me" elements. He has begun to establish a self, a unit that is both physically contained in the body's skin and that is psychologically integrated. The mother has now become—in the child's mind—a coherent image, and the term "whole object" now becomes applicable. This state of affairs, a precarious at first, could be nicknamed the "humpty-dumpty stage," the wall on which Humpty Dumpty is precariously perched being the mother who has ceased to offer her lap.

This development implies an ego that begins to be independent of the mother's auxilary ego, and there can now be said to be an inside to the baby, and therefore an outside. The body-scheme has come into being and quickly develops complexity. From now on, the infant lives a psychosomatic life. The inner psychic reality which Freud taught us to respect now becomes a real thing to the infant, who now feels that personal richness develops out of the simultaneous love-hate experience which implies the achievement of ambivalence, the enrichment and refinement of which leads to the emergence of concern.

It is helpful to postulate the existence for the immature child of two mothers—shall I call them the object-mother and the environment-mother? I have no wish to invent names that become stuck and eventually develop a rigidity and an obstructive quality, but it seems possible to use these words "object-mother" and "environment-mother" in this context to describe the vast difference that there is for the infant between two aspects of infant-care, the mother as object, or owner of the part-object that may satisfy the infant's urgent needs, and the mother as the person who wards off the unpredictable and who actively provides care in handling and in general management. What the infant does at the height of id-tension and the use of thus made of the object seems to me very different from the use the infant makes of the mother as part of the total environment. [1]

In this language it is the environment-mother who receives all that can be called affection and sensuous co-existence; it is the object-mother who becomes the target for excited experience backed by crude instinct-tension. It is my thesis that concern turns up in the baby's life as a highly sophisticated experience in the coming-together in the infant's mind of the object-mother and the environment-mother. The environmental provision continues to be vitally important here, though the infant is beginning to be able to have that inner stability that belongs to the development of independence.

In favourable circumstances, when the baby has reached the necessary stage in personal development, there comes about a new fusion. For one thing, there is the full experience of, and fantasy of, object-relating based on instinct, the object being used without regard for consequences, used ruthlessly (if we use the term as a description of our view of what is going on). And alongside this is the more quiet relationship of the baby to the environment-mother. These two things come together. The result is complex, and it is this that I especially wish to describe.

The favourable circumstances necessary at this stage are these: that the mother should continue to be alive and available, available physically and available in the sense of not being preoccupied with something else. The object-mother has to be found to survive the instinct-driven episodes, which have now acquired the full force of fantasies of oral sadism and other results of fusion. Also, the environment-mother has a special function, which is to continue to be herself, to be empathic towards her infant, to be there to receive the spontaneous gesture, and to be pleased.

The fantasy that goes with full-blooded id-drives contains attack and destruction. It is not only that the baby imagines that he eats the object, but also that the baby wants to take possession of the contents of the object. If the object is not destroyed, it is because of its own survival capacity, not because of the baby's protection of the object. This is one side of the picture.

The other side of the picture has to do with the baby's relation to the environment-mother, and from this angle there may come so great a protection of the mother that the child becomes inhibited or turns away. Here is a positive element in the infant's experience of weaning and one reason why some infants wean themselves.

In favourable circumstances there builds up a technique for the solution of this complex form of ambivalence. The infant experiences anxiety, because if he consumes the mother he will lose her, but this anxiety becomes modified by the fact that the baby has a contribution to make to the environment-mother. There is a growing confidence that there will be opportunity for contributing-in, for giving to the environment-mother, a confidence which makes the infant able to hold the anxiety. The anxiety held in this way becomes altered in quality and becomes a sense of guilt.

Instinct-drives lead to ruthless usage of objects, and then to a guilt-sense which is held, and is allayed by the contribution to the environment-mother that the infant can make in the course of a few hours. Also, the opportunity for giving and for making reparation that the environment-mother offers by her reliable presence, enables the baby to become more and more bold in the experiencing of id-drives; in other words, frees the baby's instinctual life. In this way, the guilt is not felt, but it lies dormant, or potential, and appears (as sadness or a depressed mood) if only opportunity for reparation fails to turn up.

When confidence in this benign cycle and in the expectation of opportunity is established, the sense of guilt in relation to the id-drives becomes further modified, and we then need a more positive term, such as "concern." The infant is now becoming able to be concerned, to take responsibility for his own instinctual impulses and the functions that belong to them. This provides one of the fundamental constructive elements of play and work. But in the developmental process, it was the opportunity to contribute that enabled concern to be within the child's capacity.

A feature that may be noted, especially in respect of the concept of anxiety that is "held," is that integration *in time* has become added to the more static integration of the earlier stages. Time is kept going by the mother, and this is one aspect of her auxiliary ego-functioning; but the infant comes to have a personal time-sense, one that lasts at first only over a short span. This is the same as the infant's capacity to keep alive the imago of the mother in the inner world which also contains the fragmentary benign and persecutory elements that arise out of the instinctual experiences. The length of the time-span over which a child can keep the imago alive in inner psychic reality depends partly on maturational processes and partly on the state of the inner defence organization.

I have sketched some aspects of the origins of concern in the early stages in which the mother's continued presence has a specific value for the infant, that is, if the instinctual life is to have freedom of expression. But this balance has to be achieved over and over again. Take the obvious case of the management of adolescence, or the equally obvious case of the psychiatric patient, for whom occupational therapy is often a start on the road towards a constructive relation to society. Or consider a doctor, and his needs. Deprive him of his work, and where is he? He needs his patients, and the opportunity to use his skills, as others do.

I shall not develop at length the theme of lack of development of concern, or of loss of this capacity for concern that has been almost, but not quite, established. Briefly, failure of the object-mother to survive or of the environment-mother to provide reliable opportunity for reparation leads to a loss of the capacity for concern, and to its replacement by crude anxieties and by crude defences, such as splitting, or disintegration. We often discuss separation-anxiety, but here I am trying to describe what happens between mothers and their babies and between parents and their children when there is *no* separation, and when external continuity of child-care is *not* broken. I am trying to account for things that happen when separation is avoided.

Note

1. This is a theme that has recently been developed in a book by Harold Searles: *The Non-Human Environment in Normal Development and in Schizophrenia*. New York: International Universities Press, 1960.

TWENTY-FIVE

The Child in the
Family Group

A great deal has been written recently on the subject of the child and the family, and it is very difficult to know how to contribute to this vast subject in an original way. It must be the general feeling that everything has been said and one can almost claim that the title has become meaningless simply through repeated use. A little refreshment has come recently through a change of emphasis in the directives, so that now the accent is to be not on the individual, but on the family. There is some sort of plan to change the pattern of social work so that it is the family that is under consideration and the child is thought of as part of the family.

In my opinion this means no change at all, because the child has always been studied in relationship to the family or to the lack of a family. But at any rate we can try to make use of anything which relieves monotony. I do think that if we look at the psychoanalytic contribution we can say that the emphasis which psychoanalysts have placed on the treatment of a child has been unbalanced. Psychoanalysis has been through a long phase of discussing the treatment of one child as a phenomenon seen in isolation. This could not be helped. Within psychoanalytic circles there is a change here, however—a change that has come simply through the processes of development of ideas. The recent change in directive, however, is not aimed at the psychoanalyst. It is aimed at social work in general, and I would say that social work has always looked at the family when looking at the child.

There is a danger in my mind of an over-emphasis now of the management of human difficulties in terms of family and other groups as an escape from the study of the individual, whether child, infant, adolescent or grown-up. Somewhere or other in the work involved in every case, a caseworker must meet an individual out of the grouping; it is here that the biggest difficulties lie, and also it is here that there is the greatest potential for bringing about change.

I start, therefore, with a plea: remember the individual child, and the child's developmental process, and the child's distress, and the child's need for personal help, and the child's ability to make use of personal help, while of course remembering the importance of the family and the various school groups and all the other groups that lead on to the one that we call society.

In any piece of casework a decision has to be made on who is the ill person in this case. And sometimes, although it is the child that is put forward as ill, it is someone else who is causing and maintaining a disturbance, or it may even be that a social factor is the trouble. These are special cases and social workers are fully aware of this problem, which should not blind them, however, to the fact that in the vast majority of cases, when a child shows symptoms, these symptoms point to distress in the child which can best be met by work done with the child.

I want to remind you that this is especially true in all the myriad cases that exist in the community, but that do not get to the Child Guidance Clinics, which of course tend to find themselves dealing with the much less common, more complex cases. In other words, if you look around at the children that you know in your family and social setting, you will see a vast number of children who could do with a bit of help but who will never get to a clinic. I am saying that these are the children who can be helped best and who need individual attention. The children in the clinics are not representative of the children who are in need of help in the community. I say this with confidence to this audience because it is composed of teachers, and the majority of children that you teach are not clinic cases; they are the ordinary children, or much like those who belong to your social group. There is practically no child that is not in need of help over some personal problem, yesterday, today and tomorrow. Very often you deal with these problems in the school by ignoring them or by carefully graded discipline or by teaching the child a skill or by giving opportunity for creative impulses. And it has to be admitted that, on the whole, your view of psychology must be and must remain different from the views of the social worker and of the child psychiatrist.

You will understand that there must be an overlap and that some of your children ought to be attending a clinic and some of the clinic children ought to be dealing with their difficulties with the help of aunts and uncles and school teachers and every other kind of generalized social provision.

The Group in Relation to the Individual

What I want to do in order to make use of the opportunity you have given me is to remind you in some detail of the way in which the family is a group whose structure is related to the structure of the individual personality. The family is the first grouping, and of all groupings it is the one which is the nearest to being a grouping within the unit personality. The first grouping is simply a reduplication of the unit structure. When we say that the family is the first grouping, we are quite naturally talking in terms of the growth of the individual, and this is justified by the fact that the mere passage of time has no link with human living that is comparable in strength to the link that belongs to the fact that at a certain point in time each person starts and by a growth process makes an area of time personal.

The child is beginning to separate out from the mother, and before the mother becomes objectively perceived, she is what might be called a subjective object. There is quite a jerk that the child has to experience between the use of a mother as a subjective object, that is to say an aspect of the self, and an object that is other than self and therefore outside omnipotent control; and the mother performs a most important task in adapting herself to the child's needs so that she blurs a little this terrible jerk to which I have referred and which belongs to meeting the Reality Principle. The mother-figure becomes reduplicated.

In some cultures a deliberate effort is made to prevent the mother from ever becoming one person, so that the child is ensured from the beginning against shock associated with loss. In our culture we tend to regard it as normal for the child to experience the full extent of the shock as the mother becomes an adaptive external person, but we have to admit that there are casualties. When it works with one mother, there is a richness of experience which is the main argument in its favour. Anthropological study of this area provides fascinating material for the research worker observing the results of the early and deliberate splitting of the mother-figure, socially determined.

The father comes into the picture in two ways. To some extent he is one of the people reduplicating the mother-figure, and there has been a change in orientation in this country in the last fifty years so that fathers become real to their infants much more in the role of reduplications of mother than they did, it would seem, a few decades ago. Nevertheless, it interferes with the other thing about a father, which is that he enters into the child's life as an aspect of the mother which is hard and strict and unrelenting, intransigent, indestructible, and which, under favourable circumstances, gradually becomes that man who turns out to be a human being, someone who can be feared and hated and loved and respected.

In this way a group has developed and we have to see that the group has come about in two sets of ways. The first set simply belongs to the extension of the child's personality structure and depends on growth processes. The other set depends on the mother and what she is like in her attitude to this particular child; on the other people who may be available as mother-figures; on the attitude of the mother to the surrogate mothers; on the social attitude in the locality; and then on the balance of the two aspects which I have described of the father-figure. What the father is like naturally very much determines the way in which the child uses or does not use him in the formation of this particular child's family. In any case, of course, the father may be absent or may be very much in evidence, and these details make a tremendous difference to the meaning of the word "family" for the particular child we happen to be talking about.

Incidentally, I know of one child who gave the name "Family" to her transitional object. I think that in this case there was a very early recognition of inadequacy in the parental relationship, and it was at an astonishingly early date that this child tried to remedy the deficiency that she perceived by calling her doll Family. It is the only instance I know in which this happened, and now thirty years later the person is still struggling with an inability to accept the estrangement between her parents.

What I hope to have done so far is to remind you that when we simply talk about a child and his or her family, we are ignoring the tricky stages in which that particular child acquired a family. It is not simply that there is a father and mother and that perhaps new children come along and then there is a home with parents and children enriched by aunts and uncles and cousins. This is just an observer's statement. For the five children in a family there are five families. It does not require a psychoanalyst to see that these five families need not resemble each other, and are certainly not identical.

The Reality Principle

Now that I have introduced the idea of a family along with the concept of the subjective object turning into one that is objectively perceived, I would like to continue a study in this area. There is an astonishingly big change that comes in the development of human beings just here between these two types of relationship. I personally have tried to contribute by making the most of our observations of transitional objects and transitional phenomena, that is to say, all the things employed by the individual child while he or she is passing through this phase in which there is a limited ability to make objective perceptions, and where the main experience of object-relating must continue to be relating to subjective objects. (Incidentally, it is not possible to use the words "internal object" here; the object which we can see is external and is subjectively perceived, that is to say, it comes out of the creative impulses of the child and out of the child's mind. It is a more sophisticated matter when the child, now with an inside, takes externally perceived objects in and sets them up as internal images. We are discussing a stage before this language makes sense.)

A difficulty that presents itself in a description of this kind is that when a small child in this stage relates to what I am calling a subjective object, there is no doubt that at the same time there is objective perception at work. In other words, the child could not have invented exactly what the mother's left ear looks like. And yet in this stage one must say that the mother's left ear that the child is playing with is a subjective object; the child reached out and created that particular ear that happened to be there to be discovered. This is the exciting thing about the curtain in a theatre. When it goes up, each one of us will create the play that is going to be enacted, and afterwards we may even find that the overlap of what we have created, each one of us, provides material for a discussion about the play that was enacted.

I do not know how to go any further without saying that there is an element of cheating somewhere here, cheating which is inherent in the individual's development of the capacity to relate to objects. I am reading this paper to you, to an audience that I have created. But it must be admitted that in writing the paper I have also to some extent thought about the audience that in fact is here now. I would like to think that this audience that is here now can join up to some extent with the audience that I had in mind when I was writing the paper, but there is no guarantee that the two audiences will be able to relate to each other. In writing this paper I have to play and I play about in the area which I call transitional, in which I am pretending that my audience is yourselves as you are here and now.

This phase that I am choosing to discuss and to which I have sometimes referred by using the term "transitional phenomena" is important in the development of every individual child. Time is required within an "average expectable environment"[1] so that the child may be helped by someone adapting in an extremely sensitive way while the child is in the process of acquiring a capacity to use fantasy, to call on inner reality and dream, and to manipulate toys. In playing, the child enters this intermediate area of what I am calling cheating, although I want to make it clear that just in this particular aspect of cheating there is health. The child uses a position in between himself or herself and the mother or father, whoever it is, and there whatever happens is symbolic of the union or the non-separation of these two separate things. The concept is really quite a difficult one and I think it would make a difference to philosophy if this could be grasped. It would also perhaps put religion once more into the experience of those who in fact have grown up out of the concept of miracles.

For our purpose here, the point is that the child requires a length of time in which steady experiences in relationships can be used for the development of intermediate areas in which transitional or play phenomena can become established for that particular child, established so that henceforward the child may enjoy all that is to be derived from the use of the symbol, for the symbol of union gives wider scope for human experience than union itself.

Excursions and Returns

I repeat that in healthy development the child needs *time* for this phase to be fully exploited, and here I am adding that the child needs to be able to experience the various kinds of object-relating all in the same day or even at one moment; for instance, you may see a small child enjoying relationships with an aunt or a dog or a butterfly and the observer may see not only that the child is making objective perceptions, but is enjoying the enrichment that comes from discovery. This does not mean, however, that the child is ready to live in a discovered world. At any moment the child merges in again with the cot or the mother or the familiar smells and is re-established in a subjective environment. What I am trying to say is that it is the child's family pattern more than anything else that supplies the child with these relics of the past, so that when the child discovers the world there is always the return journey that makes sense. If it is the child's own family, then the return journey does not put a strain on anyone, because it is of the essence of the family that it remains orientated to itself and to the people within it.

Although these points do not require illustrations I will take an incident from an analytic case.

A woman patient sums up the accumulated traumata of her childhood by relating one incident in the way that patients often do. In her own words she shows the importance of the time factor. "I was about two. The family was on the beach. I wandered away from mother and began to make discoveries. I found seashells. One seashell led me on to another and there was an unlimited number. Suddenly I became frightened and I can see now that what had happened was that I had become interested in discovering the world and had forgotten mother. This carried with it, as I see now, the idea that mother had forgotten me. I therefore turned round and rushed back to mother, perhaps only a few yards. Mother took me up and a process started up of re-establishment of my relationship with her. I probably seemed uninterested in her because of this fact that time is required for me to feel re-established and to lose the sense of panic. Then suddenly mother put me down."

This patient was in analysis and re-enacting this episode, and from the work done in the analysis she could add: "Now I know what happened. I have been waiting all my life till now to be able to reach the next stage because if mother had not put me down I would have thrown my arms round her neck and have burst into a flood of tears, tears of joy and happiness. As it was, I never found my mother again."

It will be understood that in giving this incident, the patient was referring to a pattern of this kind of situation based on superimposed memories of similar situations. The point about this illustration is that it shows the very delicate way in which, when all goes well, the child's confidence in the return journey is built up. This is a theme which is brought out in the three volumes, and especially the last, of Richard Church's autobiography.

In observing a child of two we can easily see the coexistence of excursions and return journeys that carry with them but little risk, and excursions and returns that are significant in that if they fail, they alter the child's whole life. Various members of the family have various parts to play and children use each other in extending their experiences to cover a wide field in the quality of excursions and returns.

In this way it often happens that a child at school is very different from a child at home. The more usual pattern is for the child at school to be excited in the discovery of new things, new aspects of reality newly perceived, while at the same time at home the child is conservative, withdrawn, dependent, near to panic, preserved from crisis by the sensitive adaptation of the mother or some other near person. It can be the other way round, but it is perhaps less normal and therefore more likely to give rise to difficulty when the child is full of confidence at school in relation to some one person, or to the setting, and at home is irritable, uncertain and prematurely independent. This could happen when there is no place in the family for the child to be, as when a second child has become the middle one of three children so that he or she has lost on all counts until someone notices that the child has altered in temperament and that, although in a good family, the child has become a deprived child.

Loyalty and Disloyalty

I would like to make a further development of the theme of the family as related to the theme of the developing individual. Of the many aspects of this phenomenon, which has so many facets, I would choose to speak of the conflicts of loyalty which are inherent in child development.

In its simplest terms, the problem can be stated in this way. There is a very great difference between a child who has walked away from the mother and reached the father and who has made the return journey, and a child who has never had this experience.

In more sophisticated language, the child is not equipped in the early stages for containing conflict within the self. This is something which we ask of the social worker, and we know what a strain it puts on mature adults when they do casework and over a period of time contain the conflicts that are inherent in a case. The caseworker puts more importance on this containment of the case than on any specific actions related to individuals in the group that comprises the case.

We must expect the immature child to need a situation in which loyalty is not expected, and it is in the family that we may hope to find this tolerance of what looks like disloyalty if it is not simply a part of the growth process.

A child moves over to a relationship to the father, and in doing so develops an attitude to the mother which belongs to relating to the father. Not only can the mother be seen objectively from where the father is, but also the child develops an in-love type of relationship to the father which involves hate of the mother and fear of the mother. It is dangerous to go back to the mother from this position. There has been a gradual build-up, however, and the child returns to the mother and in this familiar orientation sees the father objectively and the feelings of the child contain hate and fear.

This sort of thing goes on as a to-and-fro experience in the daily life of the child in the home. Of course, it need not be the father-mother relationship; it can be an experience of going from the mother to the nurse and back again, or it may be an aunt or a grandmother or a big sister. Gradually in the family all these possibilities can be met with, and experienced, and a child can come to terms with the fears associated with them. Moreover, the child can come to enjoy the excitements that belong to all these conflicts, provided they can be contained; and in the games, the children of a family introduce all the strains and stresses which belong to this kind of experimentation with disloyalties, even including the perceived tensions and jealousies that exist among the grownup people in the environment. In a sense this is a good way of describing family life in theoretical terms. Perhaps the tremendous interest that children have in playing fathers and mothers derives from a gradual widening out of the experiencing of the experimentation with disloyalties.

Sometimes one can see how important these games are when a new child arrives rather late in the family and of course cannot make use of the brothers' and sisters' games because these have evolved a complexity which has a history for the older brothers and sisters. The new child may become involved in a mechanical way and feel severely eliminated or annihilated by the involvement, which is not a creative one, since the new child would need to start again and to build up from the simplest beginnings the complexity of cross-loyalties.

I know, of course, that there are positive and libidinal features in the feelings that belong to the family game, but the content making for excitement is very much associated with this matter of cross-loyalties. In this way the family game is the perfect preparation for life.

It will be seen that the school can easily provide tremendous relief for the child living in a family. For small children who play most of the time, the games played at school are not quite basic, and very soon they pass over into games which develop skills. Then there is the matter of the group discipline, and all this is a simplification very welcome for some, very irksome for others. Too early a simplification of the kind that school gives relative to the family game of children who live in a family must be looked at as an impoverishment, at any rate for those who can stand the family game, and whose families can stand up to the fact that the children are playing at families.

By contrast, it can be seen that the only or lonely child has everything to gain from going early to a play group, where, at any rate to some extent, the playing can have interpersonal relationships and cross-loyalties which are creative for the child.

These are the sort of reasons why there can never be a satisfactory decision from above in regard to the age at which children should go to school. In these delicate matters everything has to be examined afresh in every new case if good advice is to be given, and this means that in any one neighbourhood all kinds of provisions should be available. When in doubt, the child's home is the place where the richest experiences can be reached, but one has to be always on the look-out for the child who, for one reason or another, cannot be creative in imaginative play until he or she spends a few hours each day outside the family.

Primary school education belongs to the area in which the child rather welcomes being distracted from working out the complexities that life offers by learning and by the adoption of specific loyalties and by acceptance of rules and standards along with the school uniform. Sometimes these conditions persist right through the adolescent period, but we are unhappy when the children allow such a thing to happen, however convenient it may be from the teachers' point of view. We expect in the adolescence of every boy and girl for there to reappear all the experimentation and cross-loyalties which appeared creatively in the family game, only this time the excitement comes not only from the fears roused, but also from the new and intense libidinal experiences which puberty has let loose.

The family is, of course, of tremendous value to the adolescent boy or girl, especially as each one of them is thoroughly frightened most of the time, even in health, since intense loving automatically produces intense hating. Where the family framework continues, the adolescent can act out fathers and mothers, which was the substance of the imaginative play at the 2–5-year stage of life at home.

It seems to me that the family is often thought of in terms of a structure maintained by the parents, in terms of a framework in which children can live and grow. It is thought of as a place where the children discover feelings of love and hate and where they can expect sympathy and tolerance as well as the exasperation which they engender. But what I have been saying has to do with my feeling that the part played by each child in the function of the family, in respect of the children's encounter with disloyalty, is somewhat understated. The family leads on to all manner of groupings, groupings that get wider and wider until they reach the size of the local society and society in general.

The reality of the world in which the children eventually must live as adults is one in which every loyalty involves something of an opposite nature which might be called a disloyalty, and the child who has had the chance to reach to all these things in the course of growth is in the best position to take a place in such a world.

Eventually, if one goes back, one can see that these disloyalties, as I am calling them, are an essential feature of living, and they stem from the fact that it is disloyal to everything that is not oneself if one is to be oneself. The most aggressive and therefore the most dangerous words in the languages of the world are to be found in the assertion I AM. It has to be admitted, however, that only those who have reached a stage at which they can make this assertion are really qualified as adult members of society.

Note

1. This phrase was borrowed from Heinz Hartmann (see H. Hartmann, *Ego Psychology and the Problem of Adaptation*, 1939).

TWENTY-SIX

Children Learning

I have come to speak at this conference as a human being, a children's doctor, a child psychiatrist and a psychoanalyst. If I look back forty years I can see a change of attitude. It is unlikely, forty years ago, that a psychoanalyst could be expected by those engaged in religious teaching to contribute positively. You know, I hope, that I have been invited here not as a religious teacher, nor even as a Christian, but as someone with a long experience in a limited field, one who is intensely concerned with human problems of growth, living and fulfilment. Your chairman said something about my knowing more than anyone else about childhood behaviour. He got that off the back of some book! The contribution you would like me to make is that I know about more than just the surface phenomena, or behaviour on top of the whole personality structure. The word "fulfilment" comes in here. There is a class of people who study childhood behaviour and miss out on unconscious motivation and the relation of behaviour to conflict within the person, and so get completely out of touch with anybody who is teaching about religion—I think that that is what your chairman meant, that I was interested in the developing human being in the family and the social setting.

Brought up as a Wesleyan Methodist, I suppose I just grew up out of church religious practice, and I am always glad that my religious upbringing was of a kind that allowed for growing up out of. I know that I am talking to an enlightened audience for whom religion does not mean just going to church every Sunday. May I say that it seems to me that what is commonly called religion arises out of human nature, whereas there are some who think of human nature as rescued from savagery by a revelation from outside human nature.

There are many matters of great significance we might discuss together once we have decided to look and see whether there could be a positive contribution from the psychoanalytic side to religious teaching and even to the practice of religion. Do you need miracles in this age of close, objective observation? Do you need to be addicted to the idea of an after-life? Do you need to put myth among the second-class citizens of thought? Do you need to go on robbing the individual child or adolescent or adult of his or her own innate goodness by inculcating morality?

I must keep to one subject in order to be contained within one hour and also within the limited area of my special experience. I think I may have been invited here today because of something I once said about a child's capacity to believe *in*. This leaves open the whole question of what you place at the end of the phrase. What I am doing is to separate out living experience from education. In education you can hand on to the child the beliefs that have meaning for yourself and that belong to the small cultural or religious area that you happen to be born into or to choose as an alternative to the one you were born into. But you will have success only in so far as the child has a capacity to believe in anything at all. The development of this capacity is not a matter of education, unless you extend the word to mean something that is not usually meant by it. It is a matter of the experience of the person as a developing baby and child in the matter of care. The mother comes into this, and perhaps the father and others who are in the immediate environment of the baby—but initially the mother.

You will see that for me there is always this matter of growth and development. I never think of the state of a person here and now except in relation to the environment and in relation to the growth of that individual from conception and certainly from the time around the birth date.

The individual baby is born with inherited tendencies that fiercely drive the individual on in a growth process. This includes the tendency towards integration of the personality, towards the wholeness of a personality in body and mind, and towards object-relating, which gradually becomes a matter of interpersonal relationships as the child begins to grow up and understand the existence of other people. All this comes from within the boy or girl. Nevertheless, these processes of growth cannot take place without a facilitating environment, especially at the start when a condition of dependence obtains which is near absolute. A facilitating environment must have a human quality, not a mechanical perfection, so the phrase "good-enough mother" seems to me to meet the need for a description of what the child needs if the inherited growth processes are to become actual in the development of the individual child. In the beginning the whole of the development takes place because of the tremendously vital, inherited tendencies towards development—towards integration, towards growth, the thing that one day makes the child want to walk, and so on. If there is a good-enough environmental provision, these things take place in that child. But if the facilitating environment is not good enough, then the line of life is broken and the very powerful inherited tendencies cannot carry the child on to personal fulfilment.

A good-enough mother starts off with a high degree of adaptation to the baby's needs. That is what "good-enough" means, this tremendous capacity that mothers ordinarily have to give themselves over to identification with the baby. Towards the end of a pregnancy and at the beginning of a child's life, they are so identified with the baby that they really practically know what the baby is feeling like, and so they can adapt themselves to the needs of the baby in such a way that the baby's needs are met. Then the baby is in the position of being able to make a developmental continuity of growth which is the beginning of health. The mother is laying down the basis for the mental health of the baby, and more than health—fulfilment and rich-ness, with all the dangers and conflicts that these bring, with all the awk-wardnesses that belong to growth and development.

So the mother, and the father too, though the father does not have the same physical relationship at the beginning, has this ability to identify with the baby without resentment, and to adapt to the baby's needs. The vast majority of babies in the world in the past several thousand years have had good-enough mothering at the beginning; otherwise the world would be more full of mad people than sane people, and it isn't. This identification of the woman with her baby presents a threat to some women; they won-der if they will ever get back their own individuality, and because of these anxieties some find it difficult to give themselves over to this extreme of adaptation at the beginning.

It is obvious that mother-figures meet the baby's instinctual needs. But that side of parent-infant relationship has been over-stressed in the first fifty years of psychoanalytic literature. It took a long time for the analytic world—and thought about child development has been powerfully influ-enced by the last sixty or so years of psychoanalytic thinking—to look, for example, at the importance of the way a baby is held; and yet, when you come to think of it, this is of primary significance. You could make a caricature of someone smoking a cigarette and holding the baby by the leg, swinging it round and putting it in the bath, and you know somehow that this is not what babies need. There are very subtle things here. I've watched and talked to thousands of mothers, and you see how they pick up the baby, supporting the head and the body. If you have got a child's body and head in your hands and do not think of that as a unity, and reach for a handkerchief or something, then the head has gone back and the child is in two pieces—head and body; the child screams and never forgets it. The awful thing is that nothing is ever forgotten. Then the child goes around with an absence of confidence in things. I think it is right to say that babies and little children do not remember when things went well, they remember when things went wrong, because they remember that suddenly the continuity of their life was snapped, and their neck went back or something, and it came through all the defences, and they reacted to it, and this is an extremely painful thing that has happened to them, something they cannot ever lose. And they have got to go round with it, and if that is in the pattern of their care, it builds up into a lack of confidence in the environment.

If things went well, they never say "thank you," because they did not know it went well. In families there is this great area of unacknowledged debt which is no debt. There is nothing owing, but anybody who reaches stable adulthood could not have done it if somebody at the beginning had not taken him or her through the early stages.

This question of holding and handling brings up the whole issue of human reliability. The sort of thing I have been talking about could not be done by a computer—it must be *human* reliability (that is, unreliability, really). In the development of adaptation, the mother's great adaptation to the baby gradually becomes less; accordingly the baby begins to be frustrated and to be angry and needs to identify with the mother. I remember a baby of three months who, when feeding at the mother's breast, would put his hand to her mouth to feed her before he took her breast. He was able to get an idea of what the mother was feeling like.

The child can keep the idea of the mother or father or baby-sitter alive for so many minutes, but if the mother at that stage is away for two hours, then the *image* of the mother that the child has inside him wilts and begins to die. When the mother returns, she is another person. It is difficult to bring alive the *image* inside himself. For two years or so, the child does react very badly to separation from the mother. By two years old, the child actually knows the mother or father well enough to be able to be interested not just in an object or in a situation, but in an actual person. At two years the child needs to have the mother there if, for example, he goes into hospital. But always the baby needs the environmental stability that facilitates continuity of personal experience.

I learn a lot not only from talking to mothers and watching children, but also from treating grown people; they all become babies and children in the course of treatment. I have to pretend to be more grown-up than I am to deal with this. I have a patient at the moment; she is fifty-five years old and she can keep the *image* of me alive if she sees me three times a week. Twice a week is just possible. Once a week, although I give her a very long session, is not enough. The *image* wilts and the pain of seeing all the feelings and all the meaning going out is so great that she will say to me that it is not worth it, she would rather die. So the pattern of treatment has to depend on how the *image* of the parent-figure can be kept alive. One cannot help becoming a parent-figure whenever one is doing anything professionally reliable. You are nearly all, I expect, engaged in some sort of professionally reliable thing, and in that limited area you behave much better than you do at home, and your clients depend on you and get to lean on you.

Acts of human reliability make a communication long before speech means anything—the way the mother fits in when rocking the child, the sound and tone of her voice, all communicate long before speech is understood.

We are believing people. Here we are in this large hall and no one has been worried about the ceiling falling down. We have a belief in the architect. We are believing people because we are started off well by somebody. We received a silent communication over a period of time that we were loved in the sense that we could rely on the environmental provision and so get on with our growth and development.

A child who has not experienced preverbal care in terms of holding and handling—human reliability—is a deprived child. The only thing that can logically be applied to a deprived child is love, love in terms of holding and handling. To do it later in a child's life is difficult, but at any rate we may try, as in the provision of residential care. The difficulty comes from the child's need to make tests and to see if this preverbal loving, holding, handling, and so on, stands up to the destructiveness that comes with primitive loving. When all goes well, this destructiveness becomes sublimated into things like eating, kicking, playing, competition, and so on. Nevertheless, the child is at this very primitive stage—here's somebody to love, and then the next thing is destruction. If you survive, then there is the *idea* of destruction instead. But first of all there is destruction, and if you start to love a child who was not loved in this preverbal sense, you may find yourself in a mess; you find yourself being stolen from, windows broken, the cat being tortured, and all sorts of frightful things. And you have got to survive all this. You will be loved because you have survived.

Why is it that if I stand up here and say that I had a good start, it sounds like boasting? All I am in fact saying is that nothing I am capable of is just me; it was either inherited, or else somebody enabled me to get to the place where I am. The reason it does sound like boasting is because it is impossible for me as a human being to believe that I did not choose my own parents. So I am saying that I made a good choice, aren't I clever? It seems silly, but we are dealing with human nature, and in matters of human growth and development we need to be able to accept paradoxes; what we feel and what can be observed to be true can be reconciled. Paradoxes are not meant to be resolved; they are meant to be observed. It is at this point that we begin to divide into two camps. We must observe what it is that we feel, while at the same time using our brains to work out what it is that we have feelings about. Let's take my suggestion that the whole of the preverbal expression of love in terms of holding and handling has vital significance for each developing baby. Then we can say that on the basis of what has been experienced by an individual, we may teach the concept of, say, everlasting arms. We may use that word "God," we can make a specific link with the Christian church and doctrine, but it is a series of steps. Teaching comes into place there on the basis of what the individual child has the capacity to believe in. If in the case of moral teaching we take the line that we are going to treat certain things as sinful, how far are we sure that we are not robbing the growing child of the capacity *on his own* to come to a personal sense of right and wrong, to come to this out of his own development? One can often rob an individual of a terribly important moment when the feeling is: "I have an impulse to do such and such, but I also". . . and they come to some sort of personal developmental phase, which would have been completely broken across if somebody had said, "You're not to do that, it's wrong." Then they would either comply, in which case they have given up, or else they would defy, in which case nobody has gained anything, and there is no growth.

From my point of view, what you teach can only be implanted on what capacity is already present in the individual child, based on the early experiences and on the continuation of reliable holding in terms of the ever-widening circle of family and school and social life.

Original Source of Each Chapter

Part One: Babies and Their Mothers

Note: The papers in this section were first published in 1987 (Reading, MA: Addison-Wesley) under the same title. The volume was edited by Clare Winnicott, Ray Shepard and Madeleine Davis.

1. "The Ordinary Devoted Mother." Unpublished talk given to the Nursery School Association of Great Britain and Northern Ireland, London Branch, 16 February 1966.

2. "Knowing and Learning." A BBC broadcast talk to mothers, 1950. First published in *The Child and the Family.* London: Tavistock Publications Ltd., 1957.

3. "Breast-feeding as Communication." A paper read in Winnicott's absence at a conference on breast-feeding held by the National Childbirth Trust in London, November 1968. Portions published in *Maternal and Child Care,* September 1969.

4. "The Newborn and His Mother." Lecture given at a symposium on "The Physiological, Neurological and Psychological Problems of the Neonate" in Rome, April 1964. First published under the title "The Neonate and His Mother" in *Acta Pediatrica Latina,* Vol. XVII, 1964. During the lecture the film described on page 33 was shown.

5. "The Beginning of the Individual." Written 1966 in response to a letter to the London *Times* from Dr. Fisher, then Archbishop of Canterbury. Unpublished.

6. "Environmental Health in Infancy." In this chapter the editors have combined two versions of a lecture given at a symposium with the same title held

at the Royal Society of Medicine, London, March 1967. Portions published in *Maternal and Child Care*, January 1968.

7. "The Contribution of Psychoanalysis to Midwifery." Lecture given at a course organized by the Association of Supervisors of Midwives, 1957. First published in *The Family and Individual Development*, London: Tavistock Publications Ltd., 1965.

8. "Dependence in Child Care." First published in *Your Child*, Vol. 2, 1970.

9. "Communication Between Infant and Mother, and Mother and Infant, Compared and Contrasted." Lecture in a public series about psychoanalysis, known as the Winter Lectures, Marylebone, London, January 1968. First published in *What Is Psychoanalysis?* London: Baillière, Tindall & Cassell Ltd., 1968.

D. W. W. made the following preliminary notes for this lecture on November 20, 1967, which give a slightly different perspective to the subject.

Unsatisfactoriness of current terms such as maternal instinct, symbiosis.
Limits of value of animal studies.

Contribution from psychoanalysis.
Note the word unconscious in the titles of previous lectures but not in this title.
Reason: infants not being conscious are not unconscious.
The accent is on the initial stages of development of the person who may become conscious and unconscious.
By contrast: the mother (or parent) has all the characteristics of the human mature person.
The mother has been a baby.
She has also played at being a parent and she has had ideas handed down to her.
The baby has not been a mother, nor has yet played at anything.

To get further it is necessary to make an attempt at a statement of the early stages of the development of the human baby. No time for more than a statement of:
Continuity in individual growth.

Dependence, near absolute at first.

Threat of breaks in continuity by reactions to impingements.

Impingements looked at as failures of the environment at the stage of dependence.

Gradual release of the environment due to the baby's increasing range of predicting.

Extreme example: Baby communicates by being helpless, by dependence.

There is or is not a communication according to whether the mother is or is not able to identify with the baby, to know what need is before specific needs are indicated.

This leads to a study of the changes in the mother (parent) relative to pregnancy and parenthood.

Postulate a special condition, temporary but needing abandonment as in an illness. In this condition the mother is the baby as well as herself, she does not feel a narcissistic wound when she is depleted in her own personal role by being identified with the baby.

She can be scared of this and can be helped by being told that the condition only lasts a few weeks or months, and that she will recover from it.

Without this temporary condition she cannot turn the baby's infinitely subtle needs into a communication.

The mother communicates with her baby by knowing what is needed before the need is expressed in a gesture.

From this follows naturally the gesture that expresses need, and the parent can meet this communication by appropriate response. Out of this comes deliberate communication of all kinds, not only of needs but also of wants. By this time the mother can feel free again to become herself, and to frustrate. The one state must evolve out of the other.

Frustration of "I want" produces anger. Even failure to meet deliberate "I need" gestures can produce distress, and this communication can help the mother to do what is needed, even if a little late.

By contrast, failure to meet the need that precedes deliberate gesture can only result in distortion of the infantile developmental process—nothing so good as rage can be reached.

It is to be noted that every distortion of the infantile developmental process is accompanied by unthinkable anxiety:

disintegration

falling for ever

total failure of relating to objects, etc.

Our borderline cases, those that teach us to understand these things, carry round with them experiences of unthinkable anxiety, which are failures of communication at the stage of absolute dependence.

Part Two: Talking to Parents

Note: The papers in Part Two were first published in 1993 (Reading, MA: Addison-Wesley) under the same title. The volume was edited by Clare Winnicott, Christopher Bollas, Madeleine Davis and Ray Shepard.

10. "Health Education through Broadcasting," written for *Mother and Child*, No. 28, 1957.

11. "For Stepparents." On January 3, 1955, a talk was given on the BBC's Woman's Hour by a stepmother, telling in a vivid and moving way how she was tormented by being unable to love her stepson, who had joined her household when he was seven years old. The BBC received an enormous number of letters after this broadcast, telling of like and of different experiences in stepparenting and generally indicating that the subject was worth pursuing. As a result the BBC allocated three slots to this end in the Woman's Hour of the following June 6, 7, and 9. The first of these consisted of a series of questions and answers between an expert and a stepfather. The next two were talks given by Winnicott, and are reproduced here. Both were transcribed from tapes, with the result that the punctuation has had to be added.

12. "What Do We Know about Babies as Cloth Suckers?" BBC broadcast talk given January 31, 1956.

13. "Saying 'No'." Three BBC broadcast talks given January 25 and February 1 and 8, 1960.

14. "Jealousy." Four BBC broadcast talks given February 15, 22, and 29 and March 7, 1960.

15. "What Irks?" Three BBC broadcast talks given on March 14, 21, and 28, 1960.

16. "Security." BBC broadcast talk given April 18, 1960. First published under the title "On Security" in *The Family and Individual Development*. London: Tavistock Publications, 1965.

17. "Feeling Guilty." Discussion with Claire Rayner, BBC broadcast talk given March 13, 1961.

18. "The Development of a Child's Sense of Right and Wrong." BBC broadcast talk given June 11, 1962.

19. "Now They Are Five." BBC broadcast talk given June 25, 1962. First published under the title "The Five-Year-Old" in *The Family and Individual Development*. London: Tavistock Publications, 1965.

20. "The Building up of Trust." Written in December, 1969. Never published.

Part Three

21. "Advising Parents." Lecture given at a course for midwives organized by the Royal College of Midwives. November, 1957.

22. "The Mother's Contribution to Society." The postscript to Dr. Winnicott's first collection of broadcast talks, published under the title *The Child and the Family*. 1957.

23. "The Family and Emotional Maturity." Lecture to the Society for Psychosomatic Research. November 1960.

24. "The Development of the Capacity for Concern." Paper presented to the Topeka Psychoanalytic Society. October 12, 1962.

25. "The Child in the Family Group." A talk given to the Nursery School Association Conference on "Developments in Primary Education" held at New College, Oxford, July 26, 1966.

26. "Children Learning." A paper read to a conference on Family Evangelism under the auspices of the Christian Teamwork Institute of Education, at Kingswood College for Further Education, June 5, 1968.

The Works of D. W. Winnicott

Clinical Notes on Disorders of Childhood. 1931. London: William Heinemann Ltd.

Getting to Know Your Baby. 1945, London: Heinemann.

The Ordinary Devoted Mother and Her Baby. 1949. Privately published.

The Child and the Family: First Relationships. 1957. London: Tavistock Publications Ltd.

The Child and the Outside World: Studies in Developing Relationships. 1957. London: Tavistock Publications Ltd.

Collected Papers: Through Paediatrics to Psychoanalysis. 1958. London: Tavistock Publications. New York: Basic Books, Inc., Publishers.

The Child, the Family and the Outside World. 1964. London: Penguin Books. Reading, MA: Addison-Wesley Publishing Co., Inc.

The Maturational Process and the Facilitating Environment. 1965. London: Hogarth Press and the Institute of Psychoanalysis. New York: International Universities Press. Reprinted 1990, London: Karnac Books.

The Family and Individual Development. 1965. London: Tavistock Publications Ltd.

Playing and Reality. 1971. London: Tavistock Publications Ltd. New York: Basic Books.

Therapeutic Consultations in Child Psychiatry. 1971. London: Hogarth Press and the Institute of Psychoanalysis. New York: Basic Books.

The Piggle: An Account of the Psycho-Analytical Treatment of a Little Girl. 1978. London: Hogarth Press and the Institute of Psychoanalysis. New York: International Universities Press.

Deprivation and Delinquency. 1984. London: Tavistock Publications.

Holding and Interpretation: Fragment of an Analysis. 1986. London: Hogarth Press and the Institute of Psychoanalysis. New York: Grove Press 1986. Reprinted 1989, London: Karnac Books.

Home Is Where We Start From. 1986. London: Penguin Books. New York:

W. W. Norton & Company, Inc.

Babies and Their Mothers. 1987. Reading, MA: Addison-Wesley Publishing Co., Inc.

The Spontaneous Gesture: Selected Letters of D. W. Winnicott. 1987. (Ed. F. R. Rodman) Cambridge, MA: Harvard University Press.

Human Nature. 1988. London: Free Association Books. New York: Schocken Books.

Psychoanalytic Exploration. 1989. Ed. C. Winnicott, R. Shepard, M. Davis. London: Karnac Books. Cambridge, MA: Harvard University Press.

Talking to Parents. 1993. Reading, MA: Addison-Wesley.

Thinking About Children. 1996. London: Karnac Books. 1996. Reading, MA: Addison-Wesley.

Winnicott on the Child. 2002. Cambridge, MA: Perseus Publishing.

Index

Abortion, 43, 56
Adaptation
  allowing baby to create the world, 53
  and love
    by baby, 14, 53–54
    building sense of predictability in the baby, 66
    child's needs and mother's failure to, 14, 53–54, 66
    failure of maternal, 14, 53–54, 66, 73, 76
    failures of, 51
    graduated failures of, 14, 53
    increasing complexity of, 34
    of family to child, 208–209, 234
    love and, 76
    meeting dependence, 67, 69
    of mother to baby, 6–7, 16, 21, 50, 53, 66–68, 75–76, 77–78, 99, 208, 223, 234
    to school for five-year-olds, 173–177
Adolescents, 158–159, 207, 208, 220
  defiance vs. dependence in, 209–210
  experimentation, libidinal experiences and, 230–231
Adoption, 12–13, 97
Adults
  I AM essential to, 231
  loyalty/disloyalty of, 231
  older, 236
Advice, (doctor's)
  containing problem within oneself vs., 200
  professional interview, (suffering) and, 200–201
  treatment of disease vs. life, 193–199
Aetiology, 15, 215
Affection, infant's show of, 106
Aggression, 216–218
  and forward development, 30

and love, 29–30
and survival of the object, 6, 29–30
baby's, in feeding, 5–6, 29–30
Agony (agonies). See also Anxiety
  Moro Response as, 38–40
  of childbirth, 57–58, 65
  primitive, 39–40, 67–68, 76–77, 241–242
  primitive vs. good experiences, 67–68
Ambivalence
  anxiety and, 219
  love-hate, 217
  of mother and guilt, 87, 91
  universal problem of, 184
Anger, 235
  at failures of analyst, 76
  distress vs., 241
  employing muscle erotism, 241
  jealousy and, 131, 138
  satisfaction in, vs. despair, 14
  timing of expression of, 177
  unthinkable anxiety vs., 76
Anthropology, 212–213, 223
Anxiety
  about going to school, 176–177
  adaptation, women and, 234
  ambivalence with, 219
  defenses against, 107
  experience of, in borderline cases, 242
  guilt and, 215
  'held,' in time, 219–220, 227
  in mother, and holding, 21
  jealousy and, 131
  loss of capacity for concern, disintegration and, 220
  no separation and, 220
  repression and, 72
  toleration of, 169

unthinkable, 17, 33–34, 40, 67–68, 76–77,
242
unthinkable, and distortion in development,
242
unthinkable, as fruits of privation, 76–77
unthinkable disintegration and, 17–18, 33,
38–39, 67, 220
unthinkable vs. good experience, 67–68
Arguments, annoyance over, 144, 149
Attitudes, parental
jealousy and, 135, 136–137, 229
saying 'no' and, 118–119
Autonomy
development, in infant, 5, 12
independence and, 71, 79, 208, 209, 210
Awareness, individual, 46–47

Babies and Their Mothers (Winnicott), 9
Baby (babies). See also Breast-feeding; Infants
ability to use what has been found and, 80
abnormalities of, 197–198
absence of conscious and unconscious, 70,
240
absolute dependency of, 16, 65, 67–68, 70,
71, 72, 73, 203–204, 208, 241
adaptation by, 14, 53–54
aggressiveness and destruction of, 216–218
and autonomy, 5
and capacity to know what mother is feeling,
13–14, 17
and creation of the mother, 53
and development of feelings of good and bad,
54
and experience of being born, 58
and identification with mother, 5
and memories of traumatic experience, 51
and protection of object, 30
anxiety/disintegration of, 17–18, 33, 38–39,
67, 220
as being, 17, 35
awful feelings turning to good experiences in,
67–68
becoming part of world, 30–31
birth of, brought about by the baby, 40
bodily needs of, 67
body functioning in, as a basis for health, 55
breakdown of holding/handling of, 17–18,
51–52, 236–237
breast-feeding, (aggressive) biting, inhibition
and love in, 5–6, 29–30

breast-feeding and experiences in, 28, 29
cheating of, 225–226
communication of, to mother, 78–80
creativeness vs. compliance in, 79–80
description of, at the beginning, 89–90
development needed before concern of, 216
development of 'belief in,' 75, 233, 235,
237–238
development of inside and outside, 54, 75
developmental stages of, 21–22
dreaming of, 28
ego orientation of, 16–17
excretions of, 54–55
experience of omnipotence and, 7, 14, 78,
223
false jigging on knee of, 196
fantasy of, 217, 218, 226
feeding inhibitions of, 63
feeding of, 26, 28, 31, 63, 168–169, 196–197
first gestures of, 22, 241
fusion of emotions of, 216–218
growth of trust and, 5, 75–76
holding/handling of, 20–21, 34, 51, 52, 235
human from the beginning, 34, 54, 57, 58
imago of, 219–220
instinct of, 168, 218, 219, 234–235
insults to, 51–52
integration of, 16–17, 34
integrity of, 5
irregular feeding/psychology of, 28
lack of experience in, 6, 74, 240
love of, 168–169
mental health of, 25
mother taken away from, 61–62, 63–64
mother's intuition/instinct, care for, 5, 6, 13,
50–51, 62–63
need for physical contact and, 67
newborn, 32–42, 70–71, 205
not as human being, 198
not separate from environment at the
beginning, 71
object-relating for, 18
physical contact with mother and, 67, 77–78
potential in, for realising potential, 79
premature awareness in, 38, 42
psychoanalysis, schizophrenia, emotional
development and, 35–36
reactions of, to Moro test, 37–38
reactions of, to failures of adaptation, 52
ruthless aggression in, 29–30
self-contained, 21–22

sense of predictability and, 66
storing of experiences and, 45, 52, 58, 65
surprising the environment, 22
use of mother's face and, 78
BBC, 11, 98
radio talks on, 89, 91
Beginning
of children, at birth, 46
of children, when brain is anatomically
    established, 44
of children, when psychology becomes
    meaningful, 45–46
of children, when they are conceived,
    43–44
of children, when they are conceived of, 43
of children, with development of moral code,
    47
of children, with me/not-me distinction,
    46–47
of children, with objectivity, 47
of children, with viability, 45
of continuity, 70
of individual, 34–35, 43–48
of life, and necessity for holding, 51–52
of personal psychic reality, 48
of play and cultural experience, 47–48
Being, 17, 35
and I AM, 17
and establishment of self, 17
and primary identification, 16–17
continuity of, 38, 70
giving rise to doing, 14, 17
interruption in, 38
self-experiencing, 14, 17
Belief in
beginning of, in baby, 75
capacity for in child, 48, 235, 237–238
Benzie, Isa, 11
Birth (see also Childbirth)
as beginning of the individual, 43, 46
psychologically normal, 40, 45–46
Biting, 167–168
Blame, for maternal failure, 12, 15
Bottle-feeding, 26, 31
and breaking of bottle, 31
and experience of relief, 26
and sensuous use of rubber, 29
eye contact and, 29
from medical point of view, 25, 52
problems with, 196
Bowlby, John, 184

Brain
and registering and sorting experience, 45
as an organ, 44, 45
Breast-feeding, 97, 106, 128, 130, 146. See also
    Feeding
a natural function, 24, 31, 52, 62, 63
and biting, 5–6, 29–30
and powerful gum action, 29
and propaganda, 24
and sense of achievement, in mothers, 5, 29
and sensuous experience, 5, 29
and sentimentality, 24
as communication, 5–6, 24–31, 63
baby's aggressiveness in, 29–31
baby's searching in, 53
baby's sleep and, 196–197
expert knowledge not needed for, 20
forced situation by nurses for, 61–62, 63, 196,
    199
from medical point of view, 25, 52
holding vs., 26
inability for, 27
intuitive/instinct reactions in, 5, 19, 63, 197
mother's physical intimacy beyond, 24
not a guarantee of successful object-relating,
    25–26
not absolutely necessary, 24, 25–26
not to be forced on mothers, 26, 27–28, 52,
    63
not under conscious control, 26–27, 63
positive value of, 28–31
problems with, 196–197
psychoanalysts and, 25–26
richness of experience of, for baby, 28
something that cannot be taught, 52
survival of mother, breasts and, 30–31
total personality involvement in, 29
weaning of, 31, 195–196, 219
Broadcasting, health education through, 95–98

Case material
adopted baby with abnormal feeding pattern,
    28
girl of two and birth game, 37
hysterical woman and dream of birth, 36–37
initiation of infant feeding mismanaged,
    61–62
regressed patient and reaction to Moro test,
    37–39

schizophrenic boy and game of being born
again, 36
schizophrenic woman and dream of birth,
40–42
Character
strength in, and breast-feeding, 24–25
strength in, and good-enough mothering,
25–26
warping of, through environmental failure,
68, 241
Child (children)
adaptation of family to, 208–209
and capacity for belief in 75, 233, 235,
237–238
and need to go back to earliest stages, 22–23
beginning of, 43–48
deprived, and unmended environmental
failures, 76–77, 236–237
estrangement of parents and, 224
firm setting to work out conflicts for, 16
floor time for, 192
illness of family or, 222
image of mother, age of two and, 235–236
immature, 217, 229
importance of playing of, 47–48
internal image and, 225–226
mental defect in, 44
mind nurturing of, 192
not under obligation to thanks parents,
202–203
outside advice tampering/benefit with rearing
of, 191–192
parents, same and opposite sex, 16
playing as mother/father, 73, 229, 231, 240
relationship of parent and, 191–192, 202–203
retaining primary relationship with parents
by, 211–212
return journey, objective perceptions and,
226–228
school vs. home for, 228
siblings of, 229–2230
Child Guidance Clinic, 222
Childbearing, 6
Childbirth
a natural process, 60
and change in attitude of parents, 46, 57
and natural processes, 57–58, 60
and need for continuity in care, 59–60
at home, 59
attitude of baby in process of, 58
baby and, 57

big head of baby and, 60
dependency of mothers during, 58–59, 60
dream of, 40–42
enriched by health in the participants, 61
father and, 57–58, 61
game of, 36
healthy mother and, 58–61
midwife and, 57, 58
postmature, 45–46
premature, 33, 44, 45–46, 51
process of, 46, 71
remembering of, 36–37
unhealthy mother and, 60–61
Church, Richard, 228
Circle
as diagram of infant's self, 38
becoming two instead of one, 38
Cloth sucking, 104–107
Communication
baby to others, 198–199
baby's helplessness in, 7, 79, 241
baby's, to mother, 78–80
baby's use of mother's face as, 78
between baby and mother through
management of excretions, 54–55
between infant and mother, 6–7, 70–81,
240–242
bodily, 6
breakdown of, through privation, 76–77
breast-feeding as, 5–6, 24, 3163
deliberate, arising from needs being met, 241
dichotomy of mother/child, 74
failure in, at stage of absolute dependence,
241
failure of reliability of, 76
holding as, 75
of love, through mended failures, 76
of mother's reliability, 75–76, 236
mother's verbalisation, to baby and, 75
silent, 75–76, 77–78
taking place from the beginning of life, 71
through experience of omnipotence, 78
through gestures, 241
through inflections in mother's voice, 6
through mutuality in physical experience,
77–78
through needs of the baby, 241
through playing, 7, 77
Complex, the arising out of the simple, 14, 53
Compliance
in baby, and ill-health, 79–80

in mother, and ill-health, 62
vs. creativeness, 79–80
Compulsion, cleaning, 161
Conceived of, being, as beginning of children, 43
Conception
  as accident, 43–44
  as beginning of children, 43–44
Concern
  guilt vs., 215, 219
  loss of capacity for, 220
  love-hate ambivalence leading to, 217
  responsibility with, 215
Confidence, 5, 65, 235
  infants loss of, 106–107
Confinement
  and need for mother to know those in attendance, 59
  home vs. hospital, 59
Conflict(s), 184–185, 229, 232
  inner, 102
  jealousy and, 131
  self-control and, 159
Continuity
  as basis for development, 70, 235–236
  in care of baby, 68, 220
  of baby, threatened by reactions to impingement, 235, 241
  of being, 38, 70, 75
  of child, fragmented by reactions to insult, 51–52
  of development, 75, 241
Controls, children's need vs. hate for, 159
Creativeness
  cross-loyalties for, 230
  in baby, 7, 53, 77, 79–80
  root of, 214
Cultural experience, 47–48

De-adaptation, graduated, of mother, 14
Defects, 44
Defiance
  dependence vs., 209–210, 214
Dependence
  absolute, and needs of baby, 16, 67–68, 203–204, 208
  absolute, in the womb, 65
  absolute, of the baby at the beginning, 6, 16, 46, 65, 70, 71, 72, 73, 241
  and sense of security, 65

as a fact, 65
defiance vs., 209–210, 214
developmental stages and, 208
environmental failure during, 68, 241
in child care, 65–69
met by human adaptation to need, 67, 208
moving towards independence, 46, 65, 71, 208–209, 210, 212, 213–214, 223
of mother during childbirth, 59
relative, 46, 65, 71
retaining of, 210–212
Depression
  of child, 219
  maternal, 15, 22, 78, 80n2
  school and mother/child, 174
Determinants of Infant Behaviour, 35
Development
  and positive use of destructiveness, 30–31
  backward movement in, in schizophrenia, 40
  emotional, 156
  inherited tendency towards, 179–180
  importance of along natural lines, 25
Devotion, nature of, in mothers, 11, 12, 14, 15, 18, 21, 85, 90, 203, 204
Dictator, 204
Diet
  vitamins and, 19–20
Disintegration, as unthinkable anxiety, 17, 39–40
Disloyalty, child's feeling of, for enjoying school, 177
Disorders of Childhood (Winnicott), 3
Distractions, 110, 112, 117
Doctor(s), 205
  and advice about intimacy between baby and mother, 26–27, 55
  and continuity of contact with pregnant woman, 59–60
  and demands of modern medicine, 27
  and difficulty in seeing infants as human beings, 32, 49–50
  and establishment of breast-feeding, 52
  and holding of baby, 33
  and instruction of parents, 50
  and interference with natural processes, 53, 54, 55
  and knowledge of the parents' function, 50
  containing problem within oneself (vs. solution) by, 200
  facilitate natural process of birth with, 57
  mother/child relationship lacking in, 26–27, 49–50, 54–55

mothers trust, during confinement, 59–60, 205
not experts on psychology, 194, 200
professional interview, psychology and, 200–201
solution from dynamics of family situation for, 200
suffering experienced by, 200
treatment of disease *vs.* advice about life and, 193–199
Doctoring
need of mothers for, 53
not concerned with basic needs of baby, 51–52
Doing, arising out of being, 13–14
Dreams
and conceiving of children, 43
material for, in feeding experience, 28
of baby, 28
of being born, 36–37, 40–42, 48
"Drean Child," 43
Dynamic systems theory, 191, 200, 207–208

Education. *See* School
Ego, 16–17
before (or beginning of), 33, 38
concern and development of, 216
holding sensitivity for development of, 33
independent of mother, 21
individual awareness, life and, 46–47
Ego-functioning, premature, 34
Ego-support
and facilitation of baby's ego organisation, 16
faulty, causing intolerable pain, 38–39
reliability of, in mother, 14
Electric shock, avoiding, 110, 112, 118
Emotional development, 156
baby, ego, concern and, 216
backward movement of, 35–36, 40, 42
capacity to believe by child and, 75, 233, 237–238
family, individual and, 213
forward movement of, 40
group and, 223–224
growth of, 192
individual development of increasing spheres for, 208, 209, 213–214
loyalty, disloyalty, child and, 228–231
time for, 226, 227
Empathy, 183

Enclosure
child's emergence from, 172–173, 174
child's inability to get out of, 175
Environment, 25
and dependence, 68, 73, 74, 208, 240–241
and health in infancy, 49–55
failure of, 35, 38, 39, 65, 68, 76–77, 236–237, 241
gradual release of, by baby, 240–241
groupings, 214
inherited tendencies and adequate, 70–71, 78–79, 233–234
insecurity, through early insult of, 51–52, 65
inseparable from individual at the beginning, 46, 214
let-down in, 14–15, 73
mother warding off unpredictable, 217–220
muddled, resulting in difficulty with reality, 47
must be human at the beginning, 51, 72, 75
reliability in, and growth of trust, 75, 235–236
successful, and personal growth, 78–79
surprising baby, 22
usually good enough, 73, 216, 226, 234
Environmental provisions, 156
parental knowledge of, 180–181
stress coming from, 184–185, 186
study of, 185–186
Envy
jealousy and, 127
Essays of Elia, 43
Excretions, 54–55
and interference by manipulations, 55
and training, 55
good and bad, 54
letting the baby come to terms with, 54
linked with intake by baby, 54
management of, 54–55
management of, and pattern for giving and, constructive effort, 55
mother's understanding of, 54–55
Existentialism, 17
Expectation, and frustration, 45
Experience(s)
affection and enjoyment in, through playing, 77
baby's, of breast-feeding, 5–6, 28–29
baby's, of omnipotence, 6–7, 14, 78, 223
differences in quality of, for baby, 28–29

early, remembered in analysis through, re-experiencing, 3 8–39
good and bad, 54
letting the baby come to terms with, 54
linked with intake by baby, 54
interweaving of, with dreams, 62
management of, 54–55
management of, and pattern for giving and, constructive effort, 55
memories of, of faulty holding, 51
mother's, of breast-feeding, 29
mother's, of having been a baby, 6, 13, 29, 57, 73–74, 240
mother's vs. baby's, 73–74, 240
never lost, 66, 70
of birth, 36–37, 40–42, 45, 58, 65, 71
physical, mutuality in, 67, 77–78
reliability, baby's experience of, through being held, 75, 235
sensuous, and transitional objects, 29
storing of, in baby, 45, 52, 58, 65, 71, 235
External reality
acceptance of, by child, 47
contrasted with inner reality, 47
Extremes, 145
perception of world in, 99–101
Eye contact, between mother and baby, 29

Facilitating environment
and developmental processes, 24–25
and inherited tendencies, 16, 25
failure in, and distortion of development, 38–39
human and personal, 16, 51
Failure(s)
accidental, 14–15
and blame, 15
environmental, and distortion in development, 68, 241
environmental, and premature awareness, 38, 41–42
environmental, and unpredictability, 65
graduated, of mother, 14, 53
gross, of holding, and unthinkable anxieties, 76–77
in early growth processes, and mental hospital, illness, 15
in integration, 17
in human beings, 6–7, 76
in object-relating, 18

in psycho-somatic existence, 17
maternal and autism, 11–12
maternal, and deprivation, 76
maternal depression, 15
mending of, and adding up to success, 6–7, 76
new pregnancy as, 15
of analyst, 39, 40
of facilitating environment, 38–39
of holding, 34, 51–52, 76–77
of maternal adaptation, 14, 51, 53–54, 66, 73, 76
of unmended environment and deprived child, 68, 241
of reliability, and communication, 76
relative, of environment, 14, 76
unmended, and deprivation, 76–77
Fairy godmother, stepmother as, 102
Family
adaptation to child by, 208–209, 234
adolescence and, 230–231
anthropology of, 212–213
as bridge with parental care to social provision, 213
discovery of feelings in, 231
dynamic systems theory for, 191, 200, 207–208
emotional maturity of individual and, 213–214
feedback for, 191
games, 229–231
groupings and, 223–224, 231
intact, 210–211, 212
management, 210
maternal/parental care evolving into, 208, 213
not being let down by, 210
not solver of all problems, 212
perceived differently by each person in, 224
sharing of problems, children and, 210
social work, child and, 221–222
Family and Kinship in East London (Young and Willmott), 212–213
Fantasy, 101, 131, 163, 164, 168–169, 217, 218, 226
beginning of, in destruction and survival, 30
Father(s)
and special state around baby's birthday, 12–13, 57–58
and support for mother, 20, 30–31, 57–58
and survival of infant's aggression, 30–31
as authority figure, 223–224

as 'bean ideal' of little girl, 63
as reduplicated mother-figure, 223–224
birth process and, 57–58, 61, 206
boy identification with, 212
child relationship development, love and,
    229, 234
importance of, at birth of baby, 27
in inner psychic of child, 48, 211–212
job of, 206
leaving out of, 11, 80n3
mother achievement understanding and, 204
saying 'no' by, 120, 154
Fear(s), 160, 161–162, 164, 167–168
of dependence, 204
of domination, 204
in expanding out past mother, 229
guilty, 161–162
of mother, 21, 73, 204, 229
of nurse, 62
of woman, 204
Feeding, 90, 105–106, 169
jealousy and, 127–128, 129
Fertilization, 43–44
Fetus, 44
Finger-sucking, 106. See also Cloth-sucking
Fisher, Dr. Geoffrey, Archbishop of Canterbury,
    43 (48, n.1), 46
Five-year-olds, 171–177
adapting to school for, 173–177
Flowers for church, 12
Freedom, 155–156
Freud, Sigmund, 216
Frustration(s), 157
beginning of meaning of, 45
child's need to react to, 53
experience of, arising form experience of,
    omnipotence, 78
of 'I need,' producing distress, 241
of 'I want,' producing anger, 241
in postmature infants, 45–46
of infant, 14
tolerable after arrival of first gestures, 241
Fusion, 216–218

Game(s)
family, 229–231
of childbirth, 36
school, 230
Good-enough parents, 179
Grandparents, 214

Group
individual in relationship to, 223–224
Growth, process of, 180–181
Guilt, 219
concern vs., 215, 219
feeling, 160–166
sense of, 87, 91, 169, 170

Handling
and facilitation of maturational processes, 51,
    75
and psycho-somatic existence, 17
breakdown of, 236–237
love and, 237
more important than actual breast-feeding,
    26
of baby by mother, 5, 6, 75, 235
reliability in, 75, 235
Hate
for baby, 101
for children, 146–147
for mother, 100, 101
jealousy and, 131
love, 217, 231
of mother, 229
Helplessness, of newborn baby, 7, 79, 241
Holding
and belief in reliability in inner processes,
    75–76, 235, 237–238
and establishment of personality, 75
and Moro Response, 37–38, 39, 51
and psycho-somatic existence, 17
and warding off impingement, 22
as auxiliary ego-function, 34
as communication, 75
as facilitation of maturational processes, 75
breakdown of, 17–18, 51–52, 236–237
case-work as, 51
ego development from, 33
failure of, 76–77
functioning of family unit as, 51
good enough, by mother, 34
insults and bad, 51–52
integration alternating with relaxation and,
    75
integration and, 75
love and, 237
more important than actual breast-feeding,
    26
of baby, by doctor, 33

of baby, by mother, 5, 6, 13–14, 20–21, 34, 51–52, 75
of baby, by older sister, 20–21
of a child as baby by mother, 22–23
of patient's head in psychoanalysis, 39
physical, of baby, 51
prototype of all infant care, 33
sensitivity to, in babies, 20–21
Home
value of, 203
Hot, teaching meaning of word, 111, 115–116, 117–118

I AM
arising out of primary identification, 17
as stage of development, 46–47
Id-drives, 216, 218, 219
Identification
of baby with mother, 5, 13–14, 17, 66–67, 240
of individual with others, 68
of individual with society, 68–69
of mother with baby, 5, 5, 12, 13–14, 17, 66–67, 73, 234, 240
parent and gender, 212
primary, 17, 33
Identity
and me/not-me distinction, 46–47
sense of, in baby, 16
Image
internal, 235–236
of mother, age of two and, 235–236
of older adult, 236
Imagination, 86, 105, 106
Impulses, protecting children from their own, 157
Independence
autonomy and, 71, 79, 208, 209, 210
from dependence towards, 208–209, 210, 212, 213–214, 223
in health, mixed with all sorts of needs, 65
inherited drives towards, 70–71
precocious, 210
Individual
development of increasing spheres for, 208, 209, 213–214
emotional maturity, family and, 213, 221
group in relationship to, 223–224
social/family context vs. development of, 213, 221–222

Individual life, beginning of
birth process and, 46
brain as organ and, 44
conceiving of, 43
conception of, 43–44
continuity of, 70
individual awareness and, 46–47
moral code and, 47
objectivity of world and, 47
personal psychic reality for, 48
play and cultural experience as, 47–48
psychology becoming meaningful in, 45–46
quickening (of fetus) and, 44
viability (if born premature) and, 44
Individuality
asserted by baby, 16
realised through love, 69
Infant(s) (see also Baby, babies)
big head of, at birth, 60
postmaturity in, 33, 45–46
prematurity in, 33, 44, 45–46, 51
seen as human from birth, 58
Infant feeding
and baby's creation of the mother, 53
and initiation of human relationships, 52–53
and maternal adaptation, 52–53
difficulties in, 50
forced onto baby, 52–53
initial mismanagement of, 61–62
Information seeking, 96–97
Inherited tendencies. See also Maturational Processes
actualization of, and adequate environment, 70–71, 78–79, 233–234
as external to the baby, 80n2
not enough by themselves for self-fulfillment, 73
Inner psychic reality. See Psychic reality, inner
Insecurity. See also security
defending against, 157
sense of, through early environmental insult, 51–52, 65
Instincts, 218. See also Intuition
experience of, 168–169
Instinctual life
development of, 168, 218–220, 234–235
Insult
bad holding as, 51–52, 65
interference with infant feeding as, 26
pushing nipple into baby's mouth as, 52
Integration, 169

alternating with relaxation, 75
and becoming a unit, 75
and disintegration and, 17–18
and holding and, 75
and maturation, 34
inherited drives towards, 70–71
of baby, 16–17, 34
Interaction, 181–182
Interference
an insult to mother, 26
and maiming of baby's personality, 18
and initiation of breast-feeding, 6, 26
in relationship between baby and mother, 5,
18, 53, 55, 62–63, 78–79, 205
Internal process, stress coming from, 182–185,
186
Interruptions, 152–153
Intimacy
and relationship between baby and mother,
26–27
outside the scope of professional advice, 26–7
physical, not necessarily dependent on breast-
feeding, 24, 27
Intuition
mother's, 5, 6, 13, 20, 50–51, 62–63, 66–67,
196–197, 241
mother's, vs. expert knowledge, 20
natural, 20
Irksome matters, 86, 91, 139–140, 153–154
and invasion of mother's privacy by children,
144–148
discussion of, by mothers, 139–144, 148–154
Isa Benzie, 89

Jealousy
abnormal, 137–138, 150
age of children and, 123, 124, 125–127
amongst siblings, 132–133
anger and, 131, 138
anxiety and, 131
beginning of, 127
between mother and child, 162–163
coming to terms with, 122
disappearance of, 86, 91, 130–132, 134
discussions of, by mothers, 123–127,
127–130, 130–132, 132–133, 133–138
envy and, 127
love and, 122–123, 131, 134
parental attitude and, 135, 136–137, 229
possession and, 129–130

Knowledge
from books and instruction vs. natural
mothering, 50–51
natural, in mothers, 19, 20, 23
of experts, 19–20, 23, 26
two types of, 19
useful parental, 180–181
Knowledge, vs. learning, 5, 19–23

Labour, 6, 59–60
Lamb, Charles, 43
Love
and destructiveness, 29–31
and jealousy, 122–123, 131, 134
and meeting of dependence, 68–69
as setting for child to become an individual,
69, 231
baby's, for mother, 5–6, 30
baby's fusion (of object) and, 216–217
becoming evident with loss, 83
deprived, 236–237
father and, 229
hate, 217, 231
holding/handling and, 237
inhibition, breast-feeding, and, 5–6, 29–30
mother's, almost physical, 18
mother's, for baby, 6
mother's reliability as, 75–76
new kind of, when object survives, 30
of baby, 168–169
of baby at birth, absence of, in mother, 97,
101
of mother, 12, 14, 15, 18, 21
survival and, 237
Lovelace, Richard, 155
Loyalty, 177, 192, 210
disloyalty and, 228–231
family and cross-, 230
Luck, as factor in maternal care, 15

Man
femininity in, 204
Man Who Came to Dinner, The, 12
Marriage counseling, 200
Marriage, sexual development and, 212
Matches, playing with, 110–111
Maternal function, 174
Maturational process(es)
and facilitating environment, 25, 34, 46
and genetic factors, 44

and positive use of baby's aggression, 29–30
distortion in, due to faulty holding, 34,
  38–39, 51–52
facilitation of, a vital necessity, 15
in baby, 14, 16
interweaving of with environment in playing,
  47–48
psycho-somatic existence as, 17
undone in schizophrenia, 42
Maturity, at age, 207, 210, 213–214
Me/not-me distinction
  and establishment of identity, 46–47
  as beginning of the individual, 46–47
  facilitated by the environment, 46–47
  infant's distinguishing between, 107
  not present at the beginning, 71
  perceived, 217
Memories
  for confidence, 65, 235
  of birth, 58
  of mother as baby, 13, 73–74, 240
Menstruation, 6
Mental defect, 44
Mental disorders, 18, 27, 35–38, 40–42, 55, 68,
  78, 222
Mental health, 214
  facilitating, 25, 78–79, 234
Merging, of infant with environment, 46
Midwife
  and attitude towards mother, 6
  and establishment of feeding, 63
  and importance of knowledge and skill, 56
  and/of management, 61–64
  and management of ill patients, 60–61
  and need to give health its due, 61
  and need to know her patient, 60
  and need to make psychiatric diagnosis, 58,
    60
  and practice of taking the baby away, 63–64
  as a person with human feelings, 57, 63, 64
  as employee, 61
  as persecutory figure, 62, 64
  breast-feeding by mother not overseen by, 6
  concern for personage of patient by, 56–57
  facilitate natural process of birth with, 57
  forcing of breastfeeding by, 61–62
  mother's trust in, 6, 56, 58–59
  opposite concerns of mother and, 63–64
  personal diagnosis of (healthy) mother, birth
    and, 58–59

women's genital/reproductive function
  awareness by, 6, 56
Midwifery, and psychoanalysis, 6, 56–64
Moral code, 47
  development of, as beginning of individual,
    47
  personal vs. Implanted, 47
Moral judgment, 201
Morality
  development of child's, 167–170
  mother's version of, 120
Victorian, 3
Morley, Robert, 12
Moro Response, the
  an example of not good enough mothering,
    37
  and premature awareness in infant, 38
  as example of bad holding, 51
  as insult to baby, 51
  elicited in regressed woman patient, 39
  psychology of, 39
  reaction of baby to, 37
Mother(s). See also Breast-feeding; Dependency;
  Feeding
  adaptation of, to baby, 6, 13–14, 21, 50,
    52–53, 66–68, 75–76, 77–78, 99, 208, 223,
    234
  and acting naturally, 13–14, 20, 21, 62
  and belief in persecuting woman, 62
  and change in personal life at birth of baby,
    12–13, 57
  and experience/of being a baby, 6, 13, 29, 57,
    73–74, 240
  and foundation for mental health of child,
    21, 25, 78–79
  and graduated failures in adaptation, 14,
    53–54, 66, 73, 76
  and handling of baby, 5, 6, 21, 75
  and holding of baby, 5, 6, 17–18, 20–22, 34,
    36, 51–52, 75–76, 235
  and importance of previous life experience,
    13, 29, 50, 57, 63–64, 73–74, 240
  and intuitive knowledge about feeding babies,
    52
  and loss of care of midwife, 64
  and need for space to care for baby, 21–22, 26
  and playing at mothers and fathers as a child,
    50, 57, 63, 73, 229, 230, 240
  and prevention of mental hospital illness,
    17–18, 78–79

and respect or non-respect for natural
    functions, 54–55
and satisfaction in breast-feeding, 29
and self-consciousness, 18
and self-expression, 12
and sensitive management of baby's
    excretions, 55
and state of primary preoccupation with baby,
    6, 13, 33, 57–58
and survival of ruthless attack, 29–31
and trust in midwife and doctor, 59–60, 205
and wound caused by interference, 18
anxiety in, and holding, 21
as adaptive external person, 223
as baby and baby as mother, 13–14, 17
baby taken away from, 61–62, 63–64
birth and social/psychological change of, 57,
    71
blame not necessary of, 15
breakdown of holding/handling of baby by,
    17–18, 51–52, 236–237
breaking free or being swallowed up from,
    212
capacity in, to identify with baby, 5, 6, 12,
    13–14, 17, 33, 66–67, 234, 240
child of two and image of, 235–236
child's dependence to independence from,
    208, 213–214
concern of, 192
debt to, 16
depression in, 15, 22, 78, 80n2, 174
devotion/love of, 12, 14, 15, 18, 21, 85, 90,
    203, 204
ego support of, 16–17
evolution of natural instincts, 62–63
excretions and, 54–55
face of, as mirror, 78
facilitating environment of, 25
failures in, 6–7
fear of, 21, 73, 204, 229
fear of total preoccupation with baby, 73–74,
    240
figure as reduplicated, 223–224
girl identification with, 212
grandmothers and, 195
guilt and ambivalence of, 87, 91
health or illness in, in childbirth, 58–61
holding of a child as baby by, 22–23
in inner psychic of child, 48, 211–212
intuition in, 5, 6, 13, 20, 50–51, 62–63,
    66–67, 196–197, 241

love expressed as reliability of, 75–76
maternal knowledge not taught to, 19, 23
moralistic attitude in, and verbalization,
    74–75
natural knowledge of, 5
natural sense of responsibility in, 20
need for protection while vulnerable, 73
neurotic, 40
object- and environmental-, 217–220
opposite concerns of midwifery and, 63–64
ordinary good, 85, 90, 204–206
personal difficulties in, and breast-feeding, 27
physical contact with baby and, 67, 77–78
pregnancy of, 12–13, 33
preparation of, 13
primary maternal preoccupation of, 6, 12, 15,
    33, 73–74, 218, 240
privacy, invasion of by children, 144–148
reliability of, 6, 14, 75–76
seeing 'psychology' of infant by, 32
self-confidence in, fostered by environment,
    5, 27
sensitive post-natal state in, 62–63, 66
support of understanding of, 199
surrogate mothers and attitude of, 224
survival of, 5–6, 29–31, 237
trouble for, 15
unhealthy and needs in childbirth, 60–61
with mental disorders, 27
young, 205
Mother(s), discussions by
    discussions of jealousy, 123–127, 127–130,
        130–132, 132–133, 133–138
    of irksome matters, 139–144, 148–154
    saying 'no,' 108–112, 118–121
Mothering. See also Mother(s)
    and child's creative use of the environment,
        25
    and richness of personality in child, 25
    and strength of character in child, 25
    continuity in, leading to trust, 68, 205
    good-enough, 70, 90n2, 234
    grows out of being mother, 205
    that cannot be taught or learned in books,
        13–14, 19, 20, 23, 50–51, 66

Nail-biting, 176
Nationalism, 214, 214n2
Need(s)
    bodily, of baby, 67

by fathers, 118, 120–121, 154
discussion of, by mothers, 108–112, 118–121
'No' saying, 108
of baby, for human contact, 67
of baby, to be protected from gross
    disturbance, 67–68
stages of, 86, 91, 112–113, 114–115, 118–120
Nurse(s). *See also* Midwifery
advice on health by, 193
and advice about intimacy between baby and
    mother, 26–27, 55
and continuity of contact with pregnant
    woman, 59
and demands of modern medicine, 27
and difficulty in seeing babies as human
    beings, 49–50
and establishment of breast-feeding, 52,
    61–62, 63
and instructing parents, 50–51
and interference with natural processes, 53,
    54, 55
breast-feeding forced by, 61–62, 63, 196, 199
dismissal of, 62
facilitate natural process of birth with, 57
fear *vs.* love of, 62
mother/child relationship lacking in, 26–27,
    49–50, 54–55
mothers' need for, 53
mother's trust in at time of confinement,
    59–60, 205
not concerned with basic needs of baby, 52
treatment of disease *vs.* advice about life and,
    193–199
Nursery school, 173
Nursing Couple, 32

Object(s)
adopted by infant, 106–107
child's addiction to, 176–177
constancy, 54
discovery of, and intake, 54
protection of, by baby, 30
survival of, 6, 30–31
Object-presenting, 34
Object-relating, 18, 34, 52–54
and symbolic use of objects, 18
based on instinct-drives (without
    consequence), 218, 219
cheating in relating to, 225–226
inherited drives towards, 71, 233

mother as, 217–220
mothers as subjective, 223, 225
not absolutely dependent on breast-feeding,
    25–26
objectivity to world and, 47, 225
pattern of, set through infant feeding, 53
task in primative emotional development, 34
transitional, 29–31, 77–78, 224, 225
transitional phenomena *vs.* transitional,
    225–226
Objective perceptions, 226–227, 229
Objectivity, achievement of, as beginning of
    child, 47
Oedipus complex, 212, 216
Omnipotence, baby's experience of, 7, 14, 78,
    223
Oneness, feeling of, between baby and mother,
    13–14, 16–17
Oral sadism, 218
Ordinary devoted mother, the, 5, 11–18
origin of the phrase, 11
positive value of, 15
Over protectiveness, 155

Panic, 34, 227
Paradox, 237
Paradox, of creating what is found, 53
Paranoid state in schizophrenic patient, 40–41
Parent(s)
alive in unconscious, 211–212, 213
and change in attitude at birth of baby, 46,
    240
and growing up with children, 53–54
and need to insist on self-fulfillment, 27
children, same and opposite sex, 16
containing problem within oneself *vs.* advice
    to, 200
essential nature of being, 87
estrangement of, 224
functions of, 27
importance of full-time function of, 50
maternal, then parental care evolving into
    family for, 208
professional interview *vs.* advice on life to,
    200–201
relationship between, 178–179
relationship of child and, 191–192, 202–203,
    213
surprise of conception to, 44

treatment of disease *vs.* advice on life to,
193–199
'what's irksome' about being, 86, 91
Paediatricians. *See also* Doctors
bridging gap between child development and,
4–5, 24
identifying with infant, 33
psychological training and, 3–4
understanding of child/parent relationship by,
50
Patient(s)
and need for regression in analysis, 38–39
Personality. *See also* Individual
basis of, laid down by holding, 51
development of, and continuity of line of life,
70
development of, and holding, 75
distortion of, through environmental failure,
68, 241
distortion of, through physical disease, 46
richness in, and breast-feeding, 24–25, 28–29
richness in, and good-enough mothering,
25–26
split in, owing to faulty holding, 38
Planning, 151–152
Play(ing), 47–48
and conceiving of children, 43
and cultural activity, 47–48
as mother/father, 73, 229, 231, 240
at mothers and fathers, 50, 57, 63
common ground between baby and mother,
7, 77
disloyalty, widening of experience and, 229
early good experiences re-created, 40
games in family/siblings, 229–230
games that symbolize birth, 37, 58
intense, in small children, 47–48
intermediate area of, 47–48, 77, 226
origins of affection and enjoyment in, 7, 77
vitally important to individual, 48
Poet, who stayed in bed, 13
Possession, jealousy and, 129–130
Predictability/unpredictability, 184–185, 186,
217
Pregnancy, 12–13, 33, 146–147
as period of preparation, 12–13
new, too soon after baby, 15
Premature awareness, owing to environmental
failure, 38, 41–42
Preoccupation. *See also* Adaptation;
Identification; Mothers

mother's fear of state of, 73–74, 240
primary, of mother with baby, 6, 13, 15, 33,
73, 218, 240
Primary maternal preoccupation. *See also*
Mother(s) Preoccupation). 33, 186, 187
Privacy, invasion of mother's
by children, 144–148
Privation, and unthinkable anxiety, 76–77
Prohibition, 119
Propaganda
and breast-feeding, 24
and reaction, 24
Prophylaxis, 55
Psychic reality, inner, 185, 217, 226
contrasted with external world, 47, 48
father and mother alive in, 48, 211–212,
219–220
Psychoanalysis, 182, 184
alternation of the past and, 79
and assessment of mothers as persons, 56–57
and elucidation of physical states, 56
and increase in respect for individuals, 64
birth, midwifery and, 56–58
communication of reliability in, 79
contribution of, to midwifery, 56–64
contribution of, to study of infant psychology,
35–39
contribution of, to study of psychology of
birth, 45–46, 58
dreams and, 40–42
emotional development theory from, 35–36,
40, 42
holding patient head in, 39
for internal strains/stresses, 112
non-moralistic approach and, 74
not sacrifice patient for theory of, 39
occupational therapy and, 220
origins of emotional development for, 215,
221
psychoneurotic patient's treatment by, 72
regression procedures for, 36–42
schizoid patient's treatment by, 72, 78
setting in, important for re-experiencing,
38–39
training, 4
treatment of child isolation, 221–222
unhitching of developmental hold ups and,
79
verbalisation and, 74–75
Psychology
academic, definition of, 46–47

as gradual extension of physiology, 32–33
becoming meaningful, and beginning of
    children, 45
child, instruction in, 98
doctors not expert on, 194, 200
of conception, 43–44
of the newborn, and psychoanalysis, 35–39
of the newborn, at one with physiology,
    32–33
professional interview for, 200–201
provided by holding at the beginning, 51
suffering (for limited time) agonies of case in,
    200–201
Psychoneurosis
    personal conflict and repression and, 72
    psychoanalysis and, 72
Psychosis
    distortion in early experience and, 72
    mother-infant relationship and, 78
    psychoanalysis and, 72
Psycho-somatic existence
    and good-enough holding and handling, 17
    breakdown in, 17–18
    inherited drives towards, 70–71
    rocking and, 77
    task in primative emotional development, 34
Psycho-somatic partnership, 70–71, 77
Psychotics, 35

Quarreling, in front of children, 178
Quickening, 44
Quigley, Janet, 89

Rank, Otto, 40
Rayner, Claire, 91, 160–166
Real, feeling of, in baby, 14
Reality Principle, 223, 225–226
    introducing, 119, 120
Reflex(es),
    and Moro Response, 39
    not the whole story in breast-feeding, 52
Reflex activities, 52, 106
Regression procedures, 36–39
Relationship(s)
    growth of, 192
    needs of psychotic patients in analysis,
        mother/baby and, 78
    parent-child, 191–192
Relationship between mother and baby
    and repudiation and acceptance, 53–54

and subtle natural processes, 53
as pattern for baby's relationship to the
    world, 53, 62
centered around excretion, 54–55
failure in establishment of, 62
impossible for midwife to bring about, 63
initiation of, in feeding, 52
leading to symbolic use of objects, 18
not to be interfered with, 5, 26–27, 53, 62–63
Reliability, 6, 14, 168
    as love, at beginning of life, 75–76
    baby's belief in, 75, 235, 237–238
    baby's experience of, through being held, 75,
        235
    lack of, failure of, 15, 76
    of mother, 75–76, 236
Reliability/unreliability, 184, 185, 186
Religion, 232–233, 237
Religious controversialists, 47
Repudiation and acceptance, 53–54
Resentments, 146, 148
Resilience, 171
Responsibility, parental, 118–119
    guilt and, 164–166
Responsibility, taken by child for ideas and
    actions, 47
Rhythm, adapting to each child's, 151
Right and wrong, development of child's sense
    of, 167–170
Robertson, James and Joyce
    'A Two-Year-Old Goes to Hospital,' 184–185
Rocking, 6
    as adaptation of mother to baby, 99
    as insurance against depersonalisation, 77
    reliability of communication of, 236
Romulus and Remus, 16

Sandler, Dr. J., 70
Schizophrenia, 36–37, 40–42, 72, 78
    and environmental failure at stage of absolute
        dependence, 35, 39–40
    as undoing maturational process, 42
School, 222, 228
    age for, 230
    child's adapting to, 172–175
    games, 230
    living vs. education from, 233, 237–238
    primary school education in, 230
Security, children's need for, 155–159
Self-confidence, 156

Self-control, 159
Sexual development, 207, 212
Sister
    holding of baby, 20–21
Slapping, 111, 113, 121
Social provision, 213
Social work, 221–222
    individual child *vs.* family and, 221–222,
        228–229
Space
    between baby and environment, 21–22
    potential, 77–78
Spock, Benjamin
    and interest in Winnicott's writings, 3, 4
    and psychoanalysis, 4
    and search for psychological training, 3–4
    mother's Victorian morality of, 3
    Pocket Books and, 4
    psychoanalytic training of, 4
Stepparents, 86, 99–103
Stories, bedtime, 150
Stress, 112, 178, 186
    coming from environmental provision,
        184–185, 186
    coming from internal process, 182–184,
        186
Suffering, practitioner's experiencing of,
    200–201
Suicide, 34, 38, 40, 41
Survival
    of the analyst, 76
    of the breast, 30–31
    of the mother, 5–6, 29–31, 237
    of object, 30
    of premature infants, 45
Swearing, 146

Teachers, 222
Teaching, danger of, 179–180
Temper tantrums, 147
Thumb-sucking, 15–20, 86, 176. *See also* Cloth-
    sucking
Time, 192, 219–220, 226, 227
Times, The, 43
Tiredness among mothers
    causes of, 140
Transitional object(s)
    and sensuous experiences of baby, 29
    arising in potential space between baby and
        mother, 77–78

as symbol of trust and union, 77
    family and, 224, 225
Transitional phenomena, 225–226
Trauma, memories of, due to faulty holding,
    51–52
Trauma of Birth (Rank), 40
Trauma, persecution theory of, 182–183
Triangular relationship(s), of child with parents,
    16
Trust
    arising from continuity in care, 68
    baby and growth of, 75–76, 77
    baby's, in mother, 5, 120
    building up of, 178–187
    capacity for, in child, 48
    in midwife and doctor, mother's, 59, 205
    of patient in analysis, 41
    transitional objects and, 77

Unconscious, the
    absence in baby, 70, 240
    dependence on parents, 214
    not to found in babies at the beginning, 70,
        240
    parenthood alive in, 211–212, 213
Union, symbol of, 226
Unsuccess story, value of, 101–103
Untidiness, mother's task of eternal, 117–118,
    139, 142–143

Verbalisation
    importance of attitude behind, 74–75
    in psychoanalysis, 74
    mother's, to baby, 75
    not part of infant care at the beginning, 50
Viability
    of individual, and independence, 71
    of unborn child and beginning of the
        individual, 45
Vitamins
    diet and, 19–20

War, 89–90
Wicked stepmother, myth of, 99–102
Willmott, P., 212–213
Winnicott, Clare, 91
Winnicott, D. W.
    and capacity for empathy with babies, 49–50
    and insight into mother-child relationship,
        4–7, 90

and insight into parent-infant processes, 85–86
and strength of feeling derived from experience, 49
and use of language, 7
biographical note, 249
bridging gap between paediatrics and child development by, 4–5
experience of, from forty-five years of practice, 49
importance of theory to, in work, 24
influence on, of paediatric training, 49–50
language, meaning *vs.* practical answers for, 4, 7

Woman (women). *See also* Mother(s)
and preoccupation with baby, 12
and reorientation in pregnancy, 12–13
anxiety, adaptation and, 234
fear of, 204
ordinary occupations of, 12
Wordsworth, William, 172–173, 175–176
World
infant becoming part of, 30–31
infant surprising, 22
objectivity to, 47

Young, M., 212–213

D. W. Winnicott

1896–1971

Dr. Winnicott began his medical career in paediatrics and kept an interest in the physiological side of paediatrics while becoming more and more involved in the study of child psychology. His contributions to our understanding of human development, based on extensive clinical work with mothers, babies, and young children, are internationally known and valued.

Dr. Winnicott began his medical studies at Jesus College, Cambridge, and after a period of war service continued them at St. Bartholomew's Hospital in London. Apart from his year as a resident at St. Bartholomew's, his hospital appointments were all at children's hospitals. Dr. Winnicott practiced and taught child psychiatry and psychoanalysis for over forty years and was elected President of the British Psycho-Analytical Society. He was a prolific contributor to psychoanalytic and medical journals and lectured widely on child development to many groups of professionals in this field: teachers, midwives, parents, social workers, magistrates, and physicians as well as to psychoanalysts and psychiatrists.